Human Capital Management Technology and Systems

Human Capital Management Technology and Systems

Dr. Dale J. Albrecht

Alonos®

Printed in the United States of America

First Printing: May 2024

ISBN-13: 978-1-948699-14-3

Alonos®
Dallas, Texas, United States of America

www.alonos.com

Special discounts are available on quantity purchases by corporations, associations, educators, educational institutions, and others. For details, contact the publisher.

Please contact Alonos® through our website or via email at:
information@alonos.com

Suggested bibliographical reference:

Albrecht, D.J. (2024). *Human Capital Management Technology and Systems.* Dallas, TX: Alonos Corporation.

$74.95
ISBN 978-1-948699-14-3
57495>
9 781948 699143

Table of Contents

Table of Figures

About the Author

Dr. Dale J. Albrecht is a seasoned professional with a unique blend of expertise in technology and human resources. As the CEO and Chief Human Resources Executive of Alonos Corporation, a leading management and HR consulting firm, Dale has dedicated his career to maximizing human performance and organizational effectiveness. With extensive leadership experience in industries ranging from retail and manufacturing to telecommunications and healthcare, Dale brings a wealth of knowledge and insights to his work.

In addition to his role at Alonos, Dale serves as a full-time Associate Professor of Practice at The University of Texas at Dallas, where he imparts his expertise in human resources management, organizational development, and business leadership to the next generation of professionals. With a Doctorate in Business Administration and a Master's of Business Administration specializing in HR management, Dale combines academic rigor with practical experience to deliver impactful learning experiences for his students.

Throughout his career, Dale has been at the forefront of driving strategic initiatives and leveraging technology to enhance organizational performance. From designing and implementing Human Capital Management systems to leading organizational transformations, Dale's multidisciplinary background uniquely positions him to address the complex challenges facing today's businesses.

Preface

As I embarked on the journey of writing this book, I found myself reflecting on the transformative power of technology in shaping the modern workplace. In my early career, I spent years navigating the changes that are reflected in this book. Then, when I transitioned from technical roles into human resources roles, I spent many more years navigating the intricacies of human capital management (HCM) systems and their various iterations. I realized the profound impact these technologies have on every aspect of organizational life, from recruitment and talent development to performance management and strategic planning.

My passion for exploring the intersection of technology and human resources stems from my combined professional background in both technology and human resources. I have a deep-seated belief in the power of people to drive organizational success. Throughout my career, I have witnessed firsthand the challenges and opportunities that arise when implementing and optimizing HCM systems in diverse organizational settings. I have been an active member of five implementations of Enterprise Resource Planning (ERP) systems and myriad of other implementations of smaller systems and applications. From multinational corporations to small and medium-sized enterprises, the journey has been both enlightening and enriching.

In writing this book, my aim is to share insights, lessons learned, and best practices gleaned from my experiences in the fields of human capital management and technology. It made a lot of sense to me, when writing this book about current and future technology, to incorporate the use of artificial intelligence (AI) in the authoring process. Citations for the AI tools used have been provided. By offering practical guidance, real-world examples, and thought-provoking discussions, I hope to empower readers to harness the full potential of HCM systems and unlock new opportunities for growth and innovation within their organizations. Whether you are a seasoned HR professional, a technology enthusiast, or simply curious about the future of work, I invite you to join me on this journey into the dynamic world of human capital management technology. Together, let us explore, learn, and embrace the possibilities that lie ahead.

Introduction

In today's rapidly evolving business landscape, the effective management of human capital has emerged as a critical factor for organizational success. Human Capital Management (HCM) systems have revolutionized the way businesses attract, develop, and retain talent, driving efficiency, productivity, and strategic decision-making. As organizations increasingly recognize the value of their workforce as a strategic asset, the demand for robust HCM technology solutions continues to grow.

This book serves as a comprehensive guide to navigating the complex and dynamic landscape of HCM systems and technologies. From understanding the historical evolution of HR systems to delving into the intricacies of requirements gathering, system sizing, and implementation, each chapter offers valuable insights and practical strategies for leveraging HCM technology effectively. We explore the diverse array of business uses and roles within HCM systems, examine common modules and functionalities, and provide insights into both large enterprise solutions and tailored solutions for small and medium-sized businesses.

Moreover, we delve into critical considerations such as environmental, social, and governance (ESG) factors, data privacy, and the future impact of emerging technologies on human capital management. By offering guidance on future-proofing through continuous learning and adaptation to technological advancements, this book equips readers with the knowledge and tools needed to navigate the ever-changing landscape of HCM technology and drive organizational success in the digital age. Whether you're a business leader, HR professional, or technology enthusiast, this book aims to empower you to harness the full potential of HCM systems to optimize your workforce and achieve your strategic objectives.

Chapter 1
Business Systems Overview

Chapter Table of Contents

Photo by Jopwell from pexels.com

Chapter 1: Business Systems Overview

Introduction

Business systems are the backbone of modern organizations. The word "backbone" is an understatement; most entrepreneurs won't even start operating until they have core systems in place. These commonly include office productivity systems such as accounting software and desktop office software. At a macro-level, business systems facilitate operations, which include management processes, information flow, material flow, resource utilization, and business decision making. Systems are universal in today's business world, and they're becoming more essential going forward.

In this chapter, we will explore the history of business systems, and we'll conclude with a specific focus on Enterprise Resource Planning (ERP) systems. The concept of system integration will be introduced along with the types of implementations, including on-premise, cloud-based, and Software as a Service (SaaS).

Figure 01.01
Desert Kite
Adapted from Beech, 2023. This figure is two photos. On the left is the engraving, and on the right is the actual construction of the Kite on the landscape.

History of Business Systems

Business systems have a rich history that traces back to the earliest forms of record-keeping and resource management. One of the oldest systems discovered is in Saudi Arabia at Jebel az-Zilliyat. It dates to about 9,000 years ago. Refer to Figure 01.01. The system includes documentation of structures and an implication of process and resource coordination. The term that the research community has applied to this system is the Desert Kite. (Personal opinion: I don't like the use of the word "desert," because there's other archeological evidence that this part of the world was not a desert 9,000 years ago. Maybe just "Kite" would be more appropriate for the time.)

The documentation are engravings which are scale-drawings intended to depict structures that were built on the open landscape. The Kite structures depicted are traps that are built to collect animals for domestic purposes. "The engravings illustrate desert kites—sophisticated archaeological structures composed of walls that are up to five kilometers long converging in an enclosure to trap animals. These structures, bordered by pits, can only be fully seen from the air. The necessity for this type of spatial representation was unprecedented," explains Dr. Crassard (Beech, 2023, para. 5.)

The kites were used as collection sites. People would herd wild animals from the open plain in the direction of the kite. The animals that ran into the Kite could not escape, and they were subsequently trapped. They could then more easily be repurposed for domestic use or harvested. This early system included architectural plans, facilities (Kite), materials (stones), and resource coordination (construction, herding, and harvesting.)

Over the eons, systems evolved in their complexity. Consider the water distribution system of Rome from approximately 500 B.C.E. to 476 A.D. This complex system moved water across the vast territories of Rome, through above-ground viaducts and below ground aqueducts. All with precise mathematical calculations for slope, flow rates, and volume. As humanity has progressed, these systems have evolved.

Figure 01.02
1942 Floor Waxer Plant

United States Office of War Information, Hollem, H. R., photographer. (1942). These twenty-year-old lathes are producing equipment for Uncle Sam's armed forces twenty-two hours a day. Alive to the possibilities of converting old equipment to defense usage, the owner of this small Eastern factory bought and remodeled old equipment which is proving its mettle in 1942. Note overhead power-driven machinery. Floorola Products Inc., York, Pennsylvania

Fast forward to the early part of the past century. In the late 1800's and early 1900s, some businesses adopted mechanical and electromechanical systems to automate some of their tasks. Refer to Figure 01.02, and notice the gears, pulleys, and belts in the ceiling. It was common to have a single power source for all mechanical devices in a shop, and these gears, chains, and belts would whir all day long. I like to envision the Steampunk style when I think about this era. Lots of gears, wheels, levers, steam power alongside coal power, etc. It can feel whimsical in an idealistic visual, but the reality of this era is that it was dirty and resource intensive.

Figure 01.03
First Typewriter
Bain News Service, 1915. Depiction of the first typewriter. Attributed to Christopher Latham Sholes of Milwaukee, Wisconsin.

How about a space that we never think about as a system...the printing industry. The printing industry has always been about creating forms of record keeping and disseminating information (the essence of our definition of a system.) The printing press originated in China. Then, it was popularized in western cultures in Europe in the 15th century through the Gutenberg press and the production of the Gutenberg Bible. The press reigned supreme in the printing industry for hundreds of years, with entire professions and disciplines developed around them. The typesetter being a predominant example. A Typesetter was responsible for pre-press by preparing (moveable and physical) numbers, letters, and symbols on a plate. The assembly of these would produce a mimeograph of the composite when inked and pressed onto paper. As you can imagine, producing a printed page was laborious and dirty.

Enter a revolutionary invention: the typewriter! A system to replace a system. Refer to Figure 01.03. The U.S. patent for a typewriter was issued in June of 1868 to Christopher Latham Sholes of Milwaukee Wisconsin. Consider the impact...the entire printing and typesetting system built into a single device, operated by a single person, at a single desk. It was disruptive to say the least. It didn't replace the press, but it did cause the printing industry to evolve and advance further. A few years later, Thomas Edison electrified the typewriter. Mark Twain was the first author to submit a typewritten document to a publisher. The typewriter became a common

Figure 01.04
ENIAC
Photo public domain. Photo shows part of the programming room for the ENIAC.

device in every business and many households through the middle of the 1990's! It wasn't replaced until the advent of the personal computer!

The development of computers started much earlier than many realize. Much of the early research was conducted by military organizations around the world, such as the U.S. Department of Defense. The first non-military computer was the Electronic Numerical Integrator and Computer (ENIAC,) built by researchers at the University of Pennsylvania. Refer to Figure 01.04. Early computers were massive machines that used vacuum tubes, discrete switches, patch cables, and large amounts of electricity. These early computing machines occupied thousands of square feet. Colloquially, it's often said that the entire Apollo 11 space mission (1969) had less computing power than the first smartphone.

The potential of computing systems in business became quickly evident. Large businesses invested early and did much of their own research. In the United States, the Bell telephone

Figure 01.05
Hard Disk Drives

Photos public domain. Photo on the left shows a hard disk drive by IBM, used in the 1970's and 1980's. Photo on the right shows the miniaturized version that's used today in personal computers. This has miniaturized more recently into solid state drives.

company pioneered computing research applied to telephone and telegraph communications. Motorola pioneered radio communications which initially launched as a radio in the automobile (the motored victrola, or motor-ola.) Subsequent development resulted in critical radio communications equipment used in the Second World War.

For business operations, the pivotal decades for research and development were the 1960's – 1980's. Every few years, technology would advance, and the technology became more usable. The resource requirement shrunk, sizes shrunk, and accessibility grew. My dad worked for Bell Telephone and later for American Telephone & Telegraph (AT&T.) For a few years he worked in an office in the Chicago Loop. On a few Saturdays, when he needed to go to the office, I would go along with him. We rode the train into the Loop and made a day of it. He was proud to show me the latest advances in business systems that they were trying out, and I remember him showing me a disk storage device. Refer to Figure 01.05. The disks were about 18 inches in diameter with magnetic heads that would read and write to the disks. This technology didn't last long because it seemed like only months and dad brought these disks home for us to use as toys. We spent many hours flinging these around in the back yard like frisbees. This same technology miniaturized quickly into the Hard Disk Drive (HDD) that's been used in the personal computer since the early 1990's.

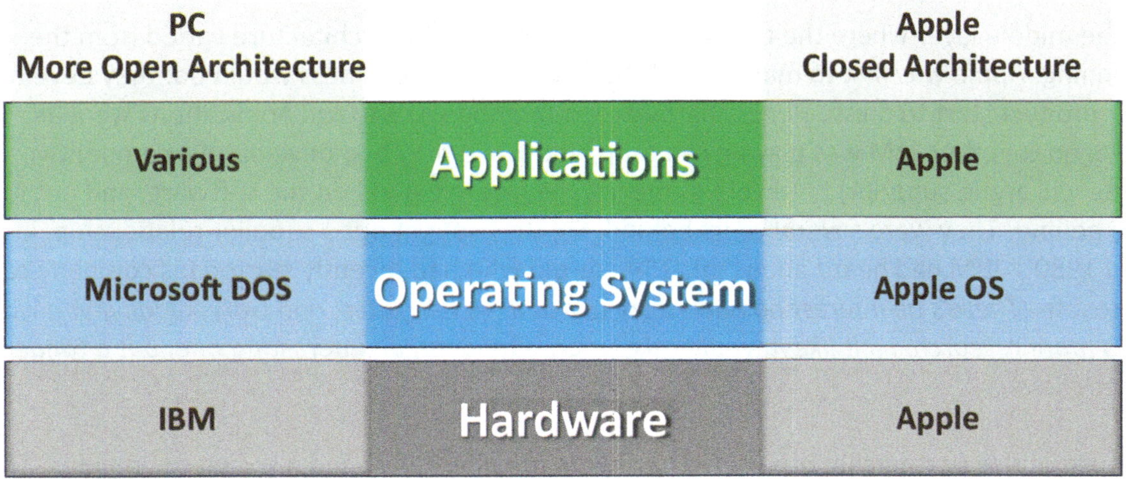

Figure 01.06
Early Architecture
Simplified illustration of the early architecture that developed. This is from the perspective of a market structure versus a technology architecture.

The ability to research, test, produce, and miniaturize is essential to technology adoption. It's this cycle that enables innovation and advancement in business practices. International Business Machines (IBM) is attributed with the first commercial version of the personal computer. IBM launched its personal computer, the IBM 5150, in August of 1981. However, few realize that Apple beat IBM from a development standpoint; they launched the Apple I in 1976, the Apple II in 1977, and the Apple II Plus in 1979. Apple lacked the financial resources of IBM, so it took them a while longer to get their product commercialized and ready for market. Apple launched its competitive product a few years later, the Macintosh in January of 1984. It was the launch of the Macintosh, with its graphical user interface, that springboarded Apple in front of IBM. Mixed in with the advent of the personal computer is the story of Bill Gates and Microsoft, whom IBM contracted with to provide the operating system. Whereas the Apple system had their graphical user interface and operating system integrated within the Apple ecosystem.

In addition to the introduction of personal computing, there was a parallel revolution taking place in business. As personal computing accelerated, the same devices became more and more prevalent in the workplace. The software development industry was beginning, producing applications that ran on top of operating and hardware systems. From a market perspective, a simple three-layer model developed as shown in Figure 01.06. At the lowest layer is the hardware, with components such as case, power supply, motherboard, central processing unit (CPU), storage devices, cabling, and human interface devices. The middle layer is the Operating System (OS). The personal computer used Microsoft's Disk Operating System (DOS), and Apple used the proprietary Apple Operating System. The top is the application layer; this is where the software products that you and I use exist. Software, like office productivity and games, are applications that reside at this top layer.

It's the middle layer where the two approaches to computing architecture varied from the beginning. Apple was first to market, and they did what any business would do: they developed their product start to finish. Hence, hardware, operating system, and applications were all packaged together. IBM was playing catch-up, and while they had developed a competitive (some will argue superior) hardware platform, they were behind on the software, and not just a little behind. They were several years behind. So, they sought out a supplier relationship. In the early 1980's, IBM had heard about this 25-year-old who had recently started his company called Microsoft. *(There's an interesting back-story about IBM, Bill Gates, and Gary Kildall if you want to do more research. I felt like it would take us on a tangent, an interesting one, but a tangent nonetheless.)*

Because of this partnership between a hardware provider (IBM) and a software provider (Microsoft,) the personal computing platform had its origins in *more* open architecture. Applications on the PC platform were built by different companies from the beginning; whereas, applications on the Apple platform were designed and developed by Apple. The open architecture of the PC enabled a rapid development of applications, and one of the benefactors of this rapid development was the business sector through packaged business systems. After a few years, Apple released specifications that enabled other companies to develop applications for their platform, but at this point the PC platform had gained a market share leadership position that it has retained since.

Packaged business systems were commonly built for specific use in a department like accounting, inventory, shipping, and manufacturing. Accounting would have an "accounting computer" with software that was designed for accounting functions. The accounting computers would be bundled with other hardware items for accounting purposes such as printers with dedicated functionality. Packaged business systems were the norm in the late 80's and early 90's. Windows 3.1 was launched in 1992, and the business computing platform evolved to include multi-functionality.

The technology evolution continued, and developers produced more integrated business systems that streamlined multiple business processes across departments. For example, sales and customer service had an Order Entry bundle. Another example, materials, procurement, order processing, and warehouse management had a supply chain planning bundle. Each of these integrated business systems, or bundles, eventually converged into a more fully integrated business system called an Enterprise Resource Planning (ERP) system.

ERP systems took shape in the late 90's, and they were the most sophisticated type of integrated business system package. They provided a single platform for managing most of a business's core processes, including accounting, supply chain management, manufacturing, customer service, and asset management. As the ERP solutions evolved in the early 2000's, capabilities such as human resources and business intelligence were added.

The business systems that we use today incorporate a wide breadth of technology, software, applications, and interfaces, which allow them to continuously evolve to our changing business needs. The evolution that we've experienced over the past several decades is rooted in our business need to keep records, track resources, and plan for effective and efficient operation.

From primitive methods such as the Desert Kite, to today's sophisticated digital databases, the progression through time is marked with key milestones. The earliest systems were manual, with etchings on rocks, later on papyrus, and more recently paper-based and then electronic. Businesses used ledgers, journals, and other handwritten records to track their financial transactions, inventory, and customer relationships. As our endeavors have grown in both size and complexity, *manual* systems have not been able to meet our needs. Our needs to track and manage have also become more complex; therefore, automation, speed, and accuracy are vitally important for the efficient and effective use of resources along with maximizing productivity.

The adoption of business systems has had a significant impact on the way that businesses operate. Business systems have helped improve efficiency, reduce costs, innovate, develop new products/services, and improve customer service. They have also made it possible for businesses to grow and expand into new markets.

The Evolution of Business Systems and the ERP Suite

The evolution of business systems can be divided into four main stages:

1. Manual Systems (Pre-1900): Early business systems were manual and paper based. Businesses used ledgers, journals, and other handwritten records to track their financial transactions, inventory, and customer relationships.
2. Mechanical and Electromechanical Systems (1900-1950): In the early 1900s, businesses began to adopt mechanical and electromechanical technologies to automate some of their tasks. For example, punch card machines were used to process accounting data and typewriters were used to generate invoices and letters.
3. Computerized Systems (1950-1990): The development of electronic computers in the mid-1900s revolutionized business systems. Computers allowed businesses to automate a wider range of tasks and to process data more quickly and efficiently than ever before.
4. Integrated Systems (1990-Present): In the 1990s, vendors began to develop integrated business systems that could automate and streamline multiple business processes across different departments. Enterprise resource planning (ERP) systems are the most sophisticated type of integrated business system.
5. *Artificial Intelligence: Could this become the fifth main stage of development?*

The Impact of Information Systems on Businesses

The birth of information systems marked a turning point in business operations. From early data processing systems to the development of intelligent personal devices, the journey toward automation and efficiency was almost inevitable. The adoption of business systems has had a significant impact on the very nature of commerce in today's world. Specifically, these systems enable:

- Efficiency: Task automation is a continuing trend. Driven to alleviate manual and mundane tasks so employees can perform more complex and strategic work.
    - Cost Reduction: Part of the efficiencies gained include reducing costs of production, thereby making products and services more accessible to a broader human population.
- Growth and Expansion: Along with integration and efficiency gains, comes the ability to replicate operations, thereby leveraging economies of scale and again making products and services more accessible to a broader human population.

Building System Capabilities through Integrations

System integrations have become a critical component of modern business operations. The ability to connect various software applications enhances the capabilities of a business system. Integrations streamline processes, reduce data silos, and enable real-time data exchange. They play a vital role in data-driven decision-making. Integrations are not merely technical solutions; they bring a multitude of benefits, including enhanced productivity, better decision-making, and a seamless user experience.

Multi-vendor integrations allow companies to connect their different business systems from different vendors. This can provide a number of benefits and advantages, including:

- Improved efficiency and productivity: By integrating their systems, companies can automate many manual tasks and processes. This can free up employees to focus on more strategic work and leads to gains in efficiency and productivity.
- Reduced costs: Multi-vendor integrations can help companies reduce costs by eliminating duplicate systems and data entry. They can also help companies streamline operations and reduce waste.
- Improved customer service: By integrating their systems, companies can get a better understanding of their customers' needs and preferences. They can also automate many customer-facing tasks, such as order processing and customer support.
- Enhanced decision-making: Multi-vendor integrations can provide companies with a single view of their data. This can help companies make better decisions about their operations, marketing, and sales strategies.

In addition to these general benefits, multi-vendor integrations provide specific advantages to companies. Overall, multi-vendor integrations provide a number of benefits and advantages to companies of all sizes. By integrating their different business systems, companies can improve their efficiency, productivity, customer service, decision-making, and agility.

Overview of the Types of Implementations Used Today

On-Premise

An on-premise system is an implementation where the hardware and software are both contained on the premises of a single company. That company can have multiple locations, and large companies can span continents and countries, but as along as the company owns and operates the equipment and software, it's considered an on-premises implementation. Refer to Figure 01.07. There are a number of reasons why a company might choose to implement an on-premise system. Some of the most common reasons include:

- Control and security: On-premise systems give companies complete control over their data and security. This is especially important for companies in regulated industries or that handle sensitive data.
- Customization: On-premise systems can be customized to meet the specific needs of a business. This is often not possible with cloud-based software, which is designed to be used by a wide range of businesses.
- Performance: On-premise systems can offer better performance than cloud-based software, especially for applications that require a lot of processing power or bandwidth.
- Cost: On-premise systems can be more cost-effective in the long run for companies that have a large number of users or that need to store a lot of data. Think size...the company must be large enough to leverage economies of scale.

There are some drawbacks to an on-premise system implementation. These include:

- Upfront costs: On-premise system implementations can require a significant upfront investment in hardware, software, and staff.
- Maintenance and support: On-premise systems require ongoing maintenance and support from staff.
- Scalability: On-premise systems can be difficult to scale up or down as needed. This can be a problem for businesses that are growing rapidly or that have fluctuating seasonal demand.

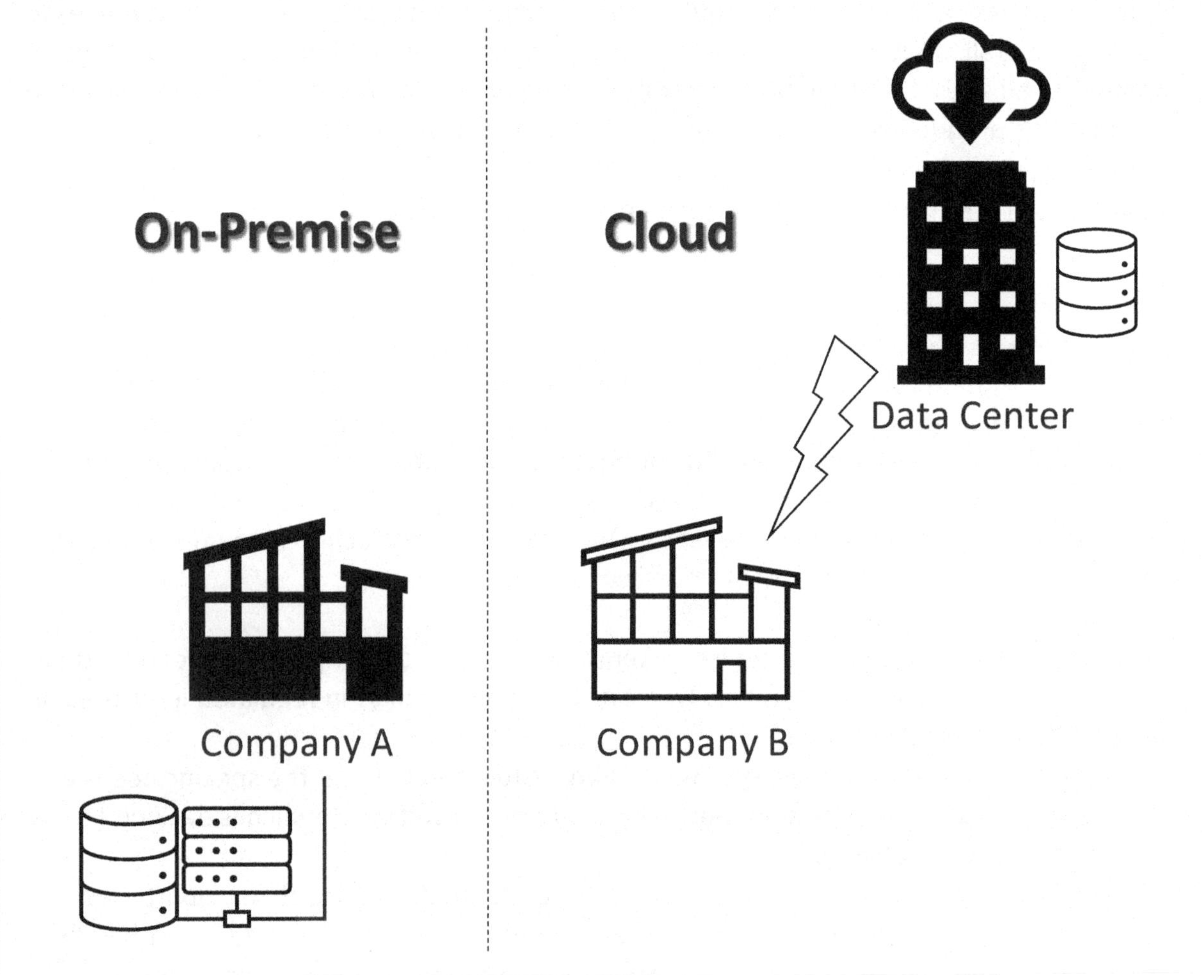

Figure 01.07
Types of Implementations
Basic illustration of on-premise versus hosted or cloud-based software-as-a-service (SAAS.)

Overall, on-premise system implementation is a good option for companies that need a high degree of control, customization, and performance. However, it is important to carefully consider the upfront costs, maintenance requirements, and scalability limitations. There are many companies whose system journey started years ago. In the 1990's and early 2000's, fewer options were available and on-premise was the only choice. As technology and software renewals are done, many companies re-examine their system needs, and they choose to move to a cloud-based/hosted environment.

Cloud – Hosted – Software As A Service

Continue to refer to Figure 01.07. Terminology first; cloud, hosted, and software-as-a-service (SAAS) are all different things. These three terms tend to get bundled together to represent the model where a third party is providing *some* of a company's technology services.

Cloud-based system implementation is the process of migrating or deploying software and data to a cloud computing platform. Cloud computing is a model for delivering IT services over the internet ("the cloud") with pay-as-you-go pricing. Instead of buying, owning, and maintaining physical data centers and servers, businesses can access technology services, such as computing power, storage, and databases, on an as-needed basis from a cloud provider like Amazon Web Services (AWS), Microsoft Azure, or Google Cloud Platform (GCP).

There are several reasons why a company might choose to implement a cloud-based system. Some of the most common reasons include:

- Cost-effectiveness: Cloud-based systems can be more cost-effective than on-premise systems, especially for businesses with limited IT resources or that need to scale their operations quickly.
- Scalability: Cloud-based systems are easy to scale up or down as needed. This is ideal for businesses with fluctuating seasonal demand or that are growing rapidly.
- Agility: Cloud-based systems can help businesses to be more agile and responsive to change. For example, businesses can quickly deploy new applications or services without having to invest in new hardware or software.
- Global reach: Cloud-based systems can be accessed from anywhere in the world with an internet connection. This is ideal for businesses with global operations or that need to provide their employees and customers wlth access to their systems from anywhere.

However, there are also some potential drawbacks to cloud-based system implementation. These include:

- Security and privacy: Businesses need to be careful to choose a cloud provider that has a strong track record of security and privacy. Businesses should also implement their own security measures to protect their data in the cloud.
- Switching Barriers: It can be difficult and expensive to switch from one cloud provider to another. Businesses need to carefully consider their needs before choosing a cloud provider.
- Performance: Cloud-based systems may not offer the same level of performance consistency as on-premise systems. Businesses need to test their applications in the cloud to ensure that they meet their performance requirements.

Overall, cloud-based system implementation is a good option for businesses that want to save money, be more agile, and have broader geographic presence. However, it's important to consider the security, privacy, switching barriers, and performance constraints before making a decision.

Summary

Business systems have evolved significantly over time, becoming more sophisticated and integrated as technology has advanced. The adoption of business systems has had a major impact on the way that businesses operate, helping them to improve efficiency, reduce costs, and improve customer service.

Discussion Questions

What are the five components of a business system?

What are some examples of business systems?

What are the benefits of using business systems?

What are the challenges of implementing and using business systems?

What are some of the latest trends in business systems?

What is the difference between on-premise and cloud-based business systems?

What are the benefits and drawbacks of on-premise business systems?

What are the benefits and drawbacks of cloud-based business systems?

When should a business choose an on-premise business system? When should a business choose a cloud-based business system?

What are some of the factors to consider when choosing between an on-premise and cloud-based business system?

What are some of the best practices for implementing and using business systems?

Chapter References

Al Hayek, W. Y., & Abu Odeh, R. A. (2020). Cloud ERP VS On-Premise ERP. *International Journal of Applied Science and Technology, 10(4).*

Bain News Service, P. (ca. 1915) *First Typewriter.*, ca. 1915. [Between and Ca. 1920] [Photograph] Retrieved from the Library of Congress, https://www.loc.gov/item/2014704116/.

Bard, Google AI. (2023). A History of Business Systems. Bard, Google AI. Accessed October 22, 2023.

Beech, S. (2023). *Ancient construction plans from 9,000 years ago unearthed: 'Oldest in human history'* (November 4, 2023). StudyFinds. Retrieved December 28, 2023 from https://studyfinds.org/ancient-construction-plans/

ChatGPT. (2023). History of Business Systems. OpenAI. Accessed October 22, 2023.

Duan, J., Faker, P., Fesak, A., & Stuart, T. (2013). Benefits and drawbacks of cloud-based versus traditional ERP systems. *Proceedings of the 2012-13 course on Advanced Resource Planning.*

Ferreira, D. (2013.). Evolution of Enterprise Systems. In Enterprise Systems Integration (pp. 3–14). Springer Berlin Heidelberg. https://doi.org/10.1007/978-3-642-40796-3_1

Hirschheim, R., & Heinz K. (2012) "A Glorious and Not-So-Short History of the Information Systems Field," Journal of the Association for Information Systems, 13(4), .
DOI: 10.17705/1jais.00294 Available at: https://aisel.aisnet.org/jais/vol13/iss4/5

Jacobs, R., & Weston, F. C. (2007). Enterprise resource planning (ERP)—A brief history. Journal of Operations Management, 25(2), 357–363. https://doi.org/10.1016/j.jom.2006.11.005

Jatav, P. K., Nagar, N., Singh, A., & Sharma, Y. Comparative study of various tools of On-Premises ERP and Cloud based ERP.

Lorincz, P. (2007). Evolution of Enterprise Systems. 2007 International Symposium on Logistics and Industrial Informatics, 75–80. https://doi.org/10.1109/LINDI.2007.4343516

Nestell, J.G., & Olson, D. L. (2018). Successful ERP systems : a guide for businesses and executives. Business Expert Press.

Prencipe. A., Davies, A., & Hobday, M. (2003). The business of systems integration. Oxford University Press.

Rashvanlouei, K.Y., Thome, R., & Yazdani, K. (2015). *Functional and technological evolution of enterprise systems: An overview.* 2015 IEEE International Conference on Industrial Engineering and Engineering Management (IEEM), Singapore, 2015, pp. 67-72, doi: 10.1109/IEEM.2015.7385610.

Sun, W., Zhang, X., Guo, C. J., Sun, P., & Su, H. (2008, September). Software as a service: Configuration and customization perspectives. In 2008 *ieee congress on services part ii (services-2 2008)* (pp. 18-25). IEEE.

United States Office Of War Information, Hollem, H. R., photographer. (1942) *Conversion. Floor waxer plant. These twenty-year-old lathes are producing equipment for Uncle Sam's armed forces twenty-two hours a day. Alive to the possibilities of converting old equipment to defense usage, the owner of this small Eastern factory bought and remodelled old equipment which is proving its mettle in . Note overhead power-driven machinery. Floorola Products Inc., York, Pennsylvania.* Pennsylvania United States York County York, 1942. Feb. [Photograph] Retrieved from the Library of Congress, https://www.loc.gov/item/2017690336/.

Weske, M. (2012.). Evolution of Enterprise Systems Architectures. In Business Process Management (pp. 25–69). Springer Berlin Heidelberg. https://doi.org/10.1007/978-3-642-28616-2_2

Wu, C., & Rajkumar, B. (2015). Cloud data centers and cost modeling : A complete guide to planning, designing and building a cloud data center (Green, Ed.; 1st edition). Morgan Kaufmann.

Zhang, L. L., Chen, X., Falkner, A. A., & Chu, C. (2014, September). Open Configuration: a New Approach to Product Customization. *In Configuration Workshop* (pp. 75-79).

Chapter 2
History of HR Systems & Technology

Chapter Table of Contents

Chapter 2: History of HR Systems & Technology

Introduction

Human resources systems and technology have evolved significantly over the past several decades. From early manual systems to today's sophisticated cloud-based solutions, HR technology has transformed the way HR professionals work and the way that businesses operate. It's easy to overlook the fact that HR systems directly impact business operations. At the transactional level, these systems facilitate workforce activities such as clocking-in/out, scheduling, pay, taxes, benefits, and more.

HR Systems & Technology Through the Decades

Like every type of system used in businesses, HR systems have evolved over time. We mentioned some of this evolution in Chapter 1, but here's a short summary focused on human resources over the past several decades:

1960s-1970s: We usually don't think of the 60's and 70's being supported by technology and systems. For human resources professionals, these two decades were filled with manual tasks and paperwork. As a matter of fact, the term "human resources" wasn't even used at this point. The current Society of Human Resources Management (SHRM) was called the American Society for Personnel Administration (ASPA.) People aspired to be "administrators," and being an effective Administrator was a noble and well-paid profession. Where technology *was* used, it

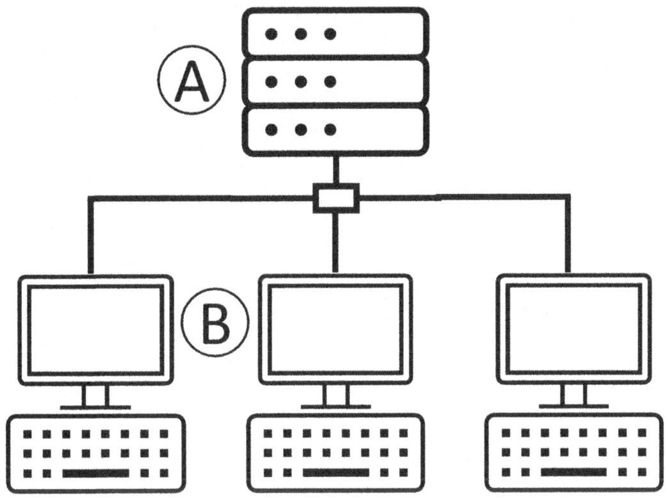

Figure 02.01
Mainframe Architecture
Simple depiction of mainframe computing architecture. A) The mainframe computer does all the processing for B) "dumb-terminals" which provide users a method of input and a display.

was deployed to automate operational record keeping and enable automated payroll processing. Payroll was the first area to receive systemic automation for human resources. Payroll then was often the responsibility of accounting, so payroll benefited from the technology investment that was being made on the financial side of businesses. Where these systems were deployed, they were predominately mainframe-based implementations. And they required significant technical expertise and monitoring to operate and maintain. Consequently, only the largest of companies were making this type of investment.

1980s: This decade was pivotal for the transition from mainframe to client-server computing. It was marked with several key technological milestones that set the stage for the decentralized architecture that we're familiar with today. Much of this was mentioned in Chapter 1. This is the decade where the competition between Apple and Microsoft really began, with the release of the Macintosh and the Personal Computer respectively. They weren't the only players though. Other significant innovations were brought to market by companies such as Sun Microsystems, Digital Equipment Corporation (DEC), Motorola, Intel, American Telephone and Telegraph (AT&T), Bell Laboratories, Novell, and Xerox. This budding technological movement occurred across all value chain and supply chain segments, and certainly included human resources (administration.) However, in the 80's much of this was still behind the scenes. The majority of the workforce was not actively using technology and systems on a daily basis. It's estimated that less than 20% of the workforce had regular use of computing systems and technology in the 1980's. (Not including office devices such as calculators and typewriters.)

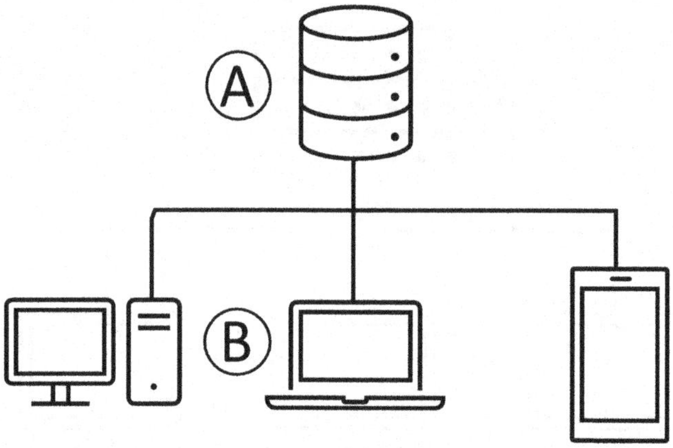

Figure 02.02
Client-Server Architecture

Simple depiction of client-server computing architecture. A) The server provides data, file storage, and application hosting for a variety of B) devices which have their own processing and storage capabilities.

Since the movement from the 70's to the 80's facilitated a shift from mainframe to client-server architecture, it's useful to provide a comparison of the differences between these architectural approaches. A **mainframe** architecture has a single/centralized computer. This mainframe computer is designed to optimize processing power, storage capacity, reliability, and security. See Figure 02.01. People use the mainframe computer through a terminal, often referred to as a "dumb-terminal." Effectively, the dumb-terminal provides the user interface such as a screen and keyboard. Everything else, including what's displayed on the screen and the processing of keystrokes on the keyboard was done centrally by the mainframe.

A **client-server** architecture distributes processing capabilities between client devices (e.g. desktop computers and laptops) and server devices (e.g. drive storage and server-hosted applications.) See Figure 02.02. In this architecture both the client devices and the server devices are "intelligent" and capable of processing. Servers are employed to host applications, manage data, and provide networking capabilities. See Table 02.01 below for a comparison of mainframe and client-server architectures.

Consideration	Mainframe	Client-Server
Architecture	Centralized computing	Distributed computing
Processing	Centralized processing	Distributed processing
Applications	Only centrally hosted applications	Mix of centrally hosted and client-run applications
Data Storage	All data is centrally stored	Mix of central and distributed storage
Security	Easier to maintain high levels of security – single point of risk	More difficult to maintain high levels of security – multiple points of risk
Costs	High initial implementation costs but lower costs on an on-going basis (compared to client-server)	Lower implementation costs, but higher costs on an on-going basis (compared to mainframe)

Table 02.01: Comparison of Mainframe and Client-Server

Early 1990's: The early 1990's was *very* different from the late 1990's. This decade needs to be split in half to better understand the evolution. The move toward client-server systems made them more affordable and accessible to smaller businesses. In the early 1990's, accessibility and affordability led to the advent of new people administration features, such as employee self-service, manager self-service, performance management, and learning management. Computing devices at both the client and server levels became prolific. These years arguably saw the most rapid technological shifts in known human history to date. For business systems, software design and more user-friendly interfaces brought systems into daily use. By the middle of the decade, the term "daily-use" was already an understatement. Businesses were dependent on systems and applications at this point. This period also saw the rapid deployment of the internet, and along with that came the trend of electronic mail as a primary means of communication.

Late 1990's: The early 90's were all about establishing availability of systems and technology. The late 90's were about exploiting its potential for business performance. This half of a decade saw a significant focus on application development in *every aspect* of running a business. This is where we see the first real introduction of systems that support human resources. HR was not alone though. The first customer relationship management (CRM) systems were launched during this time. The first salesforce automation systems were launched. Supply chain management was vastly expanded during this time. The end of the decade brought integrated Enterprise Resource Planning (ERP) systems. Today's leaders in the ERP space emerged during this time period.

2000's: This decade started with a panic, known as Y2K (the year 2000.) The concern around Y2K was date-related. Many, if not most, computing systems and applications had been built using two-digit date codes for the year. For example, "92" representing the year 1992. When the clock went from December 31, 99 to January 1, 00, what would the "00" be interpreted as by the system? Would our systems interpret "00" as 1900? Or, worse yet, would they interpret "00" as the beginning of time? What sort of calculation anomalies would manifest? Where would these anomalies be found? The fear was that Y2K would cause broad disruptions to infrastructure, global economies, and businesses. The problem was identified in the late 90's, and this caused a flurry of activity to make adjustments in systems and applications before Y2K arrived. This flurry of activity helped HR systems because one of the big areas of concern (in addition to operational continuity) was around continued and uninterrupted employment. The government and technology providers needed to ensure that the workforce could continue to function and get paid properly.

Heading into 2000, many business applications were improved. Then, it all slowed down....a lot. In 2001 many countries around the world went into an economic recession. While the recession cannot (yet) be blamed on Y2K, it can be clearly connected as a significant contributing factor. As a point of reference, in the United States at this time, it's estimated that technology related businesses comprised 10-15% of the Gross Domestic Product (GDP). In previous years (1960-1995ish,) the investment in technology, systems, equipment, and applications evolved slowly but consistently. Purchases were effectively distributed and randomized. In the few years leading up to Y2K (1995-2000) the vast majority of technology infrastructure was upgraded all at once around the world. This moved the technological economic activity from distributed and randomized to something that was synchronized. Because everyone had just upgraded at/around Y2K, there was going to be less of a need to buy technology/systems for a few years...until the technology components reached their end of life and needed to be refreshed. Think about your own devices: how often do you replace your computer? Around Y2K, a desktop computer had a lifespan of 2-4 years. Devices like servers had a lifespan of 4-7 years. With all these technology components being refreshed at one time, technology related spending plummeted in 2000-2001. Looking back, it's no surprise that many countries around the world experienced recession in 2001.

The United States officially declared a recession from March to November of 2001, as determined by the National Bureau of Economic Research (NBER.) The common experience of a recession was painful with job openings dropping 17% during the recession months. The labor market then stagnated for two years, 2002-2003. It didn't start to rebound until 2004. Here are some impacts around the world during this time period:

Europe – The Western European countries entered recession in 2002, after the United States. It is largely accepted that this was connected to the U.S. experience. The impact between countries varied. For example, Germany's recession was mild; whereas, the recessions in France and Italy were more pronounced.

Japan –Japan had been struggling economically for years leading up to Y2K; they were already in a recession. The technology issues around this time made their recession worse.

Argentina –Argentina experienced a deep economic crisis in 2001-2002. Some of which was connected to the recession that followed Y2K, but much of it was related to fiscal and trade policies. They experienced currency devaluation, high levels of inflation, and social unrest.

Mexico –Mexico had significant economic ties with the United States, especially in manufacturing and technology. As a result, they also experienced a recession in 2001, but their connection with the U.S. economy also allowed them to pull out of the recession much quicker than other Latin American countries.

These are just a few examples of the impact Y2K had around the world. There was about a 5-year lull in technology investment in the early 2000's. Granted, technology investment didn't disappear, but it did slow down. The drop in technology purchasing globally put a lot of pressure on the technology sector. Consequently, the recession drove consolidations among technology companies. Notable consolidations include the acquisition of Compaq by Hewlett-Packard, the acquisition of America Online (AOL) by Time Warner, and the blending of several semiconductor businesses. Overall, the economic downturn in technology put pressure on smaller technology companies and made them vulnerable. Today's ERP leaders, Oracle and SAP, both made significant acquisitions during this time:

Oracle: Acquired Peoplesoft in 2005, giving it a leading position in the human resources systems space. Peoplesoft also provided Oracle with CRM capabilities. A little later, in 2007, Oracle acquired Hyperion Solutions, giving them a solid place in business performance management and boosting the financial/accounting capabilities.

SAP: Made several acquisitions in the recession period. They acquired OutlookSoft in the United States which provided CRM capability. In Europe they acquired companies in the supply chain management (SCM) and business intelligence (BI) spaces. It was during the subsequent/next recession that they purchased SuccessFactors in 2012, launching them into a lead position with human resources capabilities.

2010 – Present: The rise of web-based systems/applications across business applications, including in the area of human resources. Web-based deployment enables many advantages over client-server and mainframe architectures, mostly driven by accessibility and scalability. These systems offer the convenience of accessing HR data and applications from anywhere with an internet connection. Also called cloud-based systems, these have become the "norm." We'll explore this further as we progress through the book.

HR systems and technology have come a long way from early manual approaches with paperwork and a focus on administration. Today's cloud-based solutions offer the human resources discipline a wide range of tools and capabilities. These provide task automation, efficiency improvements, workforce analytics, and a plethora of critical information which can enable effective decision making for a business.

Commonly Used Terminology

The evolution of systems and technology over the decades has provided us with an extensive lexicon of new words. We'll use this section to render definitions for the types of systems in the human resources discipline.

We'll start with the "older" term of **Human Resources Information System (HRIS.)** Because this term has been around the longest, it's common to hear HR professionals use this term for "everything technology" in HR. The term has its roots back in the 1960s and 1970s, when the focus was on automating manual HR tasks such as payroll processing and benefits administration. However, as we've already mentioned, the term "human resources" wasn't made popular until the mid-1990's. The three decades of the 1960's-1980's saw the use of systems terms such as: Personnel Information Systems (PIS), Personnel Management Information System (PMIS), and Computerized Personnel System (CPS.) We weren't short on acronyms. In the mid 1990's, and not disconnected from the rebranding of ASPA to SHRM, the term HRIS took hold, representing a bundling of personnel and administratively related capabilities. Effectively representing a collection of *information* related administrative *services*; hence the "I" in HRIS.

As we moved from the late 1990's to the early 2000's, the systems gained capabilities that took them beyond just information storage and retrieval. They were now being used to actively manage workflow and drive decision making. The technology providers chose to upgrade their branding of the systems, so they introduced a new term: **Human Resource Management Systems (HRMS).** HRMS's are a more comprehensive type of system that includes all of the features of a traditional HRIS system, plus additional capabilities such as talent management, applicant tracking, workforce planning, and analytics. The primary focus of an HRMS is the movement of work.

The term human capital has been used as a strategic organizational construct since the 1990's. Applying it to systems started later though, and it's difficult to pinpoint when. Somewhere around the 2010's and forward it came into common use, referring to **Human Capital Management (HCM)** systems. These are the most advanced type of HR system available to-date. They offer a holistic view of the employee lifecycle and provide tools to help businesses manage their human capital more strategically. HCM systems include all of the informational storage and retrieval functionality of an HRIS. HCM systems also include all of the workflow movement features of HRMS. HCM adds features and capabilities that further promote effective decision making and business intelligence such as succession planning, workforce analytics, organizational planning, and strategic alignment.

The terms HRIS, HRMS, and HCM have evolved over time reflecting iterative increases in sophistication and capabilities. You'll still hear these terms used interchangeably; however, they carry distinct and separate meanings in the technology sector.

Human Resources Information Systems (HRIS)

A human resources information system is a system that enables the storage and retrieval of key information used in the administration of tasks related to employees. In its truest definition, the word "system" refers to a combination of components such as: hardware, software, servers, devices, networks, and applications. HRIS can be implemented in either an on-premise or cloud-based environment.

HRIS systems typically include features such as:

- Employee database management: Storage and management of employee data, including contact information, job titles, salaries, and benefits information.
- Payroll processing: Facilitating the payroll process, including calculating taxes and deductions, and generating paychecks.
- Benefits administration: Managing employee benefits, such as health insurance, retirement savings plans, and paid time off. Also including the payroll deductions and adjustments associated with benefits elections.
- Time and attendance tracking: Tracking employee hours worked, clocking-in, clocking-out, and time taken for leaves of absence.
- Reporting: Generate reports on key administrative metrics, such as employee turnover, headcount, and compensation. Also sending key information to other system integrations such as a business' accounting system.

HRIS systems were, and still are, essential tools for businesses. While this type of HR system, when compared to HRMS and HCM, is the "lower-tier," it still fits the needs of many organizations. This is especially true for start-up's and small businesses. It is common for businesses to work their way through these tiers as they grow and mature, moving from HRIS, to HRMS, and then finally to HCM systems. HRIS can still help business and HR professionals improve efficiencies and productivity, reduce errors, and increase compliance. When choosing and implementing an HRIS, it is important to consider the needs of your organization and to get buy-in from all stakeholders.

Human Resources Management Systems (HRMS)

A Human Resources Management System (HRMS) is a more comprehensive HR system. In addition to the information storage and retrieval aspects of an HRIS, a HRMS facilitates the movement of workflow through an organization. The definition of the word "system" still applies and refers to a combination of components such as: hardware, software, servers, devices, networks, and applications. Likewise, HRMS' can be implemented in either an on-premise or cloud-based environment.

In addition to the HRIS capabilities, HRMS' typically include workflow related functionality such as:

- Applicant Tracking: Facilitating the recruiting process from start to finish, including requisitioning, approvals and approval routing, job posting, collecting applicants, dispositioning applicants, applicant information, interview progress tracking, hiring, and on-boarding.
- Performance Management: Facilitating the development of organizational goals, cascading and assignment of goals/objectives through the organization, capturing progress to plan throughout a performance period, measuring and reporting of progress, and input of performance appraisal data for compensation purposes.
- Compensation Management: Facilitating the definition of job families, grading structures, pay structures, application of differentials, application of incentive plans, annual compensation budgeting, compliance analytics, and approval routing.
- Benefits Management: Facilitating the definition of benefit plan designs, management of benefit funding models, tracking of claims experience data and reporting on budget impacts, employee self-service for enrollment and periodic changes to benefit selections, compliance tracking and reporting, and approval routing.

There are other areas of capability which would fall under the heading of HRMS such as Learning Management Systems (LMS.) During the timeframe when HRMS systems were prevalent in the marketplace, these other systems were also commonly viewed as standing apart from the human resources field. In the space of Human Capital Management, which we'll see next, these have since consolidated and come into the same purview. HRMS's are powerful tools that can help businesses improve workflow and processes. Workflow is the primary differentiator between HRMS and the preceding term HRIS. As such, HRMS strives to enable better business decisions, and improve the movement of work through an organization.

Human Capital Management (HCM)

Human Capital Management (HCM) is the latest terminology and to-date encompasses the broadest set of capability. A HCM system goes beyond the core features of an HRIS or HRMS and provides a holistic view of the employee lifecycle, from recruitment and onboarding to performance management and exit interviews. The primary focus of HCM systems is to facilitate the optimization of an organization's workforce as an investment to meet business goals. It culminates in decision making. At the same time, HCM systems fully include all capabilities of HRIS's and HRMS's.

In addition to the capabilities found in HRIS and HRMS's, HCM systems also include:

- Organizational Continuity: Evaluation of organizational structures, incumbent talent, and succession talent to identify continuity risks and make decisions about future talent moves.
- Talent Acquisition: Using data-rich selection tools to enable hiring decisions for organizational fit, job success, and organizational impact.

- Workforce Planning: Forecast workforce needs based on business plans, strategies, goals, and key performance indicators. Enable proactive decision making for talent sourcing strategies. Identify cost optimization opportunities based on historical and real-time data analytics.

Benefits of using an HCM system. HCM systems offer a number of benefits to businesses, including:

- Improved workforce performance: HCM systems can help businesses improve workforce performance by providing tools to manage talent, performance, and learning and development.
- Reduced costs: HCM systems can help businesses reduce costs by automating HR tasks and streamlining processes.
- Increased compliance: HCM systems can help businesses comply with complex labor laws and regulations.
- Improved employee engagement: HCM systems can help businesses improve employee engagement by providing tools to track and improve employee satisfaction and morale.
- Better decision-making: HCM systems provide businesses with access to valuable data and analytics, which can be used to make better decisions about workforce planning, strategy, and performance management.

HCM systems are the most powerful tools available to-date which help businesses optimize their workforce. They enable effective leadership decision making around performance, cost improvements, culture, and workforce planning. Since HCM systems bundle the most capabilities together, they also tend to be the highest investment. In the right application they can also pay off by helping businesses build a more productive and proactive workforce.

Technology Providers Along the Way

Here is a brief summary of some of the more significant technology providers through the past several decades:

1960s-1970s

- International Business Machines (IBM): IBM was one of the first companies to develop business systems, and its mainframe computers were used by many large businesses to automate payroll and other workforce tasks.
- National Cash Register (NCR): NCR was another early pioneer of personnel and administrative systems, and its products were popular with smaller businesses. These were referred to as Personnel Information Systems (PIS) and later Personnel Management Information Systems (PMIS). NCR was acquired by AT&T in the early 1990s.

- Automatic Data Processing (ADP): ADP was founded in 1949, and it quickly became a leading provider of payroll and other workforce services. Their systems, and business model, have focused on being an outsourced provider. (More on this later in the book.)

1980s-1990s

- PeopleSoft: PeopleSoft was founded in 1987, and it is credited with developing the first commercial HR management system (HRMS). PeopleSoft's HRMS was a breakthrough because it was based on client-server architecture, which made it more affordable and accessible to smaller businesses. (Acquired by Oracle in 2004.)
- Systems, Applications, & People (SAP): SAP is a German software company that was founded in 1972. SAP is best known for its ERP software and has developed a lot of its own capabilities through the years, moving from HRIS to HRMS, and into HCM.
- Oracle: Oracle is a multinational software company that was founded in 1977. Through the 90's, Oracle was focused on business operations and financials.

2000s-Present

- Oracle/Peoplesoft: Through its acquisition of Peoplesoft in 2004, Oracle completed a large part of its ERP capability set. Oracle also acquired the company Taleo in 2012, which provided it with applicant tracking capability. To-date, Oracle has made significant investments streamlining and integrating its suite of products into a common architecture with consistent user experience.
- SAP/SuccessFactors: Similarly, SAP acquired SuccessFactors in 2012, which completed a large part of its ERP capability set. SuccessFactors was a full HRMS suite, including applicant tracking, which initially gave SAP an edge over Oracle in terms of user experience.
- Workday: Workday came on the scene in 2005. The timing is no coincidence, one year after Oracle bought Peoplesoft. The founder of Workday was also the founder of PeopleSoft. When Oracle purchased Peoplesoft, he decided to start a new company focused specifically on Human Capital Management. What made Workday unique in the systems space was its technology architecture, built brand new...not "stitched" together through application interfaces and acquisitions. Workday was built for a cloud-based distributed computing world. This allowed for speed of processing, easy customization, lower price-points, and a unified data model across various user groups. The plan was to build out full ERP capabilities on this new architectural model, and they've been making steady progress since.

These are just a few of the many companies that have played a role in the evolution of business and workforce systems over the years. HR systems have become increasingly sophisticated, but at the same time there are many options available to businesses. Businesses can still acquire HRIS-only systems, or HRMS systems, or step all the way up to HCM systems. There continue to be options for on-premise implementations for those organizations who need to ensure a high level of control over access and security. The industry overall has moved rapidly to cloud-based and Software-As-A-Service (SAAS) models (more on this as we go forward in the book.) Today's HR systems play a vital role helping organizations manage their workforce and operate their businesses. The top-tier systems are revolutionizing business decision making.

Summary

Human resources (HR) systems and technology have evolved significantly over the past few decades. From early manual systems to today's sophisticated cloud-based solutions, HR technology has transformed the way we all work. HR systems and technology have become essential tools for businesses of all sizes. They can help businesses improve efficiency and productivity, reduce errors, increase compliance, and make better decisions. As technology continues to evolve, we can expect to see even more innovative and sophisticated systems emerge in the future.

Discussion Questions

What do you think are the future trends in HR systems and technology?

Why might a small business choose an HRIS versus a HCM system?

What's the primary difference between HRIS and HRMS?

What was the impact of Y2K on system adoption and progress in the early 2000's?

What was the global impact of the recession of 2001-2002?

Chapter References

Bard, Google AI. (2023). History of HR Systems and Technology. Bard, Google AI. Accessed October 25, 2023.

Bhuiyan, F., Chowdhury, M. M., & Ferdous, F. (2014). *Historical evolution of human resource information system (HRIS): An interface between HR and computer technology.* Human Resource Management Research, 4(4), 75-80.

Fowinkel. (2014). *Human resource management systems in new business creation : an exploratory study.* Springer Gabler. https://doi.org/10.1007/978-3-658-05982-8

Porancea-Răulea, A.S., & Cofaru, N.F. (2021). *The need and implications of the human capital management system.* MATEC Web of Conferences, 343, 5004–. https://doi.org/10.1051/matecconf/202134305004

Valcik, N.A., Sabharwal, M., & Benavides, T. J. (2021). *The History and Evolution of HRIS. In Human Resources Information Systems* (pp. 19–32). Springer International Publishing AG. https://doi.org/10.1007/978-3-030-75111-1_2

Vladimir, Yulia, Tatyana, Aleksandra, & Veronika. (2017). *Formation of Human Resource Management System in Organizations. European Research Studies, XX*(Issue 3A), 408–421. https://doi.org/10.35808/ersj/712

Chapter 3
Requirements Gathering & System Sizing

Chapter Table of Contents

Chapter 3: Requirements Gathering & System Sizing

Introduction

HCM systems are business systems, and in many cases are part of a larger Enterprise Resource Planning (ERP) system suite. In business systems, the first step in any project is to gather requirements. The business' requirements drive system sizing and selection. It's essential to understand what the system needs to provide so the business can meet its strategic and operational needs. Therefore, requirements gathering is conducted from the perspective of stakeholders. In this chapter, we'll explore the process of requirements gathering and how it impacts system sizing.

Why Requirements Gathering is Important

Requirements gathering identifies and defines the needs of different business groups, ensuring the system aligns with both operational and strategic goals. It is fundamental to successful system implementation. See Figure 3.1 for the following explanation.

Here's why requirements gathering is so important:

1. Requirements gathering ensures that *the system does what the business needs*. It might sound simple, and a bit repetitive at this point, but it's vitally important to align system

capabilities with the necessary usage needs of the stakeholders. On one end, it helps prevent buying features that nobody uses. On the other end, it ensures that key operating features aren't missing which are needed.

> One of the businesses where I fulfilled the HR leadership role had a problem with requirements gathering and their system selection. In the first two weeks on the job, I heard it loud and clear from the Board of Directors, the Chief Financial Officer (CFO), and the Chief Operations Officer (COO.) (Think Stakeholders.) The feedback went something like this, "We just spent over $250,000 on a HR system to do performance reviews, and we still can't pay people properly...we're filling out paper timecards. We thought that was going to be fixed, but it wasn't."
>
> My predecessor had gotten budget approval and sourced a system without doing any formal requirements gathering. The stakeholders weren't involved in the process. Unfortunately, the system that was purchased was completely out of alignment with the business' needs, and we ended up ripping it out and going through a new selection process. By skipping the requirements gathering the company spent twice the time, plus lost-opportunity, plus extra expense. They were both happy and upset to find out that the system they *needed* was only $50K to implement, with a much lower cost. They were happy that it was cheaper, and they were upset that they wasted resources and time.

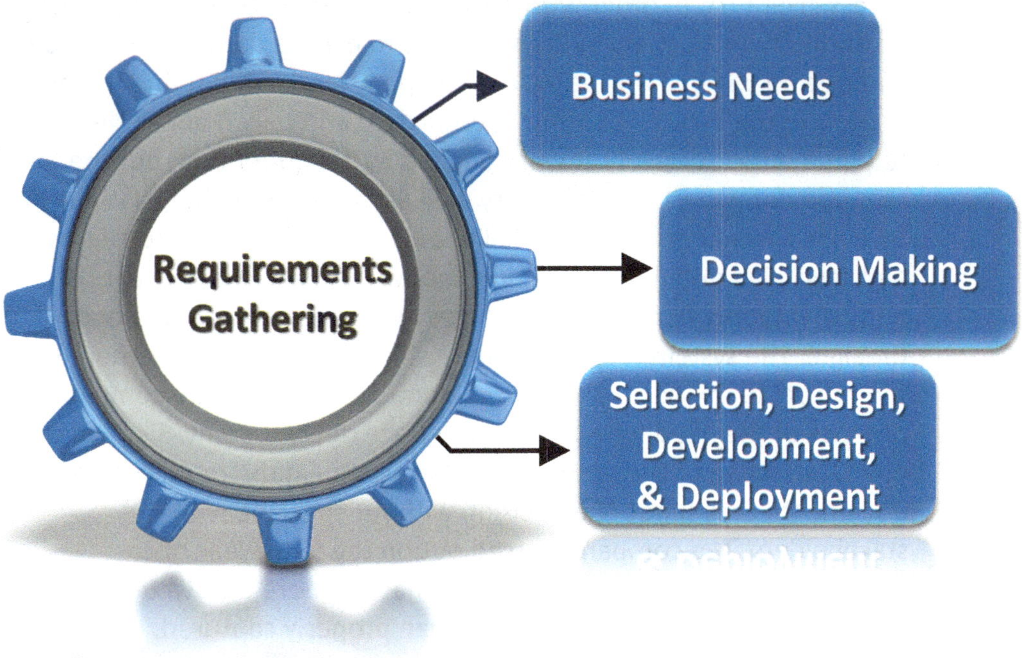

Figure 03.01
Why Requirement Gathering is Important
Requirements gathering drives three essential areas which ensure that the system aligns with business goals, both operationally and strategically.

2. Requirements gathering *enables better decision-making*. There will be choices to make along the way. When doing *selection*, common choices are around things like features, work processes, integrations, and deployment methods. When *implementing*, common choices are around things like project timeline, people resources, testing, and training. The requirements are (should be) consistently checked and verified all the way through the project to ensure that they're being met. Where trade-offs need to be made, stakeholders should be consulted to ensure that key operational requirements aren't being sacrificed which would put the business at-risk.

> I've been part of several Enterprise Resource Planning (ERP) system projects in my career. For one of them, we had a critical business requirement to achieve inventory visibility across different subsidiaries. We had spent several years making a few strategic acquisitions. These gave the company better product breadth and increased market share. During the acquisitions, the operations team identified thousands of parts where we had duplication in inventory. Each subsidiary had their own ERP system, and within each ERP system the parts were all numbered and labeled differently. It was difficult to understand how much of each part we had in inventory and even more difficult to manage the stocking costs. Operations estimated that this was costing the business $3M a year in

excess inventory. In other words, part of the return on investment (ROI) justification for the new ERP system was to extract the inventory expense and free up $3M/year in cash. The company leadership team, the project team, and the system integrator researched and talked about this requirement extensively. It was included as a requirement, but the requirement wasn't captured very well. It said something too vague like, "provide raw material parts visibility across company warehouses by unit and cost." The original project timeline was 2 years. After 3 years of implementation work, the project was overrunning its budget and timeline. The system integrator and system provider, in agreement with the project team, decided to exclude one of the subsidiary companies because of the need for extensive interface development. Since there was no ROI attached to the requirement (as written in the requirements document,) they made the decision without checking with the stakeholders. The company missed out on the $3M/year of cost reductions because the exclusion eliminated where that value was coming from. Had the requirement been properly captured, the decision would have been escalated.

3. Requirements gathering informs selection, design, development, and deployment. It is the watershed of everything that follows in a system implementation.
    a. In selection, clearly defined requirements are used to evaluate options, different system providers, approaches, and more.
    b. In design, clearly defined requirements are used to evaluate system features, functions, and the user experience.
    c. In development, clearly defined requirements are used to roadmap and plan the system build and prioritize work streams.
    d. In deployment, clearly defined requirements are used to manage stakeholder expectations, drive user adoption, and measure success.

Effective requirements gathering is crucial for the success of a project because it minimizes misunderstandings, reduces the risk of scope creep, and ensures that the end product or system aligns with the needs and expectations of the stakeholders.

Why System Sizing & Scalability are Important

The terms "sizing" and "scalability" are often used interchangeably; however, they mean different things. System **sizing** refers to selecting a system which fits the needs of the business. System **scalability** refers to the ability of the system to grow and change over time, so it continues to meet the needs of the business as it evolves. These definitions are simple to state but *doing them well* is a challenge. It's challenging because one must fully understand the business requirements of today, along with being able to accurately predict future requirements. Ideally, the system selected should fit today's needs and then scale-up with the business as it grows, optimizing price and functionality along the way.

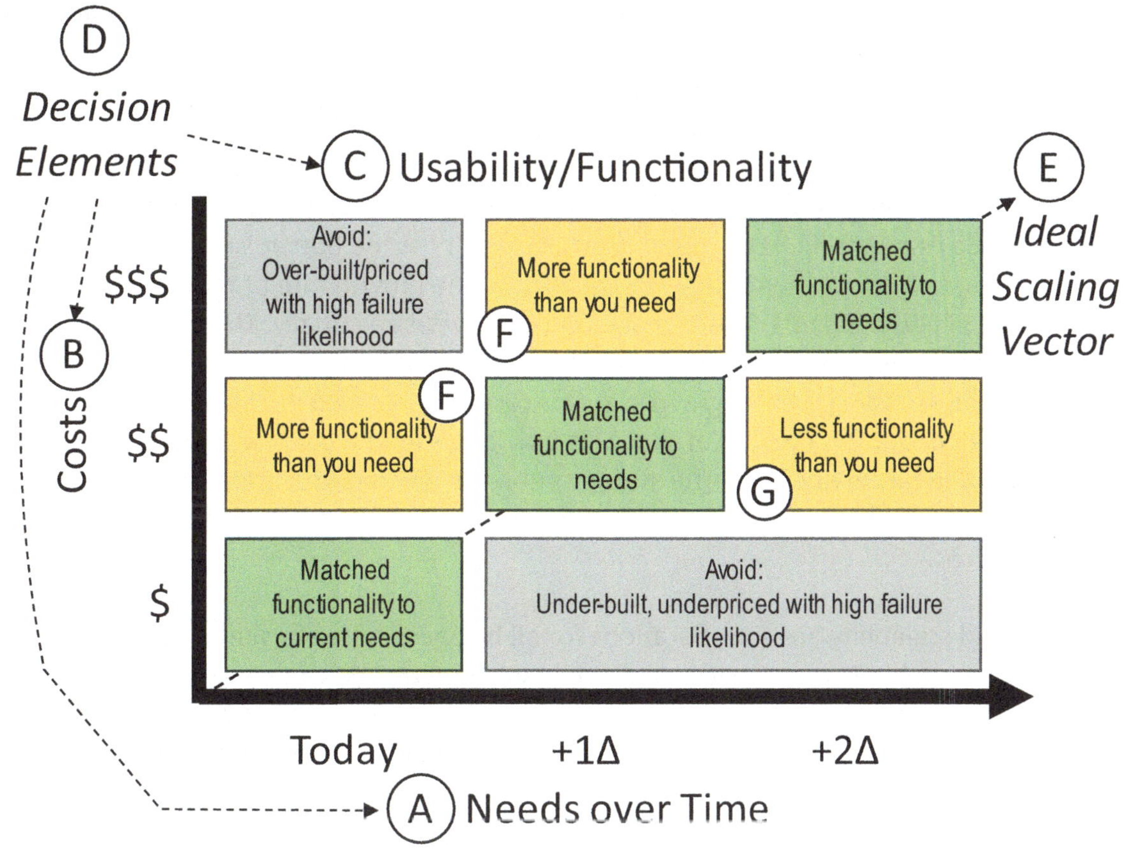

Figure 03.02
Why Sizing & Scalability are Important
Depicts the three primary decision elements, ideal scaling vector, and the usability and functionality differences associated with decision variances.

Refer to Figure 3.2. The horizontal axis (A) is time, and it starts with "today" and then represents the future at two incremental points. The increments are represented by a delta (Δ) symbol. This is the first challenge for a business: predicting their own growth. What needs to be estimated is when they expect milestones to be achieved, which in turn will warrant increases in system functionality.

The vertical axis (B) is cost, which is represented by dollar ($) signs. One $-sign being the least cost; two $$-signs being medium incremental cost; and three $$$-signs being significant incremental cost. It is reasonable to expect that increasing system functionality and usability (C) will require additional cost. The second challenge for a business is to incur the incremental cost only at a point in time where it aligns with needs. This is the (E) ideal scaling vector.

Time (A), Cost (B), and Usability/Functionality (C), become the decision elements (D) that the business must balance. Done well, the ideal scaling vector (E) is achieved. In practical language, this means:

1. The system that was initially purchased fits (sizing) the company's needs at the point of implementation.
2. As the company grows and its needs change, they are able to add capability (scale) and pay an incremental cost that makes sense.

There are alternative paths that can be taken. A company may choose to buy additional capability for today's needs (F). Having additional capability at the outset isn't necessarily a bad thing. In some cases it can be beneficial. For instance, if the growth rate of the company is such that the delta (Δ) in time is short, it may make sense to over-size initially. This can avoid additional system changes in short duration. Another option might be (G,) where the company wants to hedge its spending and lag growth. In this case, they end up with less functionality than what's needed, but for a period of time this may be desirable compared to the incremental capital and operational expenditure. The strong cautionary segments are the boxes in gray. Dramatically over or under building a system often introduces a high risk of failure and a waste of capital resources.

> Sizing and scalability are considerations for all business systems. When I started a role as head of human resources and risk management, the company had in place a separate system for performance management. The system they used for financials and core HR didn't have the ability to do performance management. As it was described to me, it made sense to buy a stand-alone system and the system had been in place for almost two years when I arrived. The performance management system was produced by a well-known company, and you would recognize the name today...except that I don't want to single them out. It had a tremendous amount of capability. We had over 1,000 employees. When I looked at the completion numbers, only 3 employees had used the performance management system. Yes, you read that right: three employees! The reason? They had purchased one of the best performance management systems on the market, which means it was in that first gray box on Figure 03.02. It was way over-built and way over-priced for what the company needed. Now that you've looked at the chart in the figure, you can see what the result was: the gray box in Figure 03.02I – over-built and over-priced with high failure likelihood.

Understanding Business Needs through Requirements Gathering

Requirements gathering is an <u>*essential*</u> process for understanding business needs. If you skip formal requirements gathering, you risk over or under sizing a system and putting your company in a position where the system won't perform effectively. Furthermore, system implementation and testing are driven by the requirements.

What is requirements gathering? **Requirements gathering** is a systematic process of collecting, documenting, and negotiating the needs of an organization relative to the functionality of a system. To perform requirements gathering requires active participation of a complete set of stakeholders.

The primary *outcome* of requirements gathering is ensuring that all stakeholders understand what the system **should do** and how it **should function**. An equally important *outcome* is that all stakeholders also understand what the system *will not do* and how it *will not function*...in other words what will be omitted as part of the selection.

The requirements gathering process involves several key activities. These can include:

- **Interviews** are a great place to start. Many stakeholders will have strong opinions about what a system needs to be able to do, and providing a one-on-one opportunity to express these opinions can make future group work more productive. It gives each individual stakeholder a "voice" and a focused opportunity to capture their input about business needs, preferences, and expectations.
- **Focus Groups** allow for open-ended discussions and encourage participants to share their experiences. They are experience-rich group discussions. They also enable a larger number of people to participate in the requirements gathering process; therefore, they help generate additional buy-in around the system specifications.
- **Surveys and Questionnaires** are used to gather information from a broader number of people in the organization. They're easy and cost-effective to deploy, so they enable a large data capture very quickly. The anonymity provided by surveys and questionnaires helps to generate more honest and transparent responses.
- **Direct Observation** of users in their natural work environment is an exceptional method for gaining unique and value insights. Sometimes what users *say* and what they *do* differs. Observing their day-to-day activities in the performance of the job can reveal preferences, unwritten processes, pain points, and contextual understanding. Of all the requirement gathering activities, this is one of more resource-intensive approaches.
- In some cases, **Document Analysis** can be used to derive requirements. This activity is useful when an organization 1) has work processes written *and* 2) the organization legitimately follows those written processes. It is uncommon for both conditions to be true. It's far more common that work processes were documented at a point in the past, but current work varies from the written documents. This is still an insightful activity to gather requirements, because it can often tell you a lot about what's intended versus what's followed.
- **Design Workshops** are another excellent collaboration technique, which allows stakeholders, clients, and users to explore system needs from a user-centered perspective. These take a lot of planning, but they can be highly illustrative for ideation, and refining requirements.
- **Use Cases** can flow out of several of the preceding requirements gather activities, especially the design workshops. A "use case" is a specific scenario that describes how a user interacts with a system to complete a work activity. These can be insightful and are often developed around commonly performed work activities.
- **User Stories** capture information from a particular user's point of view. They focus on the totality of what the user needs to accomplish, thereby informing requirements.

Once requirements are gathered, they are documented in a clear and structured format. This document often becomes the basis for a Request-For-Proposal (RFP) as part of a Bid & Quote process for system providers. The requirements document serves as a reference for all project stakeholders and forms the basis for subsequent phases of the project, such as system design, development, testing, and project management. A sample outline of a requirements document might look like this:

I. Introduction
    a. Project Overview: Describes the company and its objectives with the system project.
    b. Document Purpose: Explains the intended audience for the requirements document and how the document describes the system needs.
    c. Definitions and Acronyms: Captures company definitions and acronyms that have developed around unique workflow and activities.

II. Business Requirements and Scope
    a. Business Needs: Outlines the business problems and opportunities to be solved through a system acquisition.
    b. Business Goals: Articulates what the organization desires to accomplish through a new system acquisition.
    c. System Scope: Defines in broad terms the boundaries of the system project.
    d. Success Criteria: Directly related to the goals and scope, this section establishes criteria by which success will be measured for project completion.

III. User Requirements
    a. User Personas: Describes the user groups and their characteristics, needs, and key work processes.
    b. User Stories: Describes user needs and goals in a user-centric point of view around work product.
    c. Use Cases: Describes scenarios of how users interact with the system to achieve their work outputs.
    d. Functional Requirements: Lists all essential functions that the system needs to perform to meet user workflow and activities.

IV. System Requirements
    a. Technical Architecture: Describes the overall architecture of the system needed. It's more extensive in on-premise implementations vs. cloud implementations.
    b. Hardware and Software: Specifies any unique hardware and software needs of the business. It can also describe unique environmental context within which equipment will be used.
    c. Data Requirements: Defines the data the system will use, store, and process. It's an integral part of the next section.
    d. Security Requirements: Outlines security measures and access controls for the system. This includes data security.

   e. Interface Requirements: Vitally important, this section describes any system interfaces that will be required for the new system to connect with other existing systems that the organization has in place.

V. Implementation and Testing
   a. Project Phases: Describes the desired project rollout phases.
   b. Testing Strategy: Explains the approach that the company will use to test the system and its functionality.
   c. Acceptance Criteria: Defines how the company will conclude that the system is ready to accept such that it meets the requirements specified.

Who Does the Requirements Gathering

The smaller the business the more likely it is that internal staff will be conducting requirements gathering. The larger the business the more likely it is that an external/third party will conduct the requirements gathering.

Internally Conducted:
Having internal employees conduct requirements gathering can generate valuable insights. However, there are some nuances and factors to keep in mind.

Pros:

- Employees often have the best and deepest expertise in the business. They're intimately familiar with the work and how it is performed.
- When employees conduct requirements gathering, they automatically have a strong sense of ownership and a vested interest in seeing the project succeed.
- Having internal resources perform the requirements gathering is the most cost-effective way to complete it.

Cons:

- While employees have the best and deepest expertise in the business, they are also conditioned to do the work a certain way. This presents bias and blind spots. They may not be able to see that there are other/more effective ways to get the work done.
- Since a new system is being considered, existing employees may not have the technical expertise to fully understand both limitations and capabilities. (They don't know what they don't know.)
- Dedicating the time of internal employees to do an effective job of requirements gathering may not be possible. They have day-to-day work that needs to be completed, and it is highly likely (almost guaranteed) that they're already fully loaded or even over-loaded.

Externally Conducted:

Having an external/third party conduct the requirements gathering mitigates all of the cons listed above from an internal perspective. There are two variations to external resources that are commonly used.

Systems Integrator:

A systems integrator is a company that provides services combining hardware, software, applications, and networking into solutions for companies. They work as a "go-between" for providers and end-customers/companies. Hence the word "integrator." They act as a translator and connector between technology and business, ensuring that all the various components work together to enable production. When a company embarks upon a systems change, it's very common to first contract with a systems integrator who will be their advocate through the entire process. This starts with requirements gathering and goes all the way through implementation and acceptance testing.

Pros:

- Using the same integrator through the entire process provides the company with continuity and efficiencies. Often this means that the same people are involved through the entirety of the project.
- Having an experienced advocate working on your behalf reduces anxiety and resistance, generating more trust and buy-in through the project lifecycle.

Cons:

- Often systems integrators are experienced with a limited set of providers. This generates a bias where the integrator may prescribe a provider based on their own familiarity versus what the company really needs. This bias sub-optimizes the project and risks pushing the system outside of the optimal scaling vector described in Figure 03.02.
- System integrators can be compensated by providers using various mechanisms like revenue-sharing and commissions. This presents an addition bias in the form of a conflict of interest and may exacerbate the previous con.

Neutral 3rd Party:

This approach is used to mitigate the biases that are generated by using a systems integrator throughout the entire project. In this situation, the front-end process of 1) gathering requirements, and 2) system selection is performed by a neutral third party who is solely and exclusively contracted with the company. This neutral third party may still be a systems integrator, but in this case the neutral third-party integrator is aware up-front that they will not be part of the selection decision or able to work on the implementation.

Pros:

- This neutral 3rd party is fully an agent of the company and exclusively represents the company's interests.

- Ensures the broadest view of potential providers.
- Ensures a fair evaluation of providers against company requirements.

Cons:

- Requires the selection of another systems integrator for the implementation.
- Requires additional contracting and is likely more expensive. Since the neutral third party is not privy to revenue-sharing or commissions by the providers, they will need to charge a fee to the company that fully funds their work.
- Requires additional time for training and team development.

Evaluating a Requirements List

Prior to moving forward and using a requirements document to evaluate system providers, it's beneficial to allow the stakeholders a "final review." One technique that's beneficial is to ask the stakeholders to evaluate and score the requirements document (as a whole.) In other words, not allowing an item-by-item review, but rather asking them to interpret the composite document and whether it reflects the negotiations and choices made along the way. The following is a list of criteria in a format that *could* be constructed as a worksheet and used for scoring. The questions and scales should be adjusted to fit the needs of the organization. By accurately reflecting the business needs, the requirements document ensures that the selected system will enable the achievement of the organization's **strategic objectives**.

How well do the requirements enable our **strategic objectives** in the *near-term*?

1	2	3	4	5	6	7	8	9
Not at all		Minimally		Moderately		Significantly		Perfectly

How well do the requirements align with our *immediate* **business needs**?

1	2	3	4	5	6	7	8	9
Not at all		Minimally		Moderately		Significantly		Perfectly

How well do the requirements enable our **strategic objectives** in the *future*?

1	2	3	4	5	6	7	8	9
Not at all		Minimally		Moderately		Significantly		Perfectly

How well do the requirements align with our *forecasted* **business needs**?

1	2	3	4	5	6	7	8	9
Not at all		Minimally		Moderately		Significantly		Perfectly

Proper identification and definition of business needs allows the project to address pain points and bottlenecks in the current workflow. The right system selection will streamline operations, increase **efficiency**, and boost **productivity** in the near-term and in the future.

Given the requirements identified, what level of *improvement* do you expect in **workflow**?

1	2	3	4	5	6	7	8	9
None		Slight		Moderate		Significant		Perfect

Given the requirements identified, what level of **cost efficiency** *improvements* do you expect?

1	2	3	4	5	6	7	8	9
None		Slight		Moderate		Significant		Perfect

User acceptance and adoption are critical to system success. Polling the stakeholders about representation while constructing the requirement document is important.

How thorough have we been, ensuring that we have the **right stakeholders** involved in the requirements gathering?

1	2	3	4	5	6	7	8	9
Not at all		Minimally		Moderately		Significantly		Perfectly

Have we *missed* any critical **stakeholders**?

_______________ Yes _______________ No

If "yes," who have we missed and how should we contact them?

Name/Title	Contact Information

If we select a system that meets these requirements, what level of **user acceptance** do you think we will experience?

1	2	3	4	5	6	7	8	9
None		Minimal		Moderate		Significant		Complete

The document should clearly identify which **requirements** are **priorities** for the organization. **Prioritization** allows potential system suppliers to respond based on their importance to the business. Not all features are equally critical, and understanding the requirements prioritization helps system providers focus on what matters most.

How well does the document prioritize requirements to our organization's strategic and operational needs?

1	2	3	4	5	6	7	8	9
Not at all		Minimally		Moderately		Significantly		Perfectly

Are there any **requirements** which you believe should have an *increased* importance?

________________ Yes ________________ No

If so, which ones and why?

Requirement Needing an *Increase*	Why?

Are there any **requirements** which you believe should have a *decreased* importance?

________________ Yes ________________ No

If so, which ones and why?

Requirement Needing a *Decrease*	Why?

The requirements document should reflect the organization's data-driven **decision-making** needs. When the specific data and reporting needs of the business are well represented, the system selection process will be smoother, ensuring that the chosen provider can generate the needed **analytics** and **reporting** capabilities.

How well do the **requirements** reflect our *near-term reporting and analytics needs*?

1	2	3	4	5	6	7	8	9
Not at all		Minimally		Moderately		Significantly		Perfectly

When we select a system that meets these requirements, how confident are you that the system will meet our **data-driven decision-making needs** in the *near-term*?

1	2	3	4	5	6	7	8	9
Not at all		Minimally		Moderately		Significantly		Perfectly

How well do the **requirements** reflect our *future* reporting and analytics needs?

1	2	3	4	5	6	7	8	9
Not at all		Minimally		Moderately		Significantly		Perfectly

When we select a system that meets these requirements, how confident are you that the system will meet our **data-driven decision-making needs** in the *future*?

1	2	3	4	5	6	7	8	9
Not at all		Minimally		Moderately		Significantly		Perfectly

Understanding business needs is the foundation of selecting the right system solution. It ensures that the chosen system not only meets the immediate requirements but also supports the organization's growth and strategic direction. Starting with a clear understanding of business needs sets the stage for a successful and effective system selection process.

Which timeframes for future-needs are represented in the requirements document?

☐ 0-2 years	☐ 2-4 years	☐ 4-6 years	☐ 6-8 years	☐ 8-10 years

Select all that apply

Would you make any changes to the future timeframes?

________________ Yes ________________ No

If so, what changes would you suggest and why?

Timeframe Changes	Why?

How would these changes impact the requirements identified?

Requirements Impacted

How well do the future requirements align with our forecasted business changes?

1 Not at all	2	3 Minimally	4	5 Moderately	6	7 Significantly	8	9 Perfectly

By conducting an evaluation of the requirements, you can gain a comprehensive understanding of the stakeholders' views of the organization's needs compared to what's specified in the document. The resultant outcome serves as a solid foundation for the next step, vendor evaluation and selection.

Vendor Evaluation & Selection

This is where the process moves from planning to sourcing. Vendor evaluation and selection is the process of identifying, assessing, and choosing a supplier of the system. This process is critical for businesses to make informed decisions about which supplier to engage with, whether it involves software, hardware, services, or any other business services. Where system integrators are used to create the requirements document, they often continue through this part of the process.

There are two key documents used in this part of the process: Request For Information (RFI) and a Request for Proposal (RFP). Both documents are created from the requirements gathering. These are commonly used across disciplines. Professionals in the following areas will be familiar with them: sourcing, supply chain management, program/project management, and information technology.

A Request For Information (RFI) is often completed earlier, and it can be completed before the requirements gathering phase is finished. Doing so allows the project team to start collecting information about potential suppliers, their capabilities, and their willingness to participate in the selection process. **The purpose of an RFI is to explore potential suppliers.** It typically asks broad questions about supplier capabilities, experience, products, features, functionality, differentiation, architecture models, and pricing frameworks.

From the responses gathered with the RFI, and after requirements are completed, the Request For Proposal (RFP) can be generated. A preliminary "short-list" of suppliers are invited to respond to the RFP. As part of the RFI, it is common for the project team to invite potential suppliers to present to the organization. Since this is a preliminary stage, this is often referred to as a "vendor screening." The project team will consider factors such as reputation, financial stability, technology roadmap, and high-level usability.

A response to a Request for Proposal (RFP) is a formal application by a supplier to be considered by the company. As it's name implies, the **purpose of an RFP is to solicit proposals for the project**. RFP's are informed by the requirements gathering. They define project methodology, potential technology solutions, preliminary project timeline, migration and scaling possibilities, and the qualifications of the supplier. The output of this stage of the process is to select the supplier and system that will be used to meet the business' needs. From here the process goes into contracting.

As part of the RFP, it is common (almost essential) for the project team to invite bidding suppliers to come back and present to the organization again. In this stage, the potential suppliers are focused on system demonstrations. The suppliers will walk the organization's stakeholders through several of the prioritized requirements and workflows. This allows the stakeholders to visibly see how the systems vary in their design approaches. Demonstrations may occur in multiple successive rounds, where the organization can go deeper at each round. It is during these rounds that the organization's project team evaluates each potential supplier against all the requirements that were previously gathered. The outcome of this state of the process is a decision about which supplier will be selected.

As the process progresses through selection and contracting, it's common for organizations to use a sub-step where the suppliers compete for the contract award. This is possible when there are multiple potential suppliers who can meet the organization's requirements. When this occurs, it's beneficial for the organization to use this sub-step to optimize the costs of the system. This is where several parties engage in the negotiations process, including the project team, key stakeholders, legal, suppliers, and potentially the systems integrator. The negotiations establish terms, pricing, service level agreements (SLAs), and any customizations or modifications required.

The vendor evaluation and selection process drives critical business decisions. The chosen system is a multi-year commitment, and in many cases a multi-decade commitment. The relationship between the organization and the supplier significantly impacts the success of a project, the quality of the product, and scope of services delivered. The relationship, along with the systems and technology, should last for many years and help enable the organization's growth. Selecting the right vendor requires a thorough and systematic approach to ensure mutual alignment and maximum value for the investment.

Cost Considerations

Cost considerations are a critical piece in the supplier evaluation and selection process. It's so important, that it's worth calling out as its own section in this chapter. One of the very first considerations, see Figure 03.03, is around capital expenditures (CapEx) versus operational expenditures (OpEx). Astute finance and accounting professionals determine how much of the system costs can be capitalized. There are specific rules, regulations, and requirements by country which govern the capex and opex treatment. Nothing in this book should be regarded as tax, accounting, or legal advice; seek professional, certified, and licensed advice in each of these areas. These are some of the potential advantages to being able to capitalize costs:

- Spreading Expenses over Time: Capitalizing enables organizations to spread the costs over a system's useful lifespan. This aligns the realization of expenses during time periods where the system generates economic benefits for the organization. Part of the advantage can also include special tax treatment. For example, an organization may be able to depreciate its capital assets resulting in deductions that can reduce taxable income.
- Financial Statements: Being able to spread expenses over time improves an organization's financial statements. If they were not able to spread the costs over time, their financial statements would reflect large OpEx expenditures in the first year or two

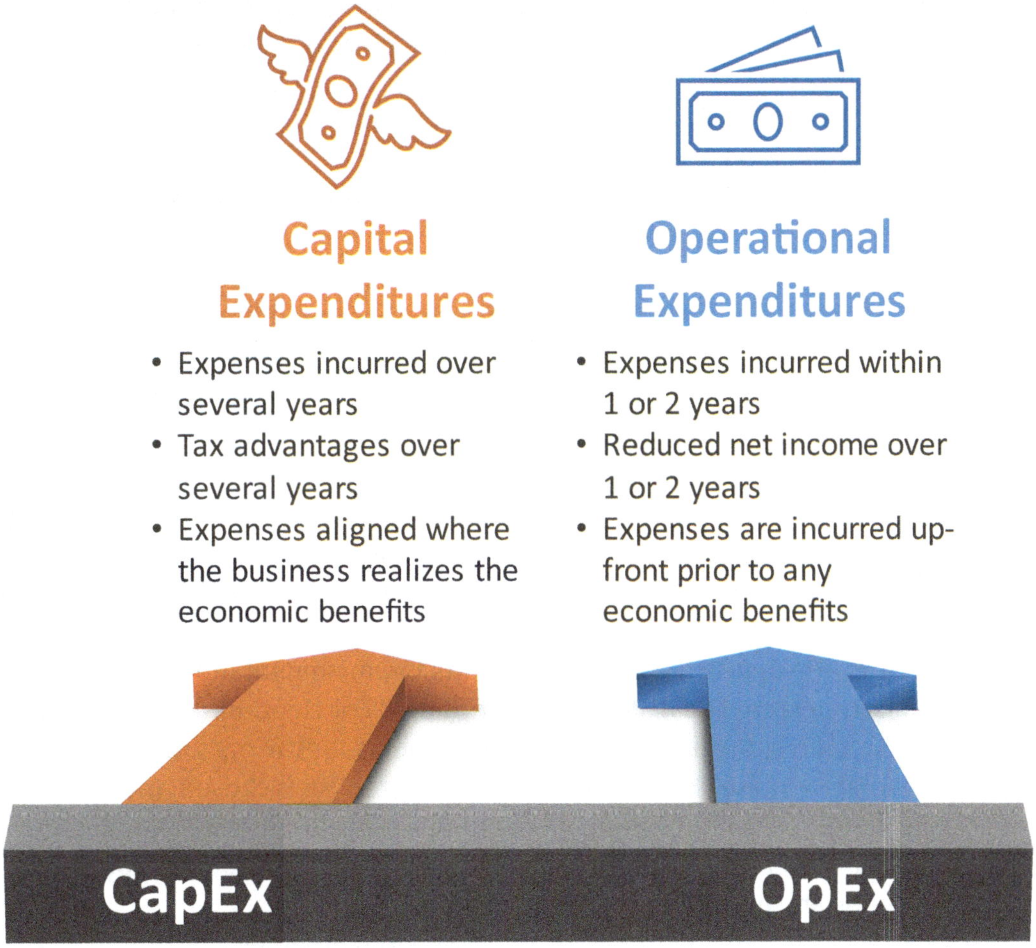

Figure 03.03
CapEx vs. OpEx

The advantages and disadvantages of cost treatment through capital expenditure versus operational expenditure.

when the system was being implemented. This could dramatically reduce net income and the creditworthiness of the organization. A couple other financial metrics impacted would include Return on Assets (ROA,) and Return on Equity (ROE.)

Implementation Costs

These costs span from supplier selection through to the point where the new system is operational and being used by the organization. These initial costs span a wide range of considerations, not all of which are intuitively obvious. These include:

- **Licensing**: Most software systems are purchased on a license basis. There are various licensing models available such as per user, per employee, usage volume, and simultaneous use. Understanding and choosing the most cost-effective licensing model is crucial. Here's a short description of each:

  - **Per User:** The company is charged for every active user that has a login to the system. In some cases, the number and levels of users have different pricing. In some organizations, not every employee requires a login to the system. When this is the case, per user licensing may have cost advantages compared to some of the other models.
  - **Per Employee:** The company is charged for every active employee headcount regardless of usage. This has become more common with the advent of employee self-service. For employee self-service to function, every employee needs to be licensed. When this happens, there's little/no difference between this model and the per user model. In effect, all employees are users.
  - **Usage Volume:** This model is based on transaction volume and can include greater economies of scale as the transaction volume increases.
  - **Simultaneous Use:** This is a licensing model that places a cap on the maximum number of people who can be actively using the system concurrently. Essentially, anyone and everyone can have an account and a login, but only a certain number of users can access the software simultaneously. This model is blended and can offer a more economical licensing structure.
- **Infrastructure:** The infrastructure requirements for implementation are dependent on the system architecture chosen by the organization. For cloud-based and software-as-a-service architectures, the infrastructure requirements for the organization are lower compared to on-premise architectures. When on-premise is chosen, the supplier's solution will likely have hardware and infrastructure requirements, and these can be significant cost drivers. These requirements can include items such as data center space, power, security, and environmental conditioning.
- **Third Parties:** For many organizations, a single system provider may not be able to deliver the complete functionality that's needed to meet the requirements. In these cases, additional third parties will be used. These additional software applications and tools will need to be procured and integrated with other systems. Integration can drive additional costs.
- **Training:** Training is often overlooked and/or underestimated. The best system in the world, combined with an under skilled user base, will not deliver the specified requirements. These costs include development of training materials, delivery of instruction, and lost productivity during the training and switchover period.
- **Historical Data Migration:** An organization's old system will likely not transport data seamlessly to the new system. Information between systems is stored and managed differently. Migrating historical data to the new system often involves custom, but temporary, application programming interfaces (API's). There can also be a lot of manual effort validating the data after it's been moved. Historical data migration can be costly, and it's common for organizations to limit the quantity of the data moved by restricting the historical period that's included.
- **Integration Services:** For larger system implementations, a systems integrator will facilitate the process of implementation. This includes consulting services related to the project. These integration services can be substantial.

- **Customization:** Customizing a supplier's system solution is usually expensive. If the organization has unique workflows and data structures that are vital to their operation, customizations may be unavoidable. Extensive customizations may increase development, implementation, and integration costs. Around the topic of customizations, the term "vanilla" is used. This means that a system is used as-is from the supplier without any customizations. In-effect, it's "vanilla" or "plain tasting" or "basic." While a vanilla implementation is usually cheapest initially, it may not be the most effective for the business. These constraints will need to be evaluated.

Post-Implementation/On-Going Costs

These costs start after the system is live and has been accepted by the organization. These can be viewed as costs that will always be present in the business and must be budgeted and planned.

- **Maintenance:** The cost of maintenance will vary by system architecture. On-premise systems will require the organization to conduct their own maintenance on hardware, software, security, and facilities. In this case, the company will have all the physical, financial, and human assets in their books. Cloud-based systems will require the same type of work, but the work is done by a third party; therefore, the cost portion will be an expense transaction between the organization and the third party.
- **Support:** The costs related to ongoing support are essential. In essence, 'who helps when there are questions and issues?' Support will also vary based on system architecture. For on-premise architectures, the organization will be responsible for supporting issues related to hardware. Security and software may be a split arrangement between the organization and the supplier. For cloud-based architectures, all support will likely go through third parties and/or the system provider.

Future Costs

Let's not forget the "ideal scaling vector" that we looked at in Figure 03.02. Scaling and growth will carry additional cost implications over time for the organization.

- **Scaling:** Consider how the system scales as the organization grows. This will primarily impact two areas. 1) As the organization grows, it will require additional *licenses* and more users in the system. 2) As the organization grows, its *needs* will change. Does the system allow the organization to turn-on modules and additional capability as the needs materialize? Have those needs been anticipated, and the terms and conditions negotiated? Or, will they need to be negotiated at a future date? These will have cost implications in the future for the organization.
- **Currency Exchange Rates:** It's common to see an organization purchase a system through a provider who operates in another country. If the supplier operates in another country, and the organization is required to pay in that country's currency, the fluctuations of exchange rates can impact costs. When this happens, it can be difficult to anticipate and predict how this will affect budgets in the future.
- **Switching Barriers:** No one likes to think about this one up-front, but it is definitely worth considering in advance. Business relationships don't last forever, so it's likely that

at some point, the organization will need to switch system providers. If this isn't planned in advance, the organization puts themselves in a restrictive bind called a "vendor lock-in." The costs associated with vendor lock-in are substantial. Planning in advance around data structures, information security, and data storage can help mitigate this future cost.

To make informed cost considerations, it's crucial to perform thorough analyses that include implementation, on-going maintenance, and long-term/future costs. The choice of systems provider should be informed by a full perspective. By understanding the all the factors that can drive costs, organizations can make the best possible decisions during the vendor evaluation and selection process.

Summary

Requirements gathering is the critical enabler to selecting a business system that fits an organization's unique profile. By thoroughly defining the organization's needs, evaluating its current processes, and understanding its long-term goals, requirements gathering ensures that the system selection is an informed decision. Effective and efficient work process are anchored in a comprehensive understanding of what the system must do and how it will enable work to be performed. This foundational process enhances effectiveness, cost-efficiency, and the overall future success of an organization.

Discussion Questions

Why is it crucial for organizations to understand their specific needs and objectives before embarking on the selection of a business system?

What are the potential consequences of selecting a business system without a thorough understanding of an organization's requirements?

How does the process of requirements gathering help align a business system with an organization's long-term strategic goals?

What steps or methodologies can organizations employ to effectively gather and document their requirements in the context of selecting a business system?

How can involving key stakeholders and end-users in the requirements gathering process contribute to the successful adoption and utilization of the selected business system?

Chapter References

ChatGPT. (2023). *Finding Business Systems Information.* OpenAI. Accessed November 2, 2023.

Curumsing, F.N., Abdelrazek, M., Vasa, R., Mouzakis, K., & Grundy, J. (2019). Understanding the impact of emotions on software: A case study in requirements gathering and evaluation. *The Journal of Systems and Software, 147*, 215–229. https://doi.org/10.1016/j.jss.2018.06.077

Lane, S., O'Raghallaigh, P., & Sammon, D. (2016). Requirements gathering: the journey. *Journal of Decision Systems, 25*(sup1), 302–312. https://doi.org/10.1080/12460125.2016.1187390

Milani. (2019). *Digital Business Analysis.* Springer International Publishing. https://doi.org/10.1007/978-3-030-05719-0

Onore, J. (2022). *Asking Effective Questions During Requirements Elicitation.* (Linked-In Learning Course.) linkedin.com.

Strause, S. (2010). Selecting and partnering with a vendor for a qualified software product. *Journal of Validation Technology, 16*(3), 43–46.

Walterbusch, M., Martens, B., & Teuteberg, F. (2013). Evaluating cloud computing services from a total cost of ownership perspective. *Management Research Review, 36*(6), 613–638. https://doi.org/10.1108/01409171311325769

Chapter 4
Business Uses of Human Capital Management (HCM) Systems

Table of Contents

Chapter 4: Business Uses of Human Capital Management (HCM) Systems

Introduction

In today's organizations, Human Capital Management (HCM) systems are part of a portfolio of systems capabilities which require formal governance. Often as part of a larger Enterprise Resource Planning (ERP) suite, HCM systems are flexible tools which are leveraged in business decision making, inextricably connected in the business ecosystem. HCM systems focus on the human elements; however, they are more than just a repository for employee data. HCM systems enable proactive workforce management and business decision making. In this chapter, we will explore the business uses of HCM systems and how they enable an organization's operation.

Strategic Asset Governance

Every organization has three fundamental asset classes that they need to govern and intentionally deploy. These are 1) Financial Assets, 2) Physical Assets, and 3) Human Assets. Effective and efficient governance of all three of these asset classes drives the ability of an

Figure 04.01
Three Types of Capital
Every organization has 3 types of capital assets: financial, physical, and human.

organization to meet its strategic objectives. Let's begin this chapter by defining each of these, see Figure 04.01.

Financial Capital
Financiers, accountants, and economists debate semantics and definitions of financial capital, and it's not our aim to try to resolve this debate. Our aim is only to render a nominal definition for the purposes of contrasting financial capital from physical and human. Financial capital comprises economic resources that a company controls and can put to use. Depending on the sources you consult, you'll find that there are different opinions about how many types of financial capital exist. In all types, financial capital is usually considered "capital" when it's being put to work for production purposes. As an example, cash would *not* be considered capital unless it's being put to use.

Physical Capital
Physical capital consists of real/tangible things that tend to have longer term value. Think of assets that have a multi-year value which might be depreciated over time. Examples include real estate, land improvements and buildings, equipment and machinery, computer and networking systems, and vehicles. Physical capital are things that have a lifespan greater than the production cycle; in other words, they are not used up when producing products and services.

Human Capital
Human capital is interesting because there are many sources which state that a business' people are an intangible asset. People can be counted, and the costs of human resources can be counted. We know that the cost of labor runs on average 20-50% of a company's revenue. We also know that without the people there is no business. You might be able to run a business with little-to-no physical or financial capital; however, you will struggle to find a business that

can run without people. (Maybe A.I. will change that though.) Not only can we count the costs of human capital, but we can also project workforce needs, volume of work, throughput of tasks, and work activities. There is a base capability, capacity, and output-expectation. Human Capital is very tangible. And, yes, it may not be a line item on a balance sheet today, but maybe it should be tomorrow!

Where human capital becomes "intangible" is in potential. It seems that financial experts like to zero-in on this aspect of people. Human skills, intelligence, training, development, growth, health, and culture set up an unknown potential. Frankly, that makes human capital far more exciting and important than either financial or physical capital! And, that makes the function of Human Resources far more valuable to a business than either Finance or Operations. One can put forward a strong argument that out of the three asset classes, human capital is the most important, for the others have no purpose absent the human purpose.

The Story of 3 Capitals

We've defined the three capitals. Let's look at their stories and how businesses have historically treated them. Financial capital consists of debt, equity, and working. Physical capital consists of facilities, assets, and equipment. Human capital consists of people, talent, capabilities, culture, and human contributions to production.

- Financial capital has a direct impact on the business operation. A business must have financial capital to invest and operate, but financial capital is a depreciating asset.
- Physical capital has a direct impact on business operations. A business must have equipment, systems, and tools to produce products and services, but physical capital is also a depreciating asset.
- Human capital has a direct impact on business operations. A business must have people to design, develop, market, sell, produce, service, and manage the business. Out of the three classes of assets, People are the only <u>*appreciating*</u> asset!

There's a caveat though: to be an appreciating asset, a business must lead, develop, and deploy its people with skill and expertise. Poor leadership, a lack of development, and unskilled deployment will make human capital a depreciating asset. This is where HCM systems play a critical role; these systems enable the proper leadership and deployment of people. In contrast, there's nothing you can do to turn financial and physical capital into an appreciating asset.

The story gets even more interesting when we examine how these three capital classes are positioned within businesses. Entrepreneurs, owners, CEO's, and Presidents treat financial and physical capital as more important than human capital. Human capital has historically been subordinated below these other two capital classes from a governance standpoint.

- **Financial capital leadership:** 64% of small businesses and 85% of medium businesses have a leader of finance/accounting. Of these, 93% report directly to the CEO (or equivalent role.) One of the biggest issues cited (about 50% of the time) by businesses, regarding their accounting leadership, is that they are more reactive than proactive.

- **Physical capital leadership:** This one is a little harder to pin down to a percentage because leadership of physical capital comes in many different forms. The simplest is if a company employs a head of operations, as operations leadership roles often manage most of the physical assets. Depending on the type of business, industry, and segment, these titles vary dramatically. Common categories of titles include operations, manufacturing, production, and service. In the case of small businesses, often the founder will fulfill the operations leadership role and manage physical capital directly. When you bundle these together, the estimate is that 98% of small-medium sized businesses have some form of an operations leader who oversees the physical capital of the organization. A similar percentage, 97%, report to the CEO or an equivalent role.

- **Human capital leadership:** Only 30% of small businesses (under 50 employees) have a human resources leader. In the cases where there is a HR leader, 65% of them report to the CFO or equivalent. Then, 70% of these small businesses add HR onto the job duties of employees who are not trained or skilled in human resources. As frightening as these statistics are, they do get better as the size of the organization increases. Medium and large businesses will target a ratio of employees to HR. Ratios will range from 150:1 to 500:1, depending on the industry and type of roles in the company. Across all sizes of companies, the reporting relationship of the HR leader is riddled with variability. The role will often report to a position other than the CEO or President, sending a clear message that the company does not believe that people are as important as money or equipment.

The story of the 3 capitals should lead you to scratch your head in puzzlement. Human capital is by far the most valuable of the three capital categories. It is the only one that has the potential to be an appreciating asset. It is the only one that can deliver incremental levels of output. It is the only one that can generate innovation. Yet, we relegate, delegate, and subjugate human resources...in businesses where this is done, a very clear message is sent that leaders do not value people as much as they value financial and physical assets. It's clear to see we have work to do to align and govern all our organizational assets in an effective and efficient manner.

How do organizations find themselves in this situation where HCM is subordinate to financial and physical capital management? Let's say you start your own web design business. At first you're doing all the work. You market yourself, sell the projects, and execute the projects. You're successful, and you have more work than you can do by yourself, so you hire another web designer. Growth continues year over year, and a couple years into the business, you have twelve employees...all doing web design/production work. Your personal work, as the owner, has evolved away from production (web design) and now includes a large percentage of back-office administration work. You recognize that the best place for you to focus your personal work is on the customer-facing part of the business such as business development, sales, and contracting. So, you hire your first back-office position, which is an accounting person. This person will handle all items related to bookkeeping, invoicing, taxes, compliance, and office administration needs. As your business continues to grow, you add resources to accounting. After that, your next addition is likely in sales and marketing, which will help you to accelerate growth. Then, after that, you add a head of operations to oversee the web design workers and all of production.

The duties that would normally be associated with a human resources department are spread among your leaders, with the bulk of the administrative duties aligned with accounting. At this point in your evolution, you realize that a professional in human resources will be beneficial for continued growth; however, your job as the CEO has evolved to high-level strategic business duties. Aligning your first human resources person to you directly doesn't make sense because you don't want to be pulled down into administrative minutia. Most of the administrative work already exists within accounting, so you have the new HR person report to your head of accounting.

There you have it: accounting and operations report directly to the CEO, and HR reports to accounting. For many businesses, it takes *much* more growth for HR to increase in size and scope enough that reporting to the CEO makes sense. However, astute CEO's realize that making human capital management a peer to financial and physical capital management can generate acceleration earlier in a company's growth cycle. It's these companies that stand the best chance of exceeding their goals while sustainably attracting and retaining the best talent. Afterall, its people that started the business. It's people that consume the output of the business. It's people that grow the business. It's people that sustain the business. Intentionally lifting the HR function up earlier in the growth cycle enables acceleration and improved governance of the organization.

Administration

As the previous story illustrates, the earliest encounter with HCM systems is often around the need to complete administrative functions. See Figure 04.02 for this section. The first of these usually centers around being able to execute payroll and taxes in an efficient manner. **Payroll** is one of the most essential functions of an HCM system. This part of the HCM system holds information about pay rates, pay differentials, tax withholding elections, garnishments, and more. It uses this stored information to calculate pay using selected pay periods such as weekly, bi-weekly, and monthly. These tasks need to be performed with precision, ensuring that employees are paid accurately and on time, and ensuring that all pay compliance items are regularly maintained. Most payroll systems today also streamline tax filing through electronic submission to local, State, and Federal organizations. By using a payroll system, businesses can save time and reduce the likelihood of errors.

Payroll can certainly be a module within a larger HCM system. It can also be a module within an accounting system. One of the more popular accounting systems for small businesses is Intuit's Quickbooks. The first system capability that most businesses go looking for is accounting. Then, when a business is ready to hire employees, they look for payroll. Turning on payroll in Quickbooks is an easy addition, and with the click of a couple buttons a small business can be running payroll. Quickbooks even provides minimal employee access and self-service. Finally,

Figure 04.02
Administration Elements of HCM Systems
The nine key administrative capabilities of HCM systems. These can be procured as either integrated or stand-alone systems.

payroll can also be a stand-alone system. This is how ADP started in the human resources space...by providing a stand-alone payroll and timekeeping solution.

Closely related to payroll is the administrative need to handle time and attendance. Most of the leading solutions in this space also enable scheduling. We'll discuss these three together: **time, attendance, and scheduling**. **Time** tracking includes capturing and storing employee data on clock-in/out time, breaks, absences, and leaves. Common methods of time tracking include 1) manual entry (e.g. employee direct entry into the system, or some form of timecard scanning,) 2) time clocks (e.g. dedicated clocks placed around a workplace used for clocking-in/out,) and 3) third-party devices/applications (e.g. other applications, or wearable devices.) **Attendance** tracking refers to the processing and sorting of the time tracking information, essentially converting it into actionable payroll processing. Time and attendance will also track, report, and process time off requests. Last is scheduling, and some HCM systems include this, and some do not. **Scheduling** is the creation of work schedules per employee, work team, department, and location. This allows managers to define work shifts and assign employees to work specific shifts and/or specific roles. The *better* approaches to scheduling enable pushing schedules out to employees electronically. The *best* approaches also enable employees to switch shifts with other employees, a process called bidding (if authorized by management.)

Human Capital Management (HCM) systems, and stand-alone systems, support a wide range of administrative duties for businesses, making their operations efficient and effective. Here are additional administrative tasks that these systems enable:

- **Tax Filing**: These systems generate tax reports and facilitate electronic tax filing, most performing the filing process automatically based on governmental deadlines.
- **Record Keeping**: These systems maintain employee records, including personal information, employment history, pay history, garnishments, immigration, evaluations, and change data.
- **Compliance Management**: These systems provide tools for completing compliance requirements with labor laws and regulations. They provide reporting, form completion, and automatic filing capabilities.
- **Document Management**: These systems commonly include document storage and management features, enabling it to become a company's system of record. Often, this enables companies to be paperless in their record keeping, which drives both ease of access and improved information/data security.
- **Benefits Administration**: These systems can help HR manage employee benefits, including health insurance, retirement plans, and other perks. This includes enrollment, tracking, and management of benefits programs.

By automating and streamlining administrative tasks, administrative systems enable businesses to accomplish these tasks in an effective and efficient manner.

Figure 04.03
Recuriting Process/Funnel
The six steps in the recruiting process depicted as a funnel, and often managed by an ATS.

Talent Acquisition

As a company grows beyond administrative uses, the next most commonly encountered need is to support the talent acquisition process. Talent acquisition is the entire process of recruitment and selection, from advertising through on-boarding. See Figure 04.03. Talent acquisition is crucial for building and maintaining a high-performing, innovative, and adaptable workforce. People are a strategic investment that impacts all aspects of a business, from product development through to customer support.

Talent acquisition is a cornerstone of organizational growth, and systems play a vital role in this process. These systems offer tools to advertise job openings, attract top candidates, and efficiently manage applicant data. By centralizing the recruitment process within a system, organizations can streamline their efforts, making it easier to hire the right candidates. It's not just in the larger suite of HCM systems that this capability can be found. Specialized systems that focus on the recruiting process are common, and these are called Applicant Tracking Systems (ATS.)

There are two common ways to acquire the ATS capability. See Figure 04.04. One way is to procure a HCM system which has ATS capability as part of its offering; shown on the left of the

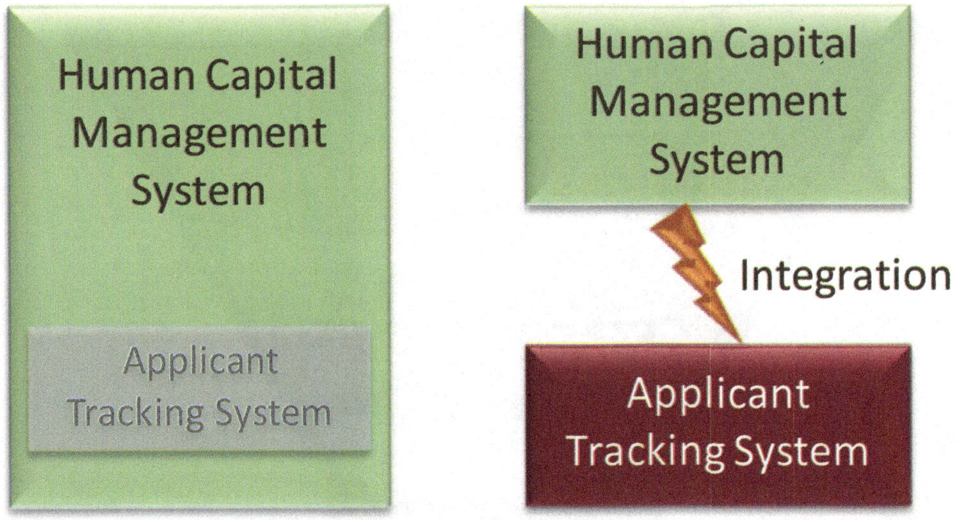

Figure 04.04
Applicant Tracking Systems
Depicts two different setups for gaining the capabilities of an applicant tracking system. On the left is an integrated ATS capability. On the right is a stand-along ATS capability requiring an integration between it and the core HCM system.

figure. The other way is to procure a stand-alone ATS; shown on the right of the figure. A stand-alone approach may require the organization to connect the ATS back to its core HCM system through an integration (if they want them to exchange data.)

Companies find themselves in situations where they need integrations between their ATS and HCM quite naturally as they evolve and grow. For example, a small company has an accounting system which has core employee records and payroll. They grow to the point where applicant tracking capabilities would be useful; however, they're not ready to spend significant monies to purchase an ATS. Instead, they decide to use the "free" ATS capabilities of one of the major job boards. This helps with the recruiting process shown in Figure 04.03; however, the free application isn't integrated. When an applicant moves to "new hire," their data does not move from the ATS to the system of record. The new employee, along with someone from accounting or HR, must now duplicate the data entry. This duplication is tolerated for a while, but continued growth will drive the need to have an integrated and seamless solution.

There are a couple other items of concern in these stand-alone system situations. One is a data and information security risk. Since the company is collecting applicant information as part of their talent acquisition process, they can be liable for any data breaches. However, the applicant data is on a third party's system. Often, the terms of use of these systems limit the provider's liability for any information security data breaches. Another area of concern is that this "free" ATS, often through a job board, restricts the company's use to the job board provider. This generates a "vendor lock-in" situation. A company's ability to advertise and attract the best quality talent can be greatly restricted.

Stand-alone/specialty ATS's can offer a higher level of functionality compared to a vendor/job bard approach. It really depends on the HCM system that a company uses. The leading HCM solutions have fully developed ATS's. As a matter of fact, both Oracle and SAP purchased ATS providers as part of their growth strategies. Oracle purchased Taleo in 2012. SAP purchased SuccessFactors in 2011. Both provided their respective companies with ATS capabilities. In contrast to large company solutions like Oracle and SAP, the HCM systems that target small to medium sized businesses may still have ATS capabilities; however, they often have a smaller set of capabilities compared to stand-alone ATS's. For example, they may lack the ability to create and deploy candidate knock-out questions. Another example is that they may not support automated interfaces to job boards for advertising, or if they do, it may be a limited number of job boards that are supported.

HCM systems with integrated ATS capabilities can provide organizations a platform for managing the entire talent acquisition process. They can also integrate with the company's own career site, popular job boards, and social media platforms. An effective ATS enables companies to reach a broader audience of potential candidates. These systems allow businesses the ability to manage applicant flow, communications, and to track the performance of their job postings.

Talent Management

As a business continues to grow, evolve, and mature, attentions turn to *talent effectiveness*. The business needs to know:

- Do we have the right people in the right jobs?
- Are we optimally deploying talent to meet our business goals?
- Where do we have talent gaps that might cause us risk with business continuity?

This is where talent management comes in. **Talent management** is one of the strategic areas of human resources, and HCM systems can provide a business with the ability to view and deploy their talent strategically. Talent management involves developing, deploying, and retaining a highly skilled and motivated workforce. It includes a wide range of activities that together maximize the potential of an organization's workforce and help align people with the organization's goals and objectives.

These are some of the activities of talent management and what a HCM system can provide:

- **Performance Management (PM):** Talent management is a broader term, and typically when it's used, it also includes the domain of performance management. A talent management module will facilitate the entire PM process from objective setting, cascading, feedback, appraisals, evaluations, and ratings.
- **Employee Development:** Talent management includes the planning and tracking of ongoing training and development objectives. It typically does not include the management of learning content or the administration of learning records; those fall under the domain of Learning Management Systems (LMS.) The talent management

module captures employee development objectives and enables the organization to report on completion, status, and to query the employee population for specific skills and experiences.

- **Succession Planning:** Extending the work of both performance management and employee development, succession planning is a *business continuity risk mitigation* function. The system provides the business with the ability to identify key positions and then to align people to those positions as potential internal successors if the job were to be vacated. In other words, it helps a business *mobilize talent* dynamically to fulfill needs. One of the outputs of succession planning can be a feedback loop to employee development, enabling advance preparation of employees for larger leadership roles within the organization. Succession planning helps ensure that the company has a pipeline of talent ready to step into key positions when needed. Succession planning helps to identify gaps when a pipeline of talent is low or absent.

It is also possible to procure stand-alone talent management systems. Many of the HCM systems for small businesses do not include talent management functionality. Those that do have a limited set of capabilities, usually limited to performance management. Much like the description of a business' evolution with ATS's, the same can happen here.

With all of the business uses, the evolution and growth process of a business can lead an organization to disparate stand-alone systems. These stand-alone systems may have limited or no integration back to the core system of record. As an organization grows, an integrated system becomes crucial for success because it enables systemic alignment of the workforce. This includes integrated oversight of the organization's goals, employee growth and development, performance, engagement, and business continuity. It helps businesses harness the full potential of their employees, ultimately contributing to sustained success and competitiveness.

Compensation and Benefits Management

Compensation and benefits management are systems needs typically encountered by mid-sized or larger businesses. Small businesses will often handle these needs through third party providers and/or through stand-alone tools. At one of the companies where I was head of HR, we managed all our compensation plans, pay grades, and incentives with spreadsheets. We were small enough that this was not only practical but more efficient. Many HCM systems have capabilities which enable organizations to manage compensation and incentives. These compensation capabilities include:

- **Job Families:** An HCM system can enable the definition, organization, and categorization of jobs, families, departments, and organizational hierarchies. This often includes being able to identify each job with associated government classification systems such as the North American Industry Classification System (NAICS,) the International Standard Classification of Occupations (ISCO,) and the European Skills and Competencies and

Occupations (ESCO.) Some of the more advanced systems can also track version changes and provide a historical record of changes.

- **Pay Structures, Grades, and Ranges**: An HCM system can provide the organization with the ability to design and implement pay grades, classify jobs, and manage the use of titles and incentive plans. Some of the more advanced HCM systems will also provide the ability to manage multiple geographic variances of each of these, enabling the organization to apply differing pay policies and strategies around the world.

Benefits management and administration is a large set of responsibilities and activities which have significant compliance requirements. It includes the design of plans, implementation/roll-out, communications, enrollment, and the management and changing of employee elections. In addition, it also includes systems connections and interfaces with medical providers and brokers to facilitate billing, collections, claims experience data, and claims validation/verification. These benefits capabilities include:

- **Program Design**: A HCM system with this capability provides an organization with the ability to design benefits programs, including: medical, dental, vision, and supplemental. Some of the more advanced systems will store historical instances of plan designs, allowing for data modeling and forecasting.
- **Administration**: An HCM system with this capability will house data structures which inform payroll and accounting of employee deductions, billing, invoicing, and accruals. It will also house legally required plan documents and provide a historical record of these.
- **Enrollment, Communication, and Education**: An HCM system with this capability will provide interactions and processing capabilities for employee enrollment choices. It will provide communications to employees and eligible dependents about the benefits calendar and tasks that need to be completed. Some will also provide the opportunity for educational modules on the plans offered, while others will provide this feature through an integration with a learning management system (LMS.)

Through effective administration and management of compensation and benefits, HCM systems help create a competitive and compelling employer value proposition. This in-turn can drive increased employee engagement and retention.

Record Keeping vs. Decision Making

While administrative needs may start an organization's journey into human capital management systems, decision making is the eventual destiny and the cornerstone of highly effective business management systems. Systems impact the direction, efficiency, and success of an organization. Effective decision making is crucial for achieving objectives, managing risks, and maintaining a competitive edge in a constantly evolving business environment.

For this section, it's best to start by understanding what makes a business *decision* <u>effective</u>. Refer to Figure 04.04. The effectiveness of a business decision is determined by examining the

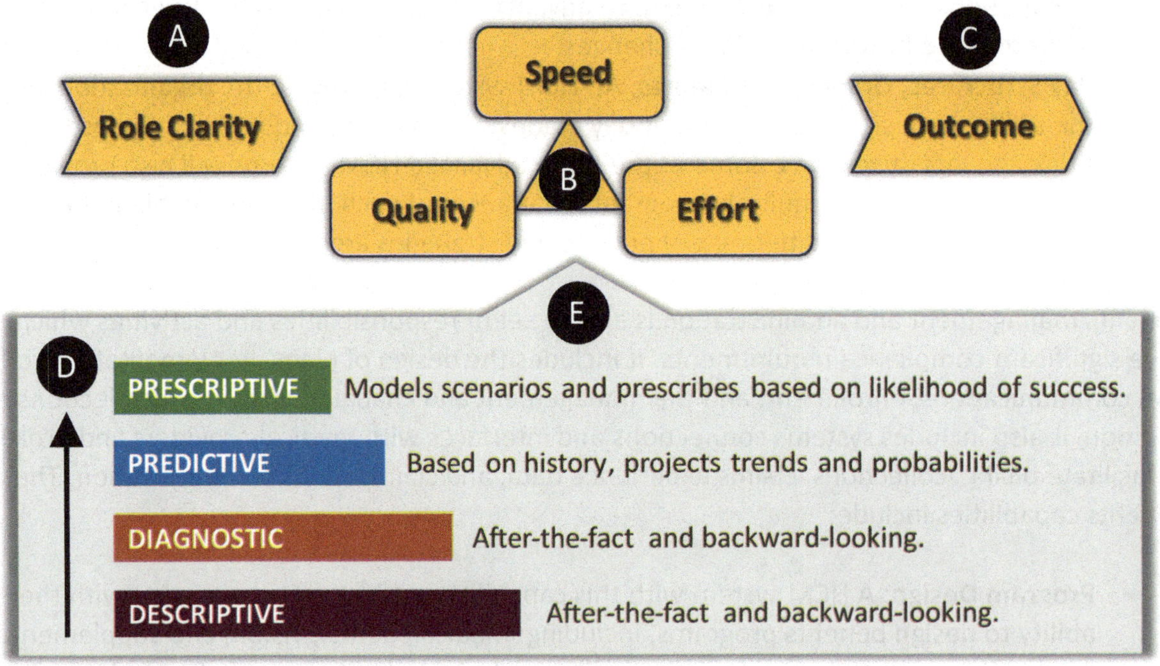

Figure 04.04
Decision Making Impact
Illustration that depicts the impact that business systems have on decision making.

(C) outcome. Just like there are thousands of different decisions, there are also many different measures of outcomes (e.g. financials, market, production, etc.) The very first enabler to effective decision making is that everyone involved in the decision-making process must understand their role (A.) The center part of the decision-making process (B) is variable. The speed at which a decision is made, the amount of effort that's applied to the decision-making process, and the quality of the decision are all interdependent. Let's look at each of these briefly:

- One of the dimensions of decision effectiveness is **speed**. It's common for people to think that faster is better, but that is not what's meant by this dimension. Faster isn't always better. Think of this dimension as "Are we moving at the right speed to succeed?" It may be faster, but it may also be slower. (Albrecht & Albrecht, 2020, p.45).
- Another dimension of decision effectiveness is **effort**. This dimension isn't necessarily about more or less, it's all about the right amount of effort. Applying more effort doesn't necessarily improve decision effectiveness. Effort is the one dimension of decisioning that looks at decision efficiency specifically. The desire in any business is to be as efficient as possible while not compromising quality, speed, yield, or clarity (Albrecht & Albrecht, 2020, p.46).
- The next dimension of decision effectiveness is **quality**. Decision quality is viewed and perceived in hindsight, answering the questions: "Did we make a good quality decision?" and "All things considered at the time, was the decision sufficiently vetted and did we

perform our due diligence before making the choice?" (Albrecht & Albrecht, 2020, pp.44-45).

It's these three dimensions of speed, effort, and quality that business/HCM systems influence directly. These (B) three dimensions are commonly referred to as the principle of "triple constraints." Sometimes also referred to as the "iron triangle," implying that it's difficult to break away from the interplay between them. The way I had these described to me when I first heard about them went like this, 'Fast, Good, or Cheap...pick two. If you want something fast & cheap, it won't be good. If you want something good & cheap, it won't be fast. If you want something good & fast, it won't be cheap.' The premise is that it's difficult to achieve all three at the same time: speed, low cost, and high quality. Hence, "iron triangle."

In decision making, having the right information at the right time can enhance all three triple constraints simultaneously! With the right system selection and implementation, (E) input can be provided which accelerates decision-making, improves the quality of the decision process, and reduces the amount of effort that's spent on decision making. It all depends on the type of analytics (D) that the chose HCM system can deliver. Types of data analytics are described in a (D) hierarchy.

- **Descriptive analytics** are the base of the model. These are after-the-fact and backward looking. They are historical and answer the question, "What happened?"
- **Diagnostic analytics** are the second level of the hierarchy. These are also after-the-fact and backward looking, but they go one step further. They answer the question, "Why did this happen?"
- **Predictive analytics** are the third level of the hierarchy. These are based on history, but they project trends and probabilities. They answer the question, "What might happen in the future?"
- The final level in the hierarchy is **prescriptive analytics**. These use the historical information to dynamically model different possible future scenarios and their respective probabilities. They answer the question, "What should we do next?"

The further up in the (D) analytics model that a system can support, the more of an impact it has on the effectiveness of business decision making. The extent to which Human Resources (HR) systems are viewed as decision enablers can vary widely among organizations. It depends on several factors, including the organization's size, industry, technology adoption, and its approach to HR management. Here are some considerations regarding the frequency with which HR systems are seen as decision enablers:

- **Size of the Organization**: Larger organizations often have more sophisticated HR systems that can provide comprehensive data and analytics. In such cases, HR systems are more likely to be viewed as decision enablers, as they can offer insights into workforce trends and support strategic decision-making.

- **Industry**: The level of emphasis on HR systems as decision enablers can differ across industries. For example, industries with high turnover or specialized labor needs, such as retail or healthcare, may rely more on HR systems for decision support.
- **Technology Adoption**: The extent to which an organization has invested in advanced technology across their enterprise plays a significant role. Organizations that have implemented advanced analytics, machine learning, or artificial intelligence are more likely to consider these systems decision enablers.
- **HR Maturity**: Organizations with a mature and strategic HR function tend to see HR systems as decision enablers. These systems help HR professionals provide valuable insights to support overall business objectives, and the organization's leaders often rely on these strategic inputs for business decision making.
- **Data Quality and Integration**: The accuracy and quality of data within HR systems are crucial. Organizations with clean, integrated data are more likely to trust their HR systems to provide reliable insights for decision-making.
- **Regulatory and Compliance Needs**: In industries with strict regulatory and compliance requirements, HR systems may be viewed as indispensable tools for operating the business.
- **Training and Skill Set of the HR Team**: The availability of HR professionals with the skills to use and interpret HR systems is critical. Organizations that invest in training and development of HR staff are more likely to utilize HR systems as decision enablers.

In recent years, there has been a growing trend towards viewing HR systems as decision enablers. This shift is driven by the recognition that data-driven HR practices can provide valuable insights into workforce planning, talent management, and other strategic HR functions. As technology and analytics capabilities continue to advance, HR systems are increasingly being leveraged to support data-informed decision-making at all levels of an organization.

Human Resources (HR) systems are becoming more accessible to small businesses. Several factors have contributed to this trend, making it easier for small organizations to adopt and benefit from HR systems such as cloud-based solutions and systems that are scalable over time. It's important for small organizations to assess their specific needs and goals before selecting a system. A tailored approach ensures that the chosen system aligns with the unique requirements and future expectations of small businesses.

Summary

Human Capital Management (HCM) systems have become integral to modern businesses, facilitating various aspects of HR management, compliance, talent acquisition, talent management, and data-driven decision making. As organizations continue to recognize the value of their workforce as a competitive advantage, HCM systems will play an increasingly critical role in their success.

Discussion Questions

When examining potential HCM system providers, what are the challenges an organization will face when trying to balance administrative needs and data-drive decision making?

In what ways do HCM systems contribute to an organization's talent strategy?

HCM systems offer features for employee development and learning. How can these tools be leveraged to enhance employee skills and performance? What are the benefits of a structured employee development program within an organization?

What are some of the key compliance challenges organizations face in HR management, and how do HCM systems help address these challenges?

Discuss the importance of diagnostic analytics in business systems. How can organizations use data and diagnostic analytics to make decisions?

Discuss the importance of predictive analytics in HR management. How can organizations use data and predictive analytics provided by HCM systems to make proactive decisions regarding their workforce?

Consider the impact of automation on HR processes within organizations. How has the adoption of HCM systems transformed HR administration and management functions, and what are the potential benefits and drawbacks of this transformation? Where do you think artificial intelligence will play a role in HCM systems?

Chapter References

Albrecht, D.J. (2021). *Strategic Human Resources: The business context. (Whitepaper).* Alonos Corporation.

Albrecht, D.J., & Albrecht, M.G. (2020). *DECIDE to Thrive: Improving business performance through decision effectiveness.* Dallas, TX: Alonos Corporation.

ChatGPT. (2023). *HCM System Business Uses.* OpenAI. Accessed November 2, 2023.

Kazakov, O.D., & Azarenko, N.Y. (2019). The Model of Human Capital Management in Decision Support Systems. *Vestnik Voronežskogo gosudarstvennogo universiteta inženernyh tehnologij, 81*(3), 290–298. https://doi.org/10.20914/2310-1202-2019-3-290-298

Miller, T. (2017). *HR analytics and innovations in workforce planning* (First edition.). Business Expert Press.

Mondal, S.R., Di Virgilio, F., & Das, S. (2021). *HR Analytics and Digital HR Practices: Digitalization Post COVID-19.* Palgrave Macmillan. https://doi.org/10.1007/978-981-16-7099-2

Rasmussen, T., & Ulrich, D. (2015). Learning from practice: how HR analytics avoids being a management fad. *Organizational Dynamics, 44*(3), 236–242. https://doi.org/10.1016/j.orgdyn.2015.05.008

Chapter 5
Common Human Capital Management (HCM) System Roles & Interactions

Chapter Table of Contents

Chapter 5: Common HCM System Roles & Interactions

Introduction

In the complex landscape of modern business operations, where organizations rely on a multitude of software systems to manage their human resources, financials, and operations, the various types of roles used in these systems have also expanded. This chapter reviews the most common roles that are used in business and HCM systems. There is special focus on the role of system integrators because they act as a bridge between system suppliers and companies. System integrators are vitally important for system selection and implementation, as they help perform requirements gathering, selection, configuration, and implementation. In the context of Human Capital Management (HCM) systems, each of the roles covered in this chapter play a critical part in making sure that HR activities are completed efficiently and effectively.

Photo by Cliff Booth from pexels.com

Employee Self Service

The Employee Self Service (ESS) role is a ubiquitous role within business systems. Each type (or area) of a business system will specify the capabilities of the employee differently. In HCM systems the ESS role allows employees to access and manage their personal information. This includes items such as pay stubs, benefits, time off requests, and personal contact information. ESS users are typically *regular employees* within the organization. Sometimes contractors can be provided with ESS access, depending on the work relationship and requirements. Employees use ESS access to view and update their own information without needing to involve HR or managers in routine tasks. This can save resources and improve efficiencies.

Benefits:

- Improves efficiency by streamlining basic employee data maintenance.
- Reduces approval routing requirements and the time needed for routine employee information tasks.
- Improves accuracy and information security by reducing the number of “touchpoints” on basic employee information. Employees directly input their information versus requesting others to make changes.
- Reduces the number of people processing employee data and places the exposure with the employee only.
- Empowers employees to take control of their own information and administrative tasks.

- Ensures that employees can make changes when they're needed and speeds up the change process, accuracy, and timeliness.

Employee Responsibilities:

- Personal contact information (e.g. address, phone, personal email).
- View work schedules, clock-in, clock-out, request schedule changes.
- Paid-Time-Off (PTO) processing. Submit and track time off requests and monitor PTO balance.
- View and print pay stubs, tax forms, and benefits enrollment information.
- Change tax withholding and exemptions.
- Change retirement plan contribution level (e.g. 401K).
- Enter and manage performance objectives, notes, and comments.
- Enter and manage development objectives.
- Access training materials and enroll for courses.

Photo by fauxels from pexels.com

Manager Self Service

The Manager Self Service (MSS) role is also a ubiquitous role within business systems. Each type of business system will specify the capabilities of the manager differently. In HCM systems the MSS role allows managers to access and manage their *team's* information. MSS in a HCM system allows managers to access and perform HR-related tasks for their team members. These actions include items such as approving time off requests, building work schedules, and conducting performance reviews. Managers can also initiate actions such as organizational changes, promotions, pay increases, and reporting relationship changes. Overall, managers use MSS access to manage team changes without needing to involve HR or higher-level managers to initiate changes. Many of these changes will require additional approvals, but the system will route the approvals automatically. In many systems, MSS actions and authority levels are configurable.

Benefits:

- Improves efficiency by enabling managers to initiate team changes and then automatically routes for additional approvals.
- Information access is enhanced by providing real-time visibility to team information and activities.
- Reduces errors processing changes by forcing actions to be completed in the system. Eliminates workarounds and potential loss of key data.
- Improves compliance by requiring accurate completion of data/information fields and automatically triggering time-driven records updates.

Manager Responsibilities:

- Approvals and denials of employee requests.
  (e.g. schedule changes, clocking, time-off requests)
- Create and manage work schedules.
- Conduct performance reviews and set objectives.
- Conduct development planning.
- Organizational maintenance.

Photo by fauxels from pexels.com

HR Professionals

There can be few or many system roles in Human Resources. The size and complexity of the organization will drive different definitions of roles for HR. The HR organization is responsible for managing the entirety of the human capital management function, and this includes duties across the employee and organizational lifecycles. HR professionals use HCM systems to do their work.

Benefits:

- Improved efficiencies can be achieved by selecting a HCM system that fits the organization. This enables streamlining of HR processes, and it can reduce administrative workload.
- Decision-making improvements can be achieved through data and informational inputs into the decision-making process.
- Compliance can be made easier by ensuring policies and practices are both aligned with regulations and automated for completion/filing with government agencies.

In this section, we're differentiating between HR Professionals and HR System Administrators. Common generalist type roles to associate with HR Professionals in this context would include HR Director, Manager, Business Partner, and Specialist. Common talent type roles would be

Figure 05.01
HR Professional Role Categories

Example of three different role categories and how they can be differentiated based on functional responsibilities.

Recruiting Manager, Recruiter, or Talent Acquisition Specialist. Common organizational development roles would include Learning Director, Manager, or Specialist.

Each of these roles can have a different set of authorities which are configured in the HCM system. See Figure 05.01. HR employees who work in organizational development have needs that center around learning and development activities. Their roles can be configured to give them access to relevant information such as on-boarding, learning records, and the management of learning content through the learning management part of the system. For HR employees in talent, they have needs which center around recruiting, selection, and hiring. Their roles can be configured to give them access to the applicant tracking part of the system. For HR employees in a generalist-type role, they have needs which facilitate the management of the overall employee lifecycle. In this example, these HR professionals would have a larger set of access, enabling them to interact with employee records, perform organizational maintenance, and process pay and promotional changes.

Being able to divide roles allows an organization to separate duties and ensure data privacy and protection. For example, a company would not want someone in the organizational development role to be able to process employee pay changes. Roles are typically set up under a "need to know" basis, meaning that unless the job *requires* access, it is not provided.

Photo by ThisIsEngineering from pexels.com

HCM System Administrators

There's usually a small number of people on a HR team who are responsible for the administration of the system itself. These are HCM System Administrators, and they are responsible for the technical and operational aspects of the system. Often these people will be part of a HR Operations or HR Information Systems (HRIS) department. They ensure the system's proper functioning, security, workflows, software updates, integration of third-party capabilities, user access and role configuration, and overall system compliance and operability. System administrators manage the HCM software, including configuration, customization, and troubleshooting, to meet the organization's needs.

Benefits:

- System Integrity: Maintains the system's reliability and performance.
- Security: Protects sensitive HR data through access control and security measures.
- Customization: Tailors the system to match the organization's unique requirements.

System Administrator Responsibilities:

- Install, configure, and maintain the HCM software.
- Manage user access and permissions.
- Resolve technical issues and provide user support.
- Perform system updates and ensure data backup.

Photo by Olia Danilevich from pexels.com

HCM Super Users

The concept of a Super User is common in business systems, and many areas of an Enterprise Resource Planning (ERP) system use this role. In human capital management (HCM,) super users are individuals within the HR organization who have an advanced understanding of the HCM system. In addition to their "normal duties" they are more technically proficient, and they may even enjoy being the first to adopt new technologies and capabilities. Their high level of technical proficiency lends itself to supporting other users through coaching and training. When a company is going through a system implementation, or an upgrade, the super users are often asked to participate in testing workflows and operability. This is often referred to as performing "use cases" and "user acceptance testing." Super Users play a crucial role helping the organization navigate and effectively implement/use the HCM system.

Benefits:

- Promote knowledge sharing and the adoption of best practices.
- Improve efficiency by assisting in the resolution of issues, especially those that may be caused by skill gaps with other members of the HR team. This can reduce the volume of technical support requests.
- Encourages user adoption and speeds up change management when transitioning to a new system and/or upgrading along the way.

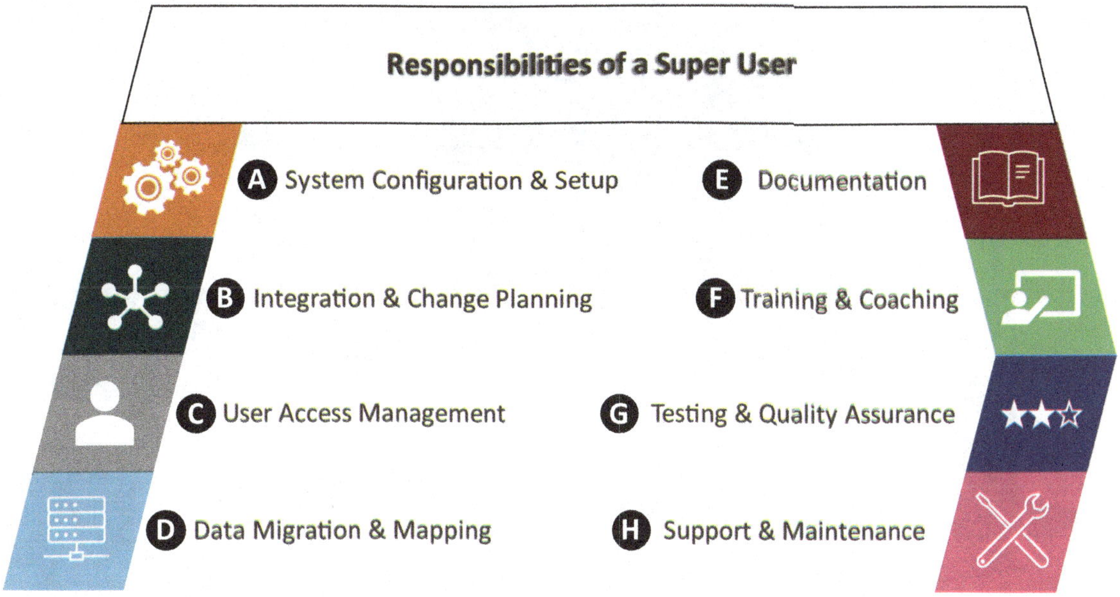

Figure 05.02
Focus Areas of a Super User
Depicts eight focus areas of a super user, often done in addition to their normal job.

Super-User Responsibilities:
(In Addition to their normal role in HR). Refer to Figure 05.02.

A. System Configuration & Setup: Assist a project team to configure a new system. May include installing software and configuring settings.
B. Integration & Change Planning: Collaborate with stakeholders to plan an integration, identify requirements, dependencies, and potential risks. This often involves assessing specific workflows of the department.
C. User Access Management: Although most often performed by System Administrators, superusers can handle user access permissions when the administrators need help.
D. Data Migration & Mapping: If the new system involves migrating data from legacy systems, superusers may be critical team participants for the data migration process. This can include mapping data fields, ensuring data integrity, and conducting migration.
E. Documentation: May be asked to create documentation such as user guides, manuals, and FAQs to support users. This is especially true for any custom workflows.
F. Training & Coaching: Provide formal and informal training to users. Super users are especially well-suited to perform live coaching with users.
G. Testing & Quality Assurance: Often active contributors in the testing phase. They ensure that the system functions correctly and meets requirements and expectations.
H. Support & Maintenance: Likely performed by System Administrators and/or the Information Technology department, super-users are often included in troubleshooting and diagnostics.

Photo by Pixabay from pexels.com

System Providers

In a treatment on common system roles, the system providers should certainly be included. Often in business we don't think of providers as having a daily/regular role once a system is operational. However, system providers play a crucial role throughout the lifecycle of a system. Refer to Figure 05.03 for this section. Providers are active in the design, development, testing, implementation, maintenance, and updating of HCM systems. Additionally, they are one of the primary entities for ongoing support of the HCM system during it operation. Here's an overview of the role they play during each of the lifecycle stages:

1) Requirements & Planning

    This is the stage where the organization defines its needs. System providers are involved in this stage by responding to requests for proposal (RFP), making presentations, and facilitating demonstrations.

2) Design & Development

    During design and development, the systems provider plays a pivotal role by translating the requirements/needs of the organization into a functional system. The team that a provider assigns at this stage and the next is usually different than the team that will support the system during operation and maintenance. Providers usually have people who specialize in design, development, testing, and implementation.

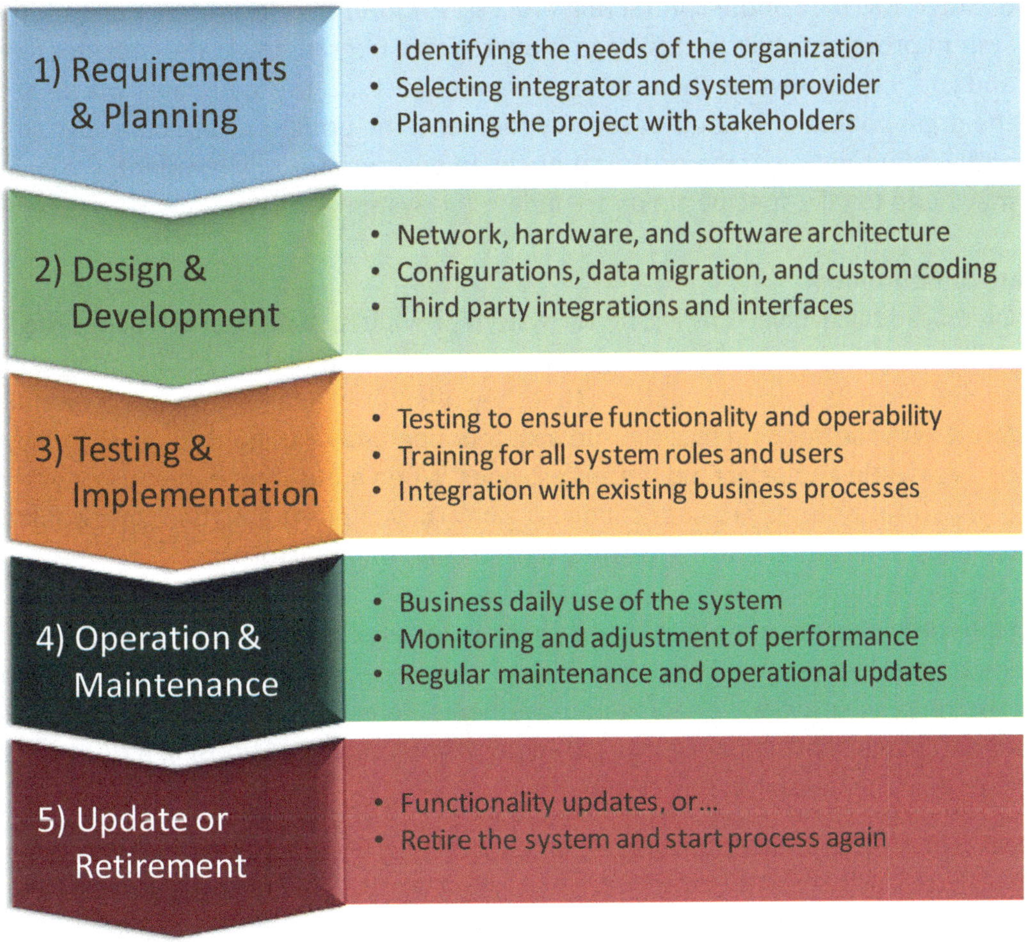

Figure 05.03
System Lifecycle Flowchart
Illustrates a five-step flowchart of a system lifecycle from requirements through end-of-life.

3) Testing & Implementation:

Testing and implementation is a transitional stage, where the provider and the organization are getting ready to go-live. The system provider's role in this stage is to facilitate and monitor use-case testing for any errors or needed changes. They make the needed changes and then provide the subject matter expertise for the organization to conduct training. It is often the responsibility of the organization to ensure that their own needs are met around training, change management, and business process integration. System providers can help with these, but they are usually added services.

4) Operation & Maintenance:

During the operation and maintenance stage, the focus of activity shifts to that of daily use by the organization. Consequently, the role of the systems provider also shifts. Their role changes to one of customer support. If the organization has operational questions or problems, the systems provider will help solve these. The support relationship is often governed by a service level agreement (SLA,) which is commonly negotiated at the end of Stage 1 as part of the contracting process. Another important function that the system provider fulfills in this stage is operational upgrading. As the provider fixes bugs and continues to evolve their own system architecture, these updates will be provided to the organization. In a cloud-based environment, the updates often occur dynamically and without notice to the organization. In an on-premises environment, the organization may need to take specific action to update the system.

5) Update or Retirement

Organizations evolve. This is true for system providers, and it's also true for the businesses they serve. This change over time can mean that an organization outgrows its system provider and the solutions that they offer. Any organization will eventually be faced with the decision to either do a system upgrade or to go through the lifecycle process again and select a different provider. When a business enters this stage, the role of a current systems provider changes again. They in effect step back into a sales role, which is reflected in Stage 1, as they try to retain their customer.

HCM system providers are integral partners in the successful implementation and ongoing management of HCM systems. They offer a range of services including system customization, support, training, security, and ongoing improvements, to help organizations optimize their HR processes and make informed decisions based on workforce data. Choosing a HCM systems provider is often a long-term commitment.

Photo by Ketut Subiyanto from pexels.com

System Integrators

System integrators play a pivotal role in the successful implementation and operation of business systems. Their primary role is to ensure that various software components and systems within an organization work seamlessly together to meet the specific needs and objectives of the organization. Referring to Figure 05.03, system integrators are involved in Stages 1-3. As an organization transitions into Stage 4, the integrator exits and their obligations are usually fulfilled. Below is a short summary of the integrator's role during the system lifecycle Stages 1-3:

1) Requirements & Planning:

- Needs Assessment: System integrators work closely with the organization to assess their HCM requirements, including existing processes and users. They identify gaps, opportunities, and challenges.
- Requirements Document: As an outcome of the needs assessment, the systems integrator will produce a comprehensive requirements document. This document will be used to make the supplier selection, configure the system, and test the system.
- Project Planning: Defining and outlining the plan for the remaining stage 2 & 3, along with a go-live transition for the organization at the beginning of stage 4.

2) Design and Development:

- Integrations: System integrators work to connect other enterprise systems together. This includes working on application programming interfaces (API's,) new system configurations, and any custom configurations and coding that are required.
- Workflow Configuration: System integrators partner with the organization and the system provider to ensure that the new system aligns with the organization's specific

workflow requirements and ensures inter-process/system compatibility. Specifies needed corrective actions to meet requirements.

3) Testing & Implementation:

- Testing: System integrators help the organization prepare to go-live and accept their new system by facilitating thorough use-case-testing. This testing is done against the requirements defined in Stage 1 and the workflow designs from Stage 2. The testing ensures that the integrated systems (all connected business systems) function correctly.
- Data Migration: This is also the stage where data migration occurs. This includes migrating data from the old system to the new system, and it includes the transfer of any/all agreed-upon historical data. Integrators oversee the migration of data from legacy systems to the new HCM system, ensuring data integrity and accuracy during the process. Any data transformations are validated as part of this effort.
- Knowledge Transfer: System integrators will transfer knowledge and documentation to the organization's IT and HR teams to ensure ongoing system maintenance and support. System integrators *may* provide training to system administrators, super users, and end-users to ensure they can effectively use the new system.

System integrators play a crucial role in ensuring that an organization's HCM system integrates effectively with other business systems, providing a seamless and efficient flow of data and processes. Their expertise is essential in achieving a well-coordinated and fully functional HCM ecosystem that supports HR operations and decision-making.

Summary

Each of the roles discussed are essential to successful implementation and daily operation. Employees, managers, HR professionals, administrators, super-users, providers, and integrators all have their part during the system lifecycle. System providers and integrators should not be overlooked when examining system roles. Both are instrumental in the successful Integration and operation of HCM systems within organizations. Their roles encompass a wide range of responsibilities, from initial assessments and strategic planning to data migration, customization, and ongoing support. They ensure that the HCM system seamlessly connects with other essential business software, optimizing HR processes, data consistency, and overall efficiency. System integrators play a crucial role facilitating knowledge transfer, which allows organizations to maintain and enhance the integrated HCM ecosystem. They are the linchpin in achieving a well-coordinated HCM system that aligns with an organization's unique needs and objectives.

Discussion Questions

How does the role of a system integrator differ from the design & development stage (2) to the testing & implementation stage (3)? What unique challenges do they face in each stage of the lifecycle?

Why is data integration and transformation such a critical aspect of system integration in the HCM context? How can organizations ensure data accuracy and consistency during the migration process?

What key functions do super-users fulfill? How would that help an organization progress through the lifecycle stages of a system?

What are some differences between employee and manager access? How do these system roles help improve the efficiency and effectiveness of the human resources department?

What strategies can organizations employ to ensure a smooth knowledge transfer from system integrators to their internal IT and HR teams?

Chapter References

ChatGPT. (2023). *HCM System Roles.* OpenAI. Accessed November 3, 2023.

Hartono, S., Tjahyadi, Td., & Cassandra, C. (2021). Analysis of Employee and Manager Self Service Module on SAP Portal (A Case Study Approach). 2021 *International Conference on Information Management and Technology (ICIMTech), 1*, 93–98. https://doi.org/10.1109/ICIMTech53080.2021.9535090

Karuppan, C.M., & Karuppan, M. (2008). Resilience of super users' mental models of enterprise-wide systems. *European Journal of Information Systems, 17*(1), 29–46. https://doi.org/10.1057/palgrave.ejis.3000728

Konradt, U., Christophersen, T., & Schaeffer-Kuelz, U. (2006). Predicting user satisfaction, strain and system usage of employee self-services. *International Journal of Human-Computer Studies, 64*(11), 1141–1153. https://doi.org/10.1016/j.ijhcs.2006.07.001

Mahdavian, M., & Mostajeran, F. (2013). Studying key users' skills of ERP system through a comprehensive skill measurement model. *International Journal of Advanced Manufacturing Technology, 69*(9-12), 1981–1999. https://doi.org/10.1007/s00170-013-5144-1

Marler, J.H., Fisher, S.L., & Weiling, KE. (2009). Employee Self-Service Technology Acceptance: A comparison of pre-implementation and post-implementation relationships. *Personnel Psychology, 62*(2), 327–358. https://doi.org/10.1111/j.1744-6570.2009.01140.x

Mayer, J.H., & Quick, R. (Editors) (2015). *Self-Service Management Support Systems: Findings from a New-Generation Manager Perspective. In Business Intelligence for New-Generation Managers* (pp. 113–136). Springer International Publishing AG. https://doi.org/10.1007/978-3-319-15696-5_9

Chapter 6
HCM System Modules

Chapter Table of Contents

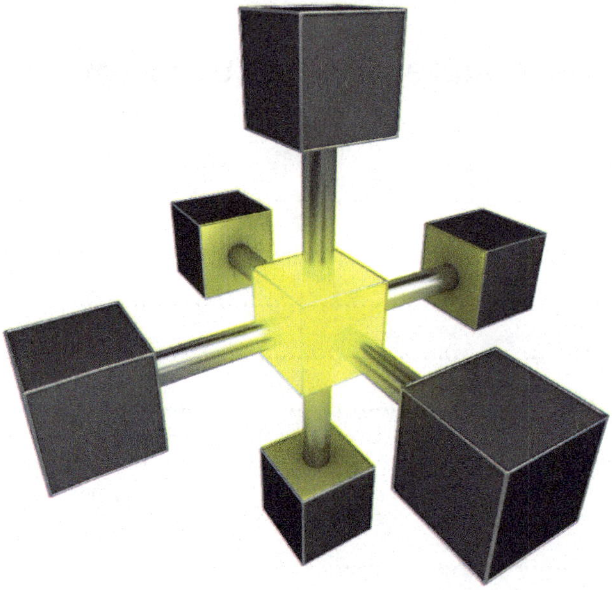

Chapter 6: HCM System Modules

Introduction

Human Capital Management (HCM) systems have revolutionized the way organizations manage their most important assets, their people. In today's businesses around the world, efficient HR processes are vital for success, and HCM system modules provide the tools needed to streamline every aspect of people management. From recruiting and onboarding to performance evaluation and talent development, HCM system modules offer comprehensive solutions that empower organizations to optimize their workforce.

In this chapter, we will explore many of the commonly available HCM system modules. Each of these are designed to address specific human resources functions and workflows. For some system providers, the use of the word "module" is excluded from their language set as it implies a separate unit of capability. Many of today's providers have constructed system architecture that leverages a cohesive and seamless set of capabilities which they turn-on or turn-off based on customer needs and licensing. The use of the word "module" does not imply separate units of capability, nor does it imply any type or modality of software development, coding, or architecture. The use of the word "module" is only meant as a convenient way to refer to distinct capabilities and workflows within the profession of human resources.

HCM system modules, from Employee Core Records to Workflow & Authorization, all play a crucial role in shaping the effectiveness and efficiency of the human resources department. The right system, with the right set of modules, contributes to an organization's overall success in the marketplace. We'll delve into what each module entails, its benefits, and its significance in the world of Human Capital Management.

Employee Core/Central Records

Employee core records is a foundational element from which all other system modules gain their functionality. Often this is referred to as employee core, employee central records, or employee master data. This foundation serves as the heart of any Human Capital Management (HCM) system. In the larger context of an enterprise resource planning (ERP) system, employee core records are part of a shared foundation of data that other enterprise functions use for deriving their capabilities. Employee Core stores crucial information about every employee within the organization (past and present,) creating a central repository of data that's essential for system workflows and processes.

These records typically contain basic personal information, employment history, contact details, and other pertinent employment data. Having accurate and up-to-date central records is fundamental for error-free transaction processing. They form the basis for various HR functions such as timekeeping, payroll, leaves of absence, performance evaluations, compensation, and more. Below is a representative listing of the types of data items that are included in Employee Core:

General Data	Demographic/Contact Data
• 1st Family Name • 2nd Family Name • Middle Name • Given/First Name • Preferred Name • Employee Identification Number • Job Title • Department • Work Location Identification Number • Manager Identification Number • Tax Identification Number	• Home Address • Home Phone Number • Home Email Address • Work Address • Work Phone Number • Work Email Address • Date of Birth • Gender Identification • Race/Ethnicity • Preferred Pronouns • Veteran/Military Status
Employment Data	**Benefits Data**
• Start Date • End Date • Employment Status • FLSA Classification • Pay Rate • Pay Frequency	• Beneficiary Information • Dependent Information • Health Plan Enrollment • Retirement Plan Enrollment • Optional Plan Enrollments • Contribution Elections
Other Data	
• Emergency Contact Information • User Identification Numbers • Work Permit/Visa Numbers • Work Permit/Visa Validity Dates	• Passport Number • Passport Validity Dates • Professional Certifications & Licenses

System providers often approach employee core records in different ways. While the concept remains consistent, managing essential employee data, they likely have variations in terms of data architecture. (Data architecture is not the focus of this book.) Here's how system providers may approach Employee Core differently:

- **Customization**: Some HCM system providers offer more extensive customization options for defining data fields within Employee Core records. This flexibility allows organizations to tailor the system to their specific needs, ensuring that they capture the precise employee information that matters most to them.
- **Integration**: The ability to integrate Employee Core records with other HR modules and external systems can differ. Some providers publish the application programming interfaces, while others require more effort to connect with other software.
- **Reporting and Analytics**: The reporting and analytics capabilities for Employee Core records can vary. Some providers offer advanced reporting tools and analytics features that allow organizations to extract valuable insights from employee data, while others may provide more basic reporting functionality.
- **Global Compliance**: For multinational organizations, differences may exist in how well various providers support global information security compliance. Some providers have a stronger global presence and are more capable of complying with international data security requirements.
- **Data Migration and Import**: The ease of data migration and importing historical employee data into the system can vary. Some providers may offer data migration services or have user-friendly import tools, while others require manual effort.

Applicant Tracking Systems

An Applicant Tracking System (ATS) is a vital module in the world of Human Capital Management (HCM). It streamlines and optimizes the recruitment process, from job posting to candidate onboarding. For many years, the ATS capabilities evolved on stand-alone platforms. More recently, these have migrated into HCM systems and are often available as an integrated module even in small business solutions.

ATS's allow organizations to post job openings, collect and manage candidate applications, schedule interviews, communicate with applicants and hiring managers, and assess candidate qualifications. It brings efficiency to the recruitment process by automating tasks, improving the candidate experience, and providing valuable insights into the effectiveness of the hiring process. ATS's are powerful tools for HR professionals, making it easier to identify the best candidates and ensuring that the hiring process is fair and compliant.

There are still some differences between stand-alone and integrated ATS's. This space continues to evolve quickly, and capabilities are blending rapidly into HCM systems. Below we'll explore these differences:

Stand-Alone Applicant Tracking Systems:

Advantages:

- Specialized Functionality: Stand-alone ATS are designed specifically for applicant tracking and recruitment. They often offer a more specialized and feature-rich set of tools tailored for the hiring process.
- Scalability: These systems can be a great choice for organizations looking for scalability and flexibility. They allow companies to select the best-of-breed ATS solution that suits their unique needs.

- Customization: Stand-alone ATS systems often provide extensive customization options, allowing organizations to adapt the system to their unique recruitment processes and branding.
- Ease of Integration: While stand-alone ATS systems are usually not part of a larger suite, they often offer various integration options with various HCM systems.

Disadvantages:

- Data Silos: The biggest drawback of stand-alone ATS is data separation. Candidate data and recruiting information may not seamlessly flow into employee core records or other HR modules. This can lead to inefficiencies and require duplication of effort on the part of the applicant and the HR professional.
- Complex Vendor Management: Organizations using multiple HR systems from different vendors may face challenges with vendor management, service contracts, and system compatibility.

Integrated ATS within HCM Suite:

Advantages:

- Seamless Data Flow: An integrated ATS/HCM suite ensures that applicant and employee data seamlessly integrate with employee core records and other HR modules.
- Unified Role Management: Roles are managed centrally, providing improved information security, and minimizing multiplying system access points.
- Reduced Duplication: With an integrated approach, there's less risk of data duplication or data inconsistencies.
- Cost and Vendor Management: Integrated systems may simplify vendor management, as organizations deal with fewer vendors and potentially reduce costs associated with multiple systems.
- Unified User Experience: Employees and HR professionals can access all HR functions from a single interface, creating a unified user experience. This is an important advantage of an integrated ATS/HCM suite. It provides benefits to candidates who transition from being applicants to new employees. This seamless transition can greatly improve the employee experience, as they don't have to re-enter information already provided during the application process. Here's an elaboration on this advantage:

  Streamlined Employee Onboarding: When an organization uses an integrated ATS within an HCM suite, the data captured during the application phase can seamlessly flow into the employee's record once they are hired. This means that the information provided by candidates during the recruitment process, such as personal details, contact information, employment history, and qualifications, is automatically populated into their new employee file.

  Benefits for New Employees: Time and Effort Savings: New employees are spared the effort of re-entering data that they've already provided during the application phase. This reduces the administrative burden on both HR professionals and the employees themselves.

Consistency and Accuracy: Data accuracy is improved because there's less manual data entry. The information is transferred consistently, reducing the risk of errors or inconsistencies in employee records.

Faster Onboarding: The onboarding process can be expedited as employees can focus on critical aspects of their new role, rather than spending time duplicating information.

Integrated ATS solutions that seamlessly transfer applicant data to core employee records benefits HR professionals by reducing administrative tasks, and they also provide a positive and efficient experience for new hires. It reflects well on the organization's commitment to a smooth onboarding process, which can contribute to improved employee satisfaction and engagement from day one.

Disadvantages:

- Limited Specialization: Integrated ATS systems may not offer the same depth of specialization as stand-alone systems. Organizations with complex or unique recruitment processes may find these features lacking.
- Less Flexibility: Integrated systems may be less flexible in terms of choosing different vendors for specific talent acquisition functions. They require a commitment to a single vendor's ecosystem.

In summary, the choice between a stand-alone ATS and an integrated ATS/HCM suite depends on an organization's specific needs, priorities, and existing system infrastructure. Stand-alone ATS's offer specialization and flexibility but may result in data silos. Integrated systems can provide a more unified user experience and seamless data flow but may lack certain specialized features. This space continues to evolve quickly, and capabilities are blending rapidly.

Performance Management

Performance Management is one of the cornerstone functions of human resources, and it's also a cornerstone module in HCM systems. Performance management is fundamentally about the conscious alignment of people to an organization's strategy and business plan. There is no other business process which strives to accomplish the degree of alignment that performance management does. Performance management is a strategic approach to enhancing employee productivity and development. It aligns individual goals with organizational objectives and provides a structured framework for evaluating and improving performance.

A well-implemented performance management module fosters employee engagement, boosts morale, and contributes to achieving business goals by ensuring that all employee's efforts are aligned with the company's mission. This module enables people to set and track objectives, review progress, provide feedback, and appraise results.

The performance management module contains a set of features which supports the entire performance process. Here are some of the key features of a comprehensive performance management module:

- Objective Setting:
  Define and set performance objectives throughout the organization. The more expansive modules enable cascading of objectives from senior leadership down to individual contributor. These also facilitate dividing objectives as they cascade and then tracking the accretive organizational results throughout the year.
- Feedback and Communication:
  The performance management module facilitates the feedback and communications process between manager and employee. It provides a place to capture the content of feedback/communications sessions so that both have an ongoing record of dialogue. These notes can be used to render more fair and accurate appraisals at the end of a performance cycle.

- Performance Appraisals:
  The performance management module captures the content and outcome of appraisals between a manager and employee. These are completed against previously defined objectives. The appraisal step can also capture comments from managers, peers, and subordinates about an individual's performance during a performance cycle. This module will also support the assignment of performance ratings based on a defined rating system.
- Automated Workflow and Notifications:
  Performance Management modules operate on a defined process. Lower tier systems may force an organization to use the provider's defined process; whereas, higher tier systems often allow organizations to customize the process and workflow. In either case, the system facilitates the automatic movement of work and approvals for both the cascading and rolling-up of objectives and results respectively.
- Data Analytics and Reporting:
  Performance management enables several other capabilities such as learning, compensation, and succession planning. Therefore, it's vital that the performance management module enables querying, dashboarding, report generation, and analytics.

Performance management is one of those modules where the capabilities can blend with other modules. It depends how the provider treats their system architecture and how they want to market and sell their system. The range of options is vast. It's still possible to purchase a stand-alone third-party system that is focused solely on performance management. At the other end of the spectrum, it's possible to purchase an integrated HCM suite that has performance management embedded in *talent* capabilities. Below are a few of the capabilities that a performance management module *may* perform, which could also be performed by another system or module:

- Development Planning:
  This is one activity that most heavily overlaps with performance management. It's natural to move from setting performance objectives to defining employee development needs. If performance objectives challenge an employee to do new things, then development is likely going to be needed. Consequently, it's common for development planning and writing development objectives to sit alongside their related performance objectives. These can feed into learning management modules where the Learning Management System (LMS) can help the employee by identifying and suggesting specific learning content.
- Competency Assessment:
  Related to development, a performance management module may support a competency-based approach. When available, it enables managers and employees to identify competencies required for success in their roles. Subsequently, they may facilitate a 360° degree competency assessment process where feedback is collected from managers, peers, subordinates, and other key work partners. This feedback can then be further incorporated into development plans.

- Talent Comparisons:
  Talent comparisons is an approach to performance management that's often referred to as "rating and ranking." It's where groups of employees are compared to each other based on their performance appraisal ratings and development potential. Where systems provide this capability, it's common to visually depict these comparisons using a matrix graph where each dot is the placement of an employee. These visualizations can be used by management to discuss their talent in terms of performance and future assignments within the organization. Some providers bundled talent comparisons inside performance management, and others will separate it under the heading of either *Talent* or *Talent Management*.

Effective performance management in an HCM system environment involves several capabilities which are designed to promote organizational alignment of people resources, energy, and effort. This helps ensure that people understand what they need to be working on, and the alignment ensures that people resources are used efficiently and effectively. The performance management module can also facilitate the process of employee development, and it can help foster a productive and engaged culture. Adaptability of the system's performance management process and workflow will depend on the scale of the solution and the provider selected.

Talent & Talent Management

When you see "Talent" used to describe a module, usually it means a larger set of capability than when you see "Talent Management" used. "TALENT" often includes performance management, applicant tracking/recruiting, development planning, succession planning, and more. Whereas, "Talent Management" is a more focused module oriented to the movement of talent within an organization. Think of "talent" as a bundle of other modules. We'll address the *talent management* module in this section. The talent management module enables employees to create and manage talent profiles, which are detailed records of an employee's skills, competencies, and career aspirations.

The Talent Management module helps an organization gain visibility and movement of their own pipeline of high-potential employees who are prepared to take on leadership roles in the future. Operationally speaking, it's the movement or mobilization of talent that has business value. Organizations mobilize people to fill operational gaps and needs, and having a talent management module facilitates a faster identification and a higher quality assignment of talent to role. Absent a talent management module, the only way to do this is based on "who you know." On their own, any given manager's knowledge of talent is limited to around 150 meaningful contacts, known as "Dunbar's Number" (Lindenfors, Wartel, & Lind, 2021.) Truer in-depth knowledge of people's capabilities is limited even further to an estimated 50-100 people. The larger the organization, the more that a talent management module is needed.

One of the leading components of a talent management module is the ability for employees to build and maintain their own talent profile. Similar in method and construct to profiles that may be constructed on various social media sites, the individual employee creates and maintains the profile. It is, however, business and professionally focused. Talent profiles provide a comprehensive view of each employee's professional career. Different sources of data can feed talent profiles, such as performance appraisal ratings, and 360° competency assessment results.

As a management team reviews their organizational talent, they can capture their own notes regarding employee strengths and needed development. These notes can be part of the employee feedback process and an input into development planning. The talent management module is focused on facilitating informed decision-making regarding talent mobilization to meet organizational needs. See Figure 06.01 for an illustrative example of a talent profile.

The talent management module typically includes a set of features designed to identify, develop, and mobilize top talent within an organization. Talent Profiles are a part of the talent management module, but they serve a distinct purpose within this broader framework. Here are the key features of talent management:

- Talent Acquisition:
  Often an integration with talent acquisition/ATS is desirable. When done, this allows for employee talent profiles to be pre-populated based on an employee's resume and application. This can save a tremendous amount of time for employees when initially building their profiles.
- Talent Development:
  Often, integration with learning and development is desirable. This enables the talent management module and profiles to include employee development achievements, and competency assessment results. It also enables the management team to be able to recommend development needs for future advancement opportunities.
- Performance Management:
  Integration with performance management is essential for an optimum talent management approach. Since the focus is around mobilizing talent to meet organization needs, having visibility to employee performance history is an essential input to decision making.
- Talent Comparisons:
  Closely related and interdependent with performance management, talent comparisons are where groups of employees are compared to each other based on their performance appraisal ratings and development potential. Also referred to as "rating and ranking." It's common to visually depict these comparisons using a matrix graph where each dot is the placement of an employee. These visualizations can be used by management to discuss their talent in terms of performance and future assignments within the organization. Again, the focus being on mobilization of talent to meet current and future organizational needs.

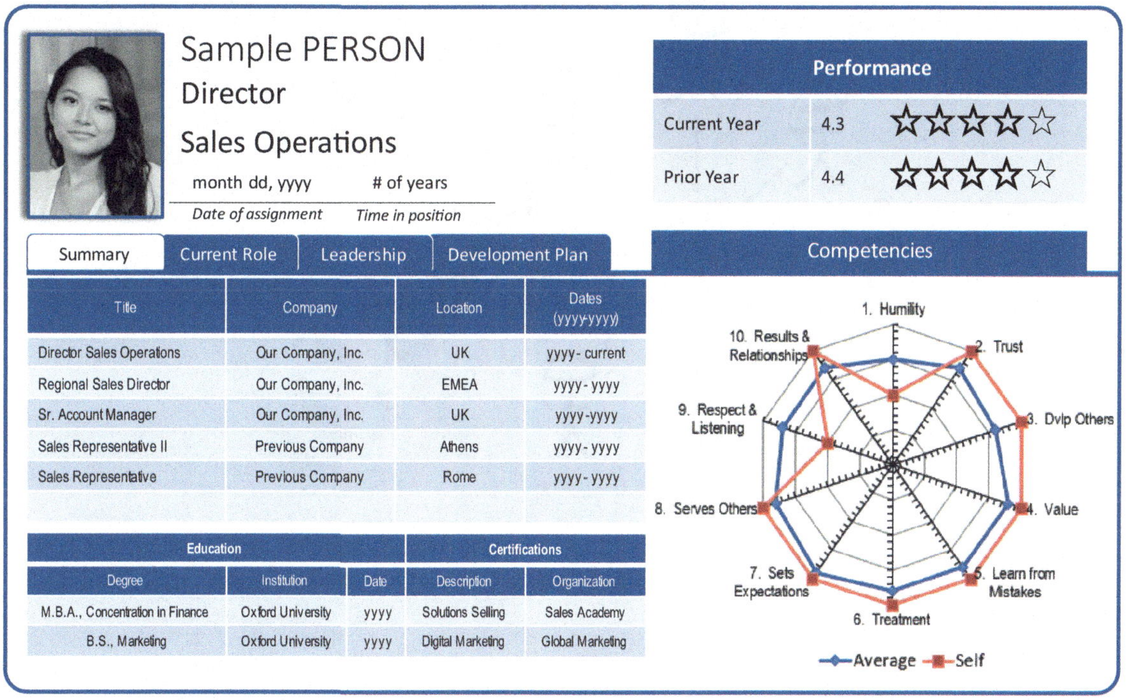

Figure 06.01
Talent Profile

Example of what a talent profile may look like in a HCM system. Photo courtesy of Christina Morillo from pexels.com

Talent Management encompasses the identification, comparison, and development of employees. It builds organizational knowledge of people. The focus of talent management is on mobilizing talent to meet organizational needs. Talent profiles are an integral part of the talent management module, which serve as a tool for capturing and managing information about employees. They facilitate organizational wide talent development and succession planning efforts.

Organization Structure

Organizational structure and organizational structure maintenance is one of the more nuanced modules within a HCM system. Providers have different ways of approaching this, and the impact can be significant on the business and on the human resources department. Organization structure depicts the hierarchy of people and positional relationships within a business. Two very important words in the previous sentence: ***people*** and ***position***. It's these two words that drive the modality of organizational structure maintenance among providers.

Understanding the difference between people-driven and position-driven structure maintenance modalities is crucial for HR professionals. It requires an astutely aware HR professional, partnering with system providers and technology representatives to help companies navigate their organizational dynamics effectively. The choices made in this regard also have a large impact on the accounting function and budgetary processes.

In a people-driven approach, the focus lies on individuals within the organization, emphasizing flexibility, personalization, and agility in adapting to changing roles and responsibilities. Conversely, position-driven approach prioritizes predefined roles and hierarchies, offering simplicity, consistency, and performance optimization at the expense of speed-of-adaptability. Each approach carries distinct implications for system architecture, coding practices, and organizational culture, shaping how businesses manage their workforce.

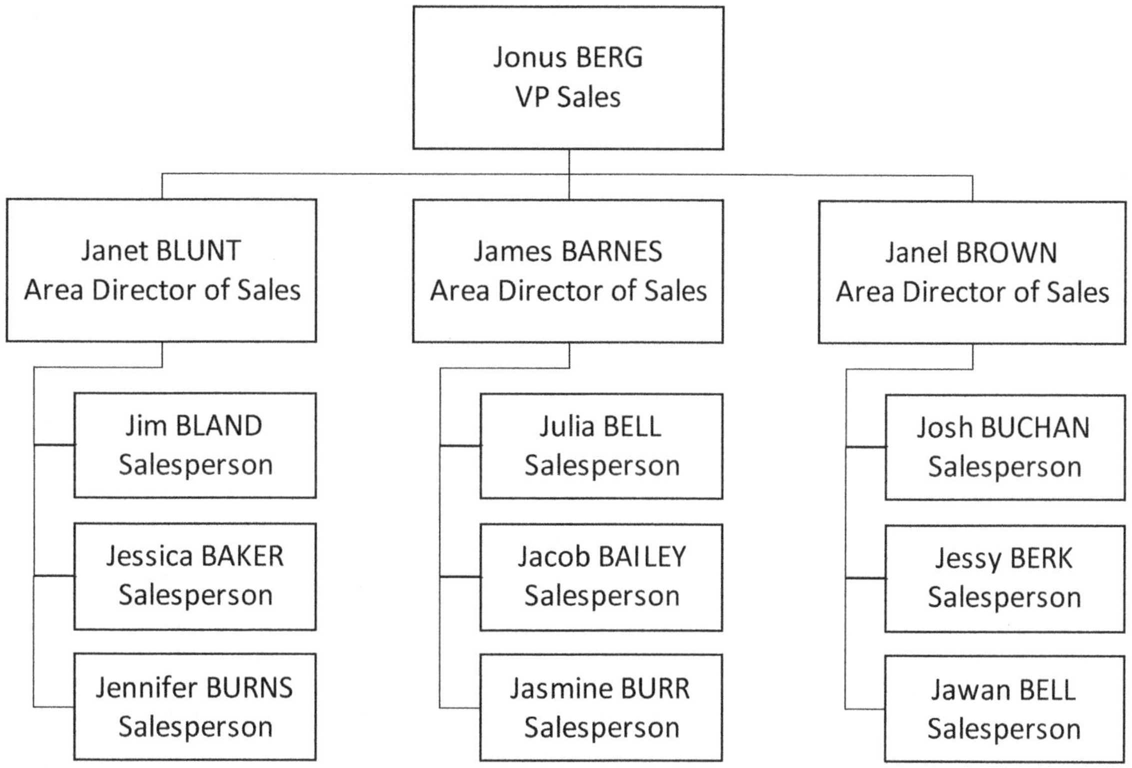

Figure 06.02
Organization Structure
An example of a simple organizational structure for a sales team with three layers depicted.

Here, in Figure 06.02, a simple organizational structure is depicted for a sales group. There's a head of sales, and underneath that are three Area Directors. Each Area Director has three Salespeople reporting to them. In total, this team has 13 people/headcount. Let's say that one of the Area Directors, Janet Blunt, has decided to leave the organization for another opportunity.

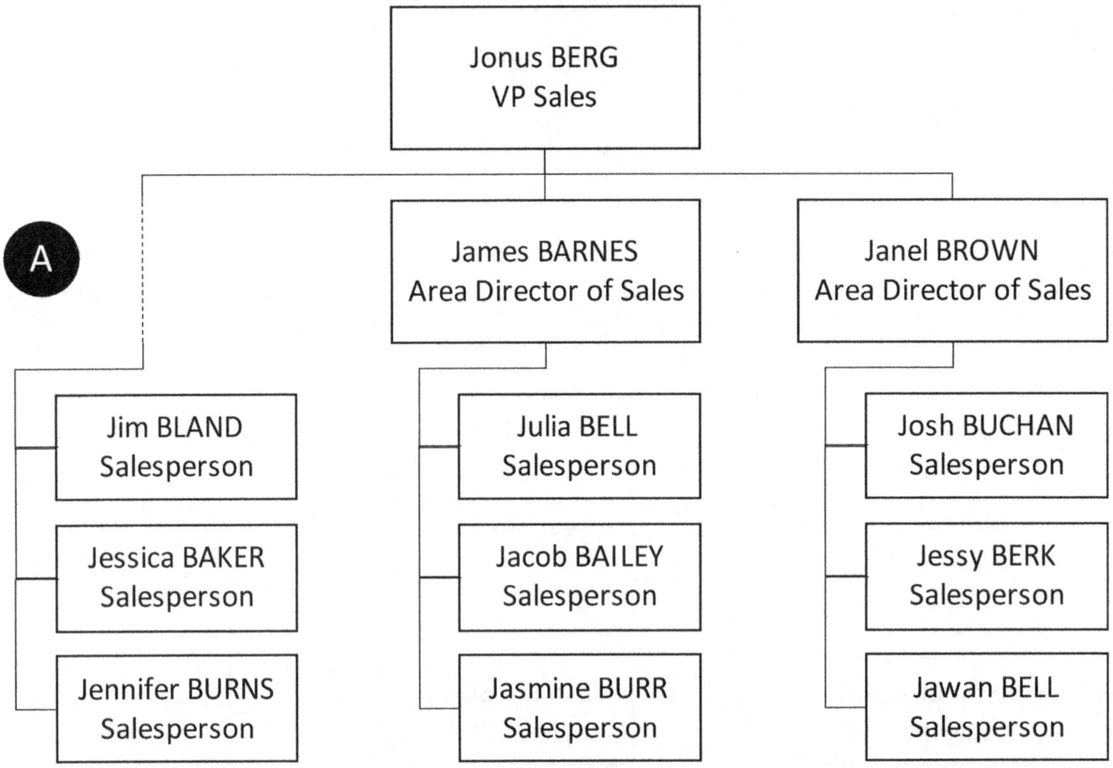

Figure 06.03
Organization Structure Maintenance, People Driven
An example of the impact of organizational structure changes when the organizational maintenance modality is people driven.

Refer to Figure 06.03. In a people-driven modality for organizational maintenance, when Janet BLUNT (A) leaves the organization, her direct reports will roll-up one level. In this case, the VP of Sales, Jonus BERG, will have three salespeople added to his responsibility. His number of direct reports will go from three to five. Additionally, in the people-driven modality, the headcount of the organization changes when someone leaves. The headcount in this example would drop from 13 to 12 because Janet BLUNT left.

Advantage

- Organizational scaling is easier to implement because the changes are simply who reports to whom.

Disadvantages

- Consistency around data integrity can be problematic especially if the organization has a high volume and frequency of role changes.
- Managing access and control can be challenging with high volume and frequency of role changes. It's easier to assign system/data authority levels to a position versus a person.

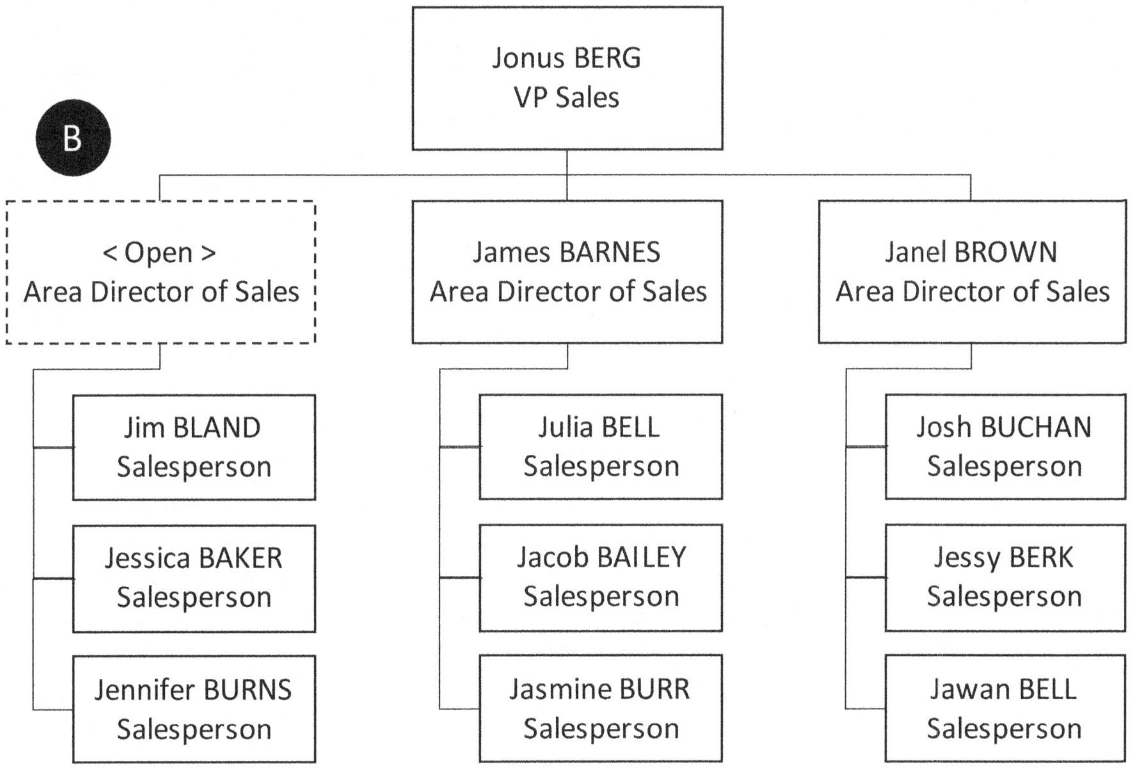

Figure 06.04
Organization Structure Maintenance, Position Driven
An example of the impact of organizational structure changes when the organizational maintenance modality is position driven.

Refer to Figure 06.04. In a position-drive modality for organizational maintenance, when Janet BLUNT (B) leaves the organization, the position that she occupied remains in place and intact. In this case, the VP of Sales, Jonus BERG, will have his direct reports drop from three to two people, but the number of positions he's responsible for stays the same. The headcount in this example still drops from 13 to 12, but there's a separate position count which remains the same.

Advantages

- Position count and budget allocation stays synchronized, which can improve budget tracking and forecasting accuracy during a fiscal year.
- Managing access and control is easier because "need to know" is driven by positional needs and positional authority.

Disadvantages

- Adds complexity to the system architecture and coding. The system must be capable of storage and retrieval of positional containers and then assigning employees (and the absence of employees) to those containers.

- Organizational scaling takes more time and effort because the organizational design itself must be created and implemented before people and reporting relationship can be added or changed. *Not* doing this isn't an option in this modality because reporting relationships will not function if it's not maintained.

Both people-driven and position-driven modalities for organizational structure maintenance have advantages and disadvantages. The choice between these approaches depends on factors such as organizational culture, business requirements, and the nature of the workforce. It's also heavily dependent on the choice of system provider. Many (if not most) systems are not capable of this level of architectural choice.

A well-defined organizational structure is essential for effective communication, decision-making, and resource allocation. It helps employees and managers understand their roles, responsibilities, and to whom they report. These enhance collaboration, workflow, and the overall efficiency of the organization. Position assignments impact decision approval authorities, and these are integrated with authorization routing across many other enterprise planning modules. The organizational structure module plays a pivotal role in shaping an business' strategy execution and day-to-day operations.

Succession Planning

Succession planning is a practice that's used to ensure business continuity and improve business responsiveness. Succession planning focuses on key leadership positions that have a significant impact on the company, its direction, performance, and success. Succession planning at its root is a business risk mitigation tool. So, it makes sense that many HCM systems providers have a module that provides succession planning and management capabilities.

The instant that a position becomes vacant, the company loses momentum and progress. The longer the gap the more risk there is of a loss of performance. By conducting succession planning, the company gives proactive thought to position-gap-scenarios and what their plan of action might be. Succession planning allows a company to anticipate talent-market changes and potential responses.

Most succession planning approaches fall short of providing companies with an effective scenario plan for talent. Most succession planning approaches are really what's called "position planning." In position planning, one identifies potential candidates for a position, if the job doesn't change. Almost all current HCM systems, which have a succession module, use this position planning approach instead of a scenario planning approach.

When conducted, and plans are put in place, succession planning minimizes the disruption that can occur during transitions. Transitions happen in organizations regularly, so it makes sense to anticipate these and identify potential internal talent proactively. Vacancies can be caused by common things like retirements, promotions, rotations, or voluntarily exits. When used, this module can be an essential component of long-term strategic organizational sustainability.

Below are some key components, features, and terminology of a succession planning module in a HCM system:

- Succession Pool Management:
  Succession pools are groups of people who have been identified as potential successors for one or more positions. These pools can be created and managed in the succession planning module.

- Integration with Talent Profiles:
  Succession planning modules will integrate with Talent/Talent Management and leverage the talent profiles created by employees. These detailed records of employees' skills, competencies, career progression, performance, and career aspirations enable leadership decision making around who will be the best/most viable candidate to assume a role. This integration ensures that potential successors' profiles are up-to-date and linked to succession planning.

Effective succession planning in an HCM system helps organizations mitigate leadership risks, ensure continuity in critical roles, and develop a strong leadership pipeline to drive long-term success. These features and components are essential to create and maintain a robust succession planning process.

Development Planning

Development Planning is another important module within a HCM system that focuses on employee growth and skill development. It involves setting individual development goals, identifying training opportunities, and tracking progress. This is one activity that most heavily overlaps with performance management. It's natural to move from setting performance objectives to defining employee development needs. If performance objectives challenge an employee to do new things, then development is likely going to be needed. Consequently, it's common for development objectives to sit alongside their related performance objectives. These can feed into learning management modules where the Learning Management System (LMS) can help the employee identify and suggest learning content. It's common to see development planning in performance management, talent management, and succession planning. Many system providers leverage a single development planning data record which shows up in multiple views, so when you look at the development objectives in performance management, they're the same ones being viewed in talent management and succession planning.

Employees benefit from development planning as it offers a clear path for advancing their careers, improving their skills, and achieving their personal and professional goals. Organizations, in turn, benefit from having a skilled and motivated workforce that's aligned with their strategic objectives. Development planning contributes to employee engagement, talent retention, and overall business performance.

Here are some of the key terminology, features, and components of the development planning module in a HCM system:

- Development Objectives:
  Allows employees and managers to partner together to define and set development objectives. Development objectives can be connected to organizational goals and business initiatives.

- Development Resources:
  Learning and development opportunities can be provided dynamically to employees. Learning Management Systems (LMS) can provide access to training courses, workshops, e-learning, and resources which are used to enhance skills and competencies. On-the-Job learning and rotational assignments can also be prescribed and tracked with this module.

It is important to note that a development planning module and a learning management system are often different things. Effective development planning empowers employees to take ownership of their professional growth while aligning their goals with the organization's strategic priorities. It also helps organizations cultivate a skilled and adaptable workforce to meet future challenges and opportunities. These features and components are essential for creating and maintaining a robust development planning process within an HCM system. A LMS is a comprehensive platform/system that's designed to deliver and manage learning content and progress to completion.

Learning Management Systems

Learning Management is a capability area that is in the process of evolving and migrating *toward* HCM systems. It is still common to find Learning Management Systems (LMS) that are stand-alone third-party systems, which require integration with a HCM system. To make things a bit more complex, there's also a difference between a LMS and a Learning Content Management System (LCMS). Let's review these terms first.

A Learning Management System (LMS) and a Learning Content Management System (LCMS) are both software systems used in the field of learning and development, but they serve different purposes and offer some distinctly different features. Below is a chart the highlights the differences between them:

Learning Management System (LMS)	Learning Content Management System (LCMS)
➢ Delivers, manages, and tracks learning activities for employees. ➢ Administration, tracking, and reporting of training programs, courses, and assessments. ➢ Facilitates user management, course enrollments, content delivery, progress tracking, assessment management, and reporting.	➢ Focused on content creation. Creating, managing, and publishing learning content. ➢ Includes content authoring tools, content repository, version control, content reuse, collaboration features, and publishing capabilities. ➢ Enables content developers to create and manage a wide range of learning materials, including courses, modules, assessments, simulations, and multimedia content.

Much of the current migration of capability toward HCM platforms is focused on the LMS features and not the content management aspects of LCMS. Effective learning management contributes to enhancing employee competencies and aligning their skills with organizational needs. It enables employees to access training resources, schedule courses, and track their progress. Learning management is pivotal for staying competitive, adapting to changing industry requirements, and fostering a culture of continuous learning within the organization.

Here are some of the key terminology, features, and components of a learning management module (*not LCMS*) in an HCM system:

- Catalogue Management:
  Enables the human resources department to maintain a catalog of available courses and programs. Allows employees to browse and enroll in courses, whether in-person, online, or through e-learning platforms.

- Scheduling and Enrollment:
  Provides the human resources department with the ability to schedule and manage training sessions, including date, time, location, and instructor information.

- Learning Paths:
  Create structured learning paths that guide employees through a sequence of content, courses, certifications, and training milestones.

- Assessment and Evaluation:
  Implement quizzes and assessments to measure learning outcomes and knowledge retention. (Many times, this capability also exists on an LCMS.)

- Learning Analytics:
  Provides reports and analytics on employee training progress, completion rates, and performance. Especially useful for compliance and other mandatory training, along with automated exception reporting.

Compensation & Benefit Planning

The compensation and benefits planning module within a HCM system manages benefit plan offerings, pay grade structures, salary/pay information, and incentive plans. It ensures that compensation is fair, competitive, complies with government regulations, and aligns with organizational objectives. Done well, compensation planning has a significantly positive impact on employee motivation, engagement, and retention. It plays a role in attracting top talent, rewarding performance, and maintaining market competitiveness. This module helps HR departments design and manage compensation and benefits, so they align with the organization's budget and business goals.

Here are some of the key terminology, features, and components of the compensation and benefits planning module in a HCM system:

- Pay Structure and Grading:
  Pay grades/bands can be created and maintained. This includes establishing grades for both hourly and salaried positions, along with other classifications that may be required around the world. It also includes managing variations of these structures based on market differences within a country and between regions.

- Compensation Management:
  Enables the human resources department to systematically analyze and price job roles in the market to determine competitive pay. This information can be tracked between markets and trended over time. Also enables the critical ability to manage, and adjust base pay, incorporate merit-based increases, and to differentially reward based on performance, skill,

and/or tenure. It also incorporates the ability to administer variable pay programs, such as bonuses, incentives, and commission structures.

- Total Rewards and Benefits:
  Administer employee benefits, such as healthcare/medical plans, retirement plans, and other fringe benefits. May also provide total rewards statements for employees, allowing them to see a regular and comprehensive view of their total compensation package, including salary, bonuses, benefits, and other perquisites.

- Budgetary and Accounting Support:
  Enables the planning cycles for compensation reviews, such as annual, semi-annual, or quarterly reviews. Includes organizational budgeting and forecasting. Facilitates approval workflows so managers and HR professionals can review and approve compensation and budgetary adjustments.

- Market Data and Benchmarking:
  May connect to third party benchmarking providers, enabling integrated access to external pay survey data. Used to compare the organization's compensation levels with industry and location practices, helping the organization to attract and retain talent.

- Compliance & Pay Equity:
  Analyzes and ensures pay equity within the organization, addressing pay disparity between protected classes. Helps identify and address over-pay (red circle) and under-pay/compression (green circle) issues.

Effective compensation planning in an HCM system is essential for attracting and retaining top talent, aligning compensation with performance and market standards, and ensuring a competitive and fair compensation structure within the organization. These features and components help organizations manage and optimize their compensation practices and attract and retain talent.

Document Management

The document management module in a HCM system handles the storage, retrieval, and organization of employment related documents. This includes contracts, performance reviews, policies, and other important records. Effective document management ensures compliance with legal and regulatory requirements, data security, and streamlined document retrieval. It saves time and resources, reduces the risk of errors, and helps maintain a complete and accurate HR history for each employee. Document management is critical for maintaining a well-organized and compliant HR environment.

HCM systems often include document management capabilities, which encompass the handling of various HR-related documents, acknowledgments, approvals, and routing. Here are some of the common terminology, features, and capabilities of the documentation management module:

- Employment Relationship:
  Central repository for the storage and active management of employment related documents for employees. Includes documents such as hiring, immigration, payroll, employment contracts, resumes, performance appraisals, discipline, and safety records. Where the documents have expirations, the module will also do version control, helping the organization complete timely updates and ensure ongoing compliance. An equally valuable feature, many of these modules will support dynamic document search capabilities which provide human resources professionals with the ability to quickly locate specific documents based on keywords, filters, and metadata.

- Acknowledgments:
  Acknowledgment tracking is important for organizations around key documents and policies. As these are updated, it's also important to collect and store acknowledgement

updates from employees. Supporting an electronic signature process enables digital records and reduces the need for physical space for paper record storage.

- Document Security:
  Implements digital access controls to safeguard sensitive and confidential information, ensuring that only authorized individuals can view or edit sensitive information on a "need to know" basis. Document access and changes are tracked, helping to ensure compliance, and protecting against the damage that can be caused by data breaches.

It's important to note that most HCM systems provide some level of document management. However, there are specialized solutions available. These third-party specialized solutions can be implemented in a stand-alone or integrated environment. While document management modules in HCM systems are suitable for many organizations, specialized document management systems can offer more advanced capabilities for organizations with specific and complex document management needs. The choice depends on an organization's unique requirements, compliance demands, and industry-specific needs.

Summary

Human Capital Management (HCM) is a complex ecosystem that demands efficiency and precision in every task and capability set. The described modules provide organizations with a structured approach to managing their workforce, ensuring employees are engaged, developed, and well-supported. These modules collectively form a cohesive system, providing a holistic approach to HR management, enabling organizations to align their workforce with their strategic goals and thrive in a dynamic and competitive business environment.

Discussion Questions

How can effective utilization of HCM modules benefit an organization's HR strategy and overall business performance?

In your opinion, which HCM module do you believe is the most critical for talent retention and why?

What challenges or obstacles might organizations face when implementing or upgrading HCM modules, and how can these be overcome?

Can you provide examples of organizations that have successfully leveraged HCM modules to achieve their HR and talent management goals? What strategies did they employ?

In what ways do you think emerging technologies, such as artificial intelligence and analytics, are influencing the development and functionality of HCM modules? How might this impact the future of HR management?

Chapter References

Athanur, A., Ingram, M., & Wellens, M. A. (2022). *Innovative SAP SuccessFactors Recruiting : A Guide to Creating Custom Integration and Automation* (1st ed. 2022.). Apress. https://doi.org/10.1007/978-1-4842-7425-5

ChatGPT. (2023). *HCM Modules.* OpenAI. Accessed November 3, 2023.

Elbardan, H., & Kholeif, A. O. (2017). *Enterprise Resource Planning, Corporate Governance and Internal Auditing : An Institutional Perspective.* Springer International Publishing. https://doi.org/10.1007/978-3-319-54990-3

Lindenfors, P., Wartel, A., & Lind, J. (2021). *'Dunbar's Number" deconstructed.* Royal Society Publishing. https://doi.org/10.1098/rsbl.2021.0158

Nestell, J.G., & Olson, D. L. (2018). *Successful ERP systems : a guide for businesses and executives.* Business Expert Press.

Sharma, C., Sakshi, Sharma, S., & Kondal, N. (2023). Role and impact of human resource information system (HRIS) on organizational activities. *AIP Conference Proceedings, 2558(*1). https://doi.org/10.1063/5.0123335

Valcik, N.A., Sabharwal, M., & Benavides, T. J. (2021). *Human Resources Information Systems : A Guide for Public Administrators* (1st ed. 2021.). Springer International Publishing. https://doi.org/10.1007/978-3-030-75111-1

Chapter 7
Large Business Solutions

Table of Contents

Photo by fauxels from pexels.com

Chapter 7: Large Business Solutions

Introduction

Our focus in this chapter will be on the large multinational enterprises (MNEs) who operate on a global scale. There certainly are many businesses which are considered large and operate in a single country, and these are not excluded from this discussion. The reader will need to interpret and adjust this content for large/single-country operations. Don't get caught up in the numbers used in this section, such as number of employees, number of countries, etc. As a previous chapter emphasized, an organization should let their requirements gathering determine system sizing and scalability.

In the realm of Human Capital Management (HCM), large MNEs grapple with a unique set of challenges and opportunities. Operating on a global scale, these organizations, often with over 10,000 employees and a presence in at least four countries, demand specialized HCM systems that cater to their unique needs. This discussion explores the intricacies of HCM for large businesses, with a focus on international and multi-national business operations. From managing global workforces to ensuring data security and navigating international compliance, we delve into the multifaceted world of HCM designed to empower these industry leaders.

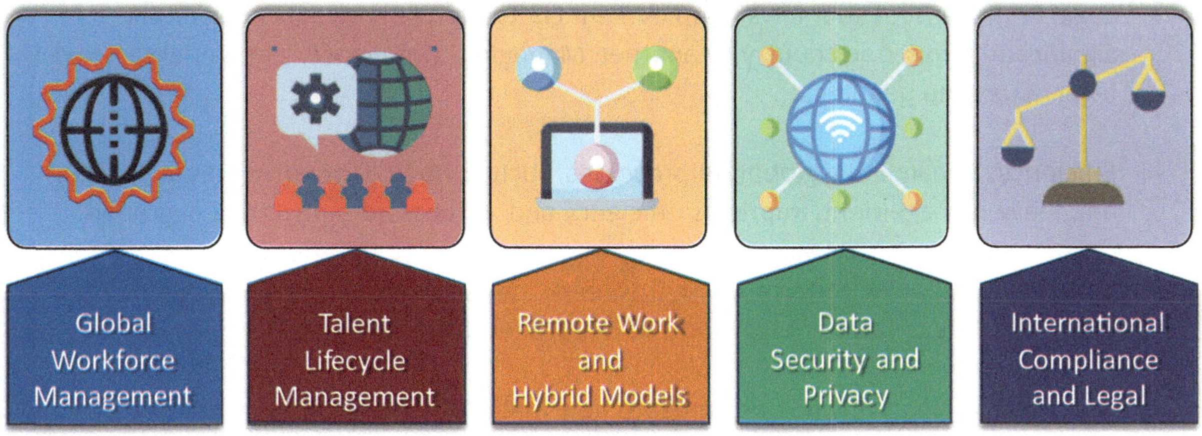

Unique Needs of Large Businesses

Large businesses operate on a grand scale, with a footprint that often extends globally across multiple countries and regions. As they grow and diversify, they encounter a unique set of challenges and opportunities that demand specialized system solutions. To be considered "large," these organizations often employ 10,000 or more employees. This is certainly not the rule. A company could have 3,000 employees and require large system capabilities. Likely, one of the primary drivers is that large companies operate multi-nationally, and they have employees and business operations in several countries. They face a more complex landscape in HR and workforce management that goes far beyond the capacities of smaller systems. In this section, we delve into the unique needs that large MNEs encounter in the realm of Human Capital Management (HCM). From navigating international compliance and cultural diversity to implementing global workforce strategies and ensuring data security across borders, we explore the requirements of HCM tailored to the operating needs of these industry leaders. Understanding these unique needs is the first step toward enabling large businesses to thrive in today's dynamic global landscape.

Global Workforce Management

Global Workforce Management involves optimizing a MNE's workforce across multiple countries and regions. It's important for large MNEs because it allows them to maximize the productivity, efficiency, and engagement of their diverse workforce while adhering to local labor laws and cultural differences. Here's why it's important and some key system considerations:

- Diverse Workforce: MNEs often have employees from various national and cultural backgrounds, each with different expectations and work styles. Effective global workforce management helps ensure inclusivity and cultural sensitivity.

- Legal Compliance: Labor laws, employment contracts, and regulations can vary significantly from one country to another. Managing compliance is essential to avoid legal issues and penalties.

- Efficiency: Streamlining global HR processes, such as payroll, benefits administration, and leave management, improves efficiency and reduces administrative overhead.

- Talent Retention: By understanding the needs and aspirations of employees in different regions, MNEs can better retain and develop their talent, reducing turnover.

- Global Expansion: As MNEs expand into new markets, workforce management systems must be flexible enough to adapt to local practices and regulations.

- Multi-Country Payroll: The HCM system should support payroll processing that complies with local tax laws and regulations in each country of operation. It should also handle multiple currencies, languages, and banking system integrations.

- Time and Attendance Tracking: The system should offer features for tracking work hours, leave, and attendance in compliance with relevant labor laws and overtime regulations.

- Benefits Administration: Benefits packages can vary greatly by country. The system should support diverse benefits offerings and ensure compliance with local laws and regulations.

- Global Recruitment: The system should facilitate international recruitment, including multilingual job postings, candidate tracking, and onboarding for all company hires in their respective locations.

- Performance Management: A flexible system should allow for both global and localized performance processes, ensuring that employees' objectives align with the company's business plan and strategies, while accommodating regional areas of focus.

- Learning and Development: Offer a comprehensive learning and development module that can cater to the diverse learning needs and preferences of a multinational workforce.

- Language and Localization: The system should be available in multiple languages and should support localization of content, such as training materials and communications.

- Data Security and Compliance: Robust data security measures need to be in place to protect sensitive employee data in accordance with local data protection laws. The different requirements from various governments adds complexity.

- Cultural Awareness: The system should help HR professionals navigate cultural differences and provide resources and best practices for creating an inclusive work environment.

- Support and Training: Access to 24/7 support and comprehensive training resources is crucial for a system that's used by HR professionals worldwide.

- Analytics and Reporting: Advanced analytics need to be available to provide insights into the global workforce's performance and engagement.

- Mobile Accessibility: A mobile-friendly system is essential for a global workforce, many of whom may be remote or frequently on the move.

Global workforce management is essential for large MNEs with a presence in multiple countries to ensure compliance, efficiency, productivity, and a positive employee experience. The right HCM system should provide the necessary features and flexibility to meet the unique requirements of such a workforce.

Talent Lifecycle Management, Internationally and Interculturally

Talent Lifecycle Management in the context of large MNEs involves the strategic and holistic management of the employee journey from recruitment to retirement, considering both international and intercultural dimensions. This approach recognizes the diverse backgrounds and needs of employees in various regions and is crucial for the success and sustainability of large MNEs. Here's why it's important and key system considerations:

- Diverse Workforce Engagement: It ensures that employees from different cultures and countries are engaged, motivated, and aligned with the company's mission and values.

- Talent Attraction and Retention: In a competitive global job market, attracting and retaining top talent is vital. Talent lifecycle management helps create an appealing work environment.

- Cultural Sensitivity: Recognizing and respecting cultural differences is essential for an inclusive work environment, reducing cultural conflicts, and promoting collaboration.

- Compliance: Managing the talent lifecycle while adhering to regional labor laws, tax regulations, and compliance requirements is crucial to avoid legal issues.

- Global Mobility: Many MNE employees may be assigned to work in different countries. Talent lifecycle management ensures smooth transitions and support for such assignments.

System Considerations for Talent Lifecycle Management:

- Global Recruitment and Onboarding: The system should facilitate international recruitment, including job postings in multiple languages and a streamlined onboarding process for international hires.

- Learning and Development: Offer comprehensive learning and development with a diverse range of training materials and resources to cater to various needs and preferences.

- Performance Management: The system should support both global and localized performance processes, allowing for flexibility in objective-setting, feedback, and performance appraisals.

- Succession Planning: Identify and develop high-potential employees for leadership roles across different regions, ensuring leadership continuity.

- Career Development: Enable employees to explore career paths within the company, offering international assignments or transfers to promote growth and global experience.

Talent lifecycle management that considers both international and intercultural dimensions is vital for large MNEs to effectively manage their diverse workforce, promote engagement, and ensure long-term success. The right HCM system should provide the necessary features and adaptability to meet the unique requirements of talent management in a global and culturally diverse context.

Remote Work and Hybrid Models

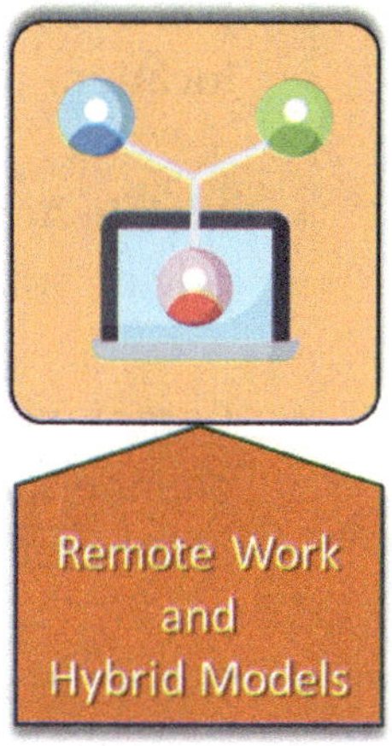

Remote Work and Hybrid Work models have gained significant importance in recent years, offering flexibility and adaptability to large multinational enterprises (MNEs) with diverse and geographically dispersed workforces. These models are crucial for several reasons, and specific system considerations are necessary to enable them effectively.

Importance of Remote and Hybrid Work Models:

- Work-Life Balance: Remote work allows employees to better balance their work and personal lives, which can lead to improved job satisfaction and well-being.
- Global Talent Acquisition: MNEs can tap into a global talent pool and hire the best candidates, regardless of their location.
- Cost Savings: Remote work can reduce overhead costs associated with physical office space, such as rent, utilities, and office supplies.
- Business Continuity: These models provide greater resilience in the face of unexpected disruptions, such as natural disasters and geo-political conflicts.
- Employee Retention: Offering remote or hybrid options can be a key factor in retaining top talent, especially as more professionals seek flexible work arrangements.
- Environmental Impact: Reducing the need for commuting can contribute to environmental sustainability by decreasing carbon emissions.

System Considerations for Remote and Hybrid Work Models:

- Data/Network Connectivity: To extract the value of remote work and hybrid models, organizations must ensure that all employees have access to data/information services where they live. While this is not a consideration specific to the HCM system, it is a general need that cannot be overlooked.
- Collaboration Tools: Effective use of collaboration tools is essential to facilitate communication and collaboration among remote and on-site teams. These tools should be integrated with the HCM system for seamless workflows.
- Remote Attendance and Time Tracking: The system should enable employees to log their hours, track attendance, and submit leave requests from remote locations.

- Access Control and Security: Robust access control and security measures should be in place to protect sensitive data, especially when employees are working from various locations.

- Mobile Accessibility: A mobile-friendly application is essential for remote workers who rely on smartphones and tablets.

- Communication Channels: The system should support a range of communication channels, including video conferencing, chat, and email, to facilitate remote team collaboration.

- Hybrid Work Policies: The HCM system should enable the management of hybrid work policies, ensuring that employees understand and adhere to the guidelines.

Incorporating these system considerations enables large MNEs to successfully implement and manage remote and hybrid work models, providing employees with flexibility while maintaining productivity and security.

Data Security and Privacy

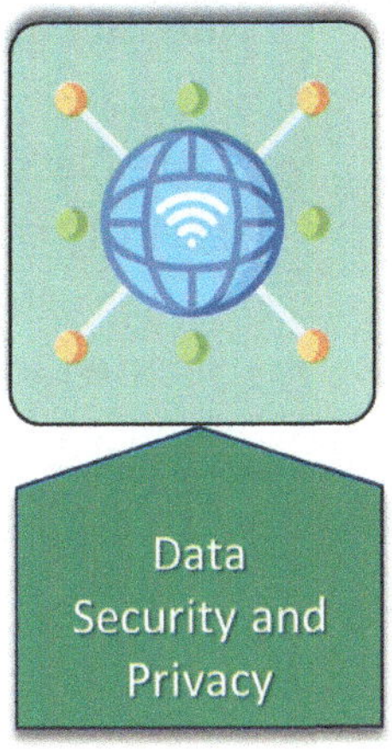

Data Security and Privacy are of paramount importance for large multinational enterprises (MNEs) with operations in multiple countries. Ensuring the confidentiality, integrity, and availability of sensitive employee and organizational data is essential for several reasons, and specific system considerations play a critical role in the achievement of security and privacy.

Importance of Data Security and Privacy:

- Legal and Regulatory Compliance: Compliance with data protection laws and regulations, such as the General Data Protection Regulation (GDPR) in the European Union, is a legal requirement. Non-compliance can result in significant fines and penalties.

- Reputation Management: A data breach or privacy violation can severely damage an MNE's reputation, eroding trust among employees, customers, and stakeholders.

- Data Integrity: Ensuring the accuracy and reliability of data is vital for making informed decisions and preventing data manipulation or corruption.

- Protection of Sensitive Information: Safeguarding sensitive employee information, such as personal identification data, financial records, and health information, is essential to prevent identity theft and fraud.

- Business Continuity: Data security and privacy measures help protect an organization from cyber threats and data loss, ensuring business continuity.

System Considerations for Data Security and Privacy:

- Access Control: Implement intentional access controls to ensure that only authorized personnel can access sensitive data. Use role-based access and authentication processes for added security.

- Encryption: Encrypt data both in transit and at rest. This includes data stored in databases, servers, transmissions, and backups.

- Data Masking: Use data masking or anonymization techniques to protect sensitive information while allowing authorized users access to relevant data.

- Audit Trails: Maintain detailed audit logs of data access and changes, enabling tracking of user actions for accountability and forensic analysis.

- Regular Security Audits: Conduct regular security audits and vulnerability assessments to identify and address potential weaknesses in the system.

- Data Classification: Categorize data based on its sensitivity and apply appropriate security controls and access levels accordingly.

- Secure Cloud Solutions: If the HCM system is cloud-based, choose a reputable cloud service provider that complies with all relevant security and privacy standards.

- Vendor Security Assessments: Assess the security and privacy practices of the HCM system provider, ensuring they adhere to industry best practices and standards.

- Data Retention Policies: Establish and enforce data retention policies to determine how long data is kept and when it should be securely disposed.

- Data Portability: Ensure that employees can access their data and request its transfer, as required by relevant data protection laws.

- International Data Transfers: If data is transferred across borders, consider legal contractual mechanisms to ensure compliance with data protection regulations.

Data privacy laws and regulations vary from country to country and even within regions, making it important for multinational enterprises to be aware of and comply with the laws relevant to their operations. Here are some notable data privacy laws and a brief description of each, along with the countries they impact:

General Data Protection Regulation (GDPR)

- **Description:** The GDPR is a comprehensive data protection regulation that governs the processing of personal data for residents of the European Union (EU) and European Economic Area (EEA) countries. It establishes strict requirements for data protection, privacy, and consent.
- **Impacted Countries:** All EU and EEA member states, affecting 27 countries.

California Consumer Privacy Act (CCPA)

- **Description:** The CCPA is a data privacy law in California, USA, granting residents the right to know what personal information is collected about them and to request the deletion of their data. It applies to businesses that meet certain criteria and interact with California consumers.
- **Impacted Countries:** United States, with a focus on California residents.

Personal Information Protection Law (PIPL)

- **Description:** China's PIPL regulates the processing of personal information and data protection, similar to GDPR. It includes provisions on consent, data transfer, and the rights of data subjects.
- **Impacted Countries:** China, and it may have implications for international businesses processing Chinese residents' data.

Personal Data Protection Act (PDPA)

- **Description:** Singapore's PDPA is designed to govern the collection, use, and disclosure of personal data by organizations. It includes requirements for consent, data transfer, and data subject rights.
- **Impacted Countries:** Singapore, and international companies may be affected if processing data from Singapore residents.

General Data Protection Law (LGPD)

- **Description:** Brazil's LGPD is similar to GDPR and establishes rules for the processing of personal data. It grants rights to data subjects and imposes obligations on data controllers and processors.
- **Impacted Countries:** Brazil, and global companies processing data from Brazilian citizens will likely need to comply.

Personal Information Protection and Electronic Documents Act (PIPEDA)

- **Description:** PIPEDA is Canada's federal law governing the collection, use, and disclosure of personal information. It addresses privacy concerns related to commercial activities and data transfers.
- **Impacted Countries:** Canada, and it has implications for international companies handling Canadian residents' data.

Protection of Personal Information (POPI) Act

- **Description:** South Africa's POPI Act regulates the processing of personal information and establishes principles for data protection, including consent and data subject rights.
- **Impacted Countries:** South Africa, and international businesses processing data from South African individuals must comply.

Personal Data Protection Act (PDPA)

- **Description:** Thailand's PDPA outlines principles for the collection, use, and disclosure of personal data. It includes consent requirements, data subject rights, and cross-border data transfer rules.
- **Impacted Countries:** Thailand, and it may affect international companies handling Thai residents' data.

Data Protection Directive

- **Description:** The Data Protection Directive is a framework for data protection within the European Union, preceding the GDPR. It required EU member states to implement national laws in line with its principles.
- **Impacted Countries:** EU member states (replaced by GDPR in 2018).

Personal Information Protection Act (PIPA)

- **Description:** PIPA is a data protection law in Japan that regulates the handling of personal information, including consent, data subject rights, and cross-border data transfers.
- **Impacted Countries:** Japan, and international businesses processing data from Japanese individuals should comply.

It's important to note that these data privacy laws are constantly evolving, and compliance may require adjustments in data handling, security practices, and consent mechanisms. Large MNEs with global operations must stay informed about the applicable data protection laws and take appropriate measures to ensure compliance.

By implementing these system considerations and adhering to best practices in data security and privacy, large MNEs can protect sensitive data, reduce the risk of data breaches, and maintain compliance with regional regulations. These practices protect an MNE's reputation and trustworthiness.

International Compliance and Legal Considerations

International Compliance and Legal Considerations for Human Capital Management (HCM) systems encompass a range of regulations and laws that MNEs need to consider when managing their workforce across different countries. These considerations are important to ensure that organizations operate within the bounds of the law, avoid legal issues, and maintain a positive reputation. System capabilities that enable compliance include:

- Labor Laws and Employment Regulations: Different countries have varying labor laws, including regulations related to working hours, overtime, breaks, and employee rights. HCM systems should be capable of accommodating and automating compliance with these diverse labor regulations.

- Work Authorization and Visa Compliance: If the organization employs foreign workers or expatriates, the system should help track and manage work authorizations, visas, and related compliance documents.

- Tax Compliance: HCM systems must address the complexities of international taxation, including payroll tax regulations, tax withholdings, and tax reporting requirements across different countries.
- Anti-Discrimination and Equal Opportunity Laws: Ensuring that the HCM system helps monitor and enforce anti-discrimination and equal opportunity laws is vital to maintaining a diverse and inclusive workforce.
- Termination and Severance Laws: The system should enable organizations to comply with various rules governing employee terminations, including notice periods, severance payments, and other legal requirements in different countries.
- Employee Records and Documentation: Many countries have specific requirements for maintaining employee records and documentation. The HCM system should facilitate record-keeping to meet these requirements.
- Trade Union and Labor Relations: In some countries, engaging with labor unions or works councils is mandated. HCM systems should enable communication and collaboration with these bodies while adhering to local labor laws.
- Global Mobility and Immigration Compliance: For companies with international relocations or assignments, the system should manage global mobility processes, including immigration compliance, work permits, and cross-border employee transfers.
- International Payroll Management: Managing payroll in various countries involves compliance with complex tax and labor laws. HCM systems should offer international payroll capabilities to automate calculations and ensure compliance.

International compliance and legal considerations for HCM systems are critical to protect the organization from legal risks, maintain a harmonious and compliant workforce, and ensure a positive corporate image. Implementing an HCM system with the capabilities mentioned above can help multinational enterprises navigate the complex landscape of international labor and employment regulations effectively.

System Provider Characteristics for Large Businesses

When selecting an HCM system provider for large MNEs, global compatibility and scalability are critical factors. To ensure that the system can effectively meet the unique needs of MNEs, the following system provider characteristics should be present:

Global Coverage & Scalability

The provider should offer services and support in multiple countries and regions. This includes having local teams or partners who understand regional nuances and can assist with implementation and ongoing support. The system should be capable of scaling to accommodate the organization's growth. Whether the MNE expands to new countries or acquires additional business units, the HCM system should be flexible enough to handle increased data and user loads.

Multi-Lingual Capabilities

The HCM system should be available in multiple languages to accommodate the diverse linguistic needs of a global workforce. It should also support regional variations in terminology and data input.

Integration Capabilities

The system should easily integrate with other enterprise systems, such as Enterprise Resource Planning (ERP), financial & accounting, and salesforce automation. Integration is crucial for sharing data and ensuring a cohesive ecosystem. The system should offer international payroll capabilities to accommodate various tax regulations, currencies, and payment methods in different countries. Financial aspects, including compensation and benefits, should be able to handle multiple currencies and exchange rate fluctuations.

Customization and Flexibility

The system should be highly customizable to adapt to the unique needs and practices of each region and business unit within the MNE. It should accommodate variations in HR processes, policies, and reporting.

Global Support and Customer Services

The provider should offer 24/7 global support with an understanding of regional time zones and languages. Support should be responsive to the needs of users around the world.

Accessibility

In a global context, many employees may work remotely or in different time zones. Therefore, a mobile-friendly interface is essential for easy access and usability across different devices.

Future-ability

The provider should demonstrate a commitment to ongoing development and keeping the system up to date with technological advances and changing HR practices worldwide. Advanced reporting and analytics features should be available to provide insights into the global workforce, track performance, and facilitate data-driven decision-making.

By evaluating HCM system providers based on these characteristics, MNEs can ensure that they have the tools and support needed to effectively manage their global workforce, maintain compliance, and adapt to the ever-evolving challenges of operating across borders.

Comparing the Current Leaders

The inclusion of these three providers is based on a review by the research and consulting firm Gartner (NewsRX, 2022 & Acquisdata, 2019). This section is not intended to be exhaustive, and there are certainly other providers for HCM solutions to large MNEs. Oracle and SAP have arguably been in this space the longest. The newer entrant of those presented here is Workday, who launched their first HR system in 2006.

System Usability

Oracle/PeopleSoft, SAP/SuccessFactors, and Workday are all prominent HCM system providers, each offering a different approach to usability. Here's a comparison from a usability standpoint:

Oracle/PeopleSoft:

- User Interface (UI): Oracle/PeopleSoft has historically been criticized for having a complex and less user-friendly interface. However, they have made improvements in recent years with the introduction of the Fluid User Interface, which offers a more modern and responsive design.

- Customization: Oracle/PeopleSoft is highly customizable, allowing organizations to tailor the system to their specific needs. While this offers flexibility, it can also make the system complex to navigate for some users.

- Learning Curve: Due to its extensive customization capabilities, Oracle/PeopleSoft can have a steeper learning curve for administrators and users. Training is often required for effective use.

- Global Compatibility: It offers global compatibility but may require more configuration for international operations, making it suitable for large MNEs with dedicated IT resources.

- Integration: Oracle/PeopleSoft can integrate with other Oracle products seamlessly, providing a unified ecosystem. However, third-party integrations may require additional effort.

SAP/SuccessFactors:

- User Interface (UI): SuccessFactors provides a more modern and user-friendly interface. It features a responsive design and intuitive navigation.

- Customization: While it offers customization options, SuccessFactors is generally considered to be less customizable compared to others. This can simplify usability for some.

- Learning Curve: SuccessFactors tends to have a shallower learning curve, making it accessible to a broader range of users. It requires less training for administrators and employees.

- Global Compatibility: SuccessFactors is designed with global compatibility in mind, with built-in support for various languages, currencies, and compliance requirements.

- Integration: It offers robust integration capabilities, especially with other SAP solutions. Additionally, third-party integrations are also well-supported, making it adaptable to diverse IT ecosystems.

Workday:

- User Interface (UI): Workday is known for its user-friendly and modern UI, with a focus on a consumer-grade experience. Its design is often praised for its simplicity and intuitive use.

- Customization: While Workday is customizable, it follows a more opinionated approach that encourages best practices. This leads to a more straightforward and standardized user experience.

- Learning Curve: Workday is often considered one of the easiest HCM systems to learn and use, with intuitive navigation and minimal training required for most users.

- Global Compatibility: Workday is built with global compatibility in mind and is designed to handle the complexities of multinational enterprises, making it a suitable choice for large MNEs.

- Integration: Workday offers strong integration capabilities and has a growing ecosystem of partner applications. Integrations are often straightforward to implement.

From a usability standpoint, Workday is often lauded for its user-friendly design and streamlined user experience, making it a strong choice for MNEs looking for a straightforward and accessible HCM system. SuccessFactors offers a good balance of usability and customization, while Oracle/PeopleSoft is highly customizable but may require more effort in terms of usability and training. Choosing among providers should align with an organization's specific needs, resources, and objectives.

Competitive Differentiators

Oracle/PeopleSoft, SAP/SuccessFactors, and Workday differentiate themselves in various ways, and each has a unique value proposition to stand out from their top competitors. Here's a comparison of some of their competitive differentiators:

Oracle/PeopleSoft:

- Comprehensive Suite: Oracle/PeopleSoft offers an extensive suite of applications, including HCM, ERP, and CRM, providing a one-stop solution for enterprises seeking a unified platform.

- Customization and Flexibility: Oracle/PeopleSoft is known for its ability to be customized, allowing organizations to tailor the system to their specific needs and processes. It appeals to large enterprises with complex requirements.

- Deep Industry Expertise: Oracle is often marketed as a solution for various industries, particularly highly regulated sectors like finance, healthcare, and public sector organizations.

- Global Compatibility: Oracle/PeopleSoft emphasizes its ability to handle complex global operations and international compliance, targeting multinational enterprises.

- Integration with Oracle Products: Oracle promotes seamless integration with other Oracle products, creating an end-to-end ecosystem that appeals to organizations already invested in Oracle technologies.

SAP/SuccessFactors:

- Cloud Focus: SuccessFactors is marketed as a cloud-first solution, emphasizing scalability and accessibility from anywhere. It positions itself as an agile, cloud-based platform.
- User Experience: SAP/SuccessFactors has made significant efforts to enhance user experience and usability, promoting a more modern and intuitive UI. It emphasizes user-centric design.
- Global-Ready: SuccessFactors is designed with global compatibility in mind, offering multilingual and multicurrency support and highlighting its readiness for international operations.
- Integration with SAP Solutions: SAP markets SuccessFactors as part of its broader suite of SAP solutions, emphasizing seamless integration with other SAP products like ERP and CRM.
- HR Analytics and Workforce Planning: SuccessFactors focuses on HR analytics and workforce planning, using data-driven insights to enhance talent management and decision-making. Of these three, SuccessFactors is the only one that can do a position planning modality for organizational management.

Workday:

- User-Friendly Design: Workday differentiates itself through its user-friendly and consumer-grade UI, designed to simplify and improve the user experience.
- SaaS-Based Model: Workday is often seen as a pioneer in the Software as a Service (SaaS) model for HCM, highlighting the benefits of reduced IT overhead, automatic updates, and scalability.
- Mobile-Centric: Workday emphasizes mobile accessibility, enabling users to access the system from any device, which aligns with the growing trend of remote work.
- Simplified Customization: Workday takes a more opinionated approach to customization, aiming to provide best-practice solutions while allowing some flexibility for specific business needs.
- Global and Multinational Focus: Workday is positioned as a system ready for global operations, with support for multiple languages, currencies, and compliance requirements.

In summary, Oracle/PeopleSoft differentiates itself with its extensive suite, customization capabilities, and deep industry expertise. SAP/SuccessFactors highlights its cloud focus, user experience, and integration with SAP solutions. Workday stands out for its user-friendly design, SaaS model, and mobile accessibility. Each system has its unique strengths and caters to different needs, which should be considered when making a choice.

Ultimately, the choice between Oracle/PeopleSoft, SAP/SuccessFactors, and Workday depends on an organization's specific needs, resources, and objectives. Large MNEs should carefully evaluate their requirements and consider factors such as usability, customization, industry expertise, global compatibility, integration, and overall cost when selecting an HCM system solution.

Summary

Large multinational enterprises (MNEs) face a complex landscape of human capital management (HCM) that demands tailored solutions. This chapter covered various facets of HCM for MNEs, including global workforce management, talent lifecycle management, remote and hybrid work models, data security, and international legal compliance. Understanding these components and the nuances of HCM system providers like Oracle/PeopleSoft, SAP/SuccessFactors, and Workday, provides MNEs with the tools and insights needed to navigate the challenges of global HR and optimize their workforce management strategies.

Discussion Questions

In the context of HCM for MNEs, what are some key considerations when selecting an HCM system provider to ensure global compatibility and scalability?

How do large MNEs effectively manage global workforces, considering factors like cultural diversity, compliance with international labor laws, and varying HR practices?

What are the system considerations and capabilities needed to ensure data security and privacy in the context of HCM for large MNEs with a global footprint?

Can you share examples of how Oracle/PeopleSoft, SAP/SuccessFactors, and Workday differentiate themselves from their top competitors in the HCM system market?

In a rapidly changing global workforce landscape, what emerging trends and technologies do you foresee having a significant impact on HCM systems and strategies for large MNEs in the coming years?

Chapter References

Aquisdata, Inc. (2019). SAP (NYSE: SAP) - SAP SuccessFactors Solutions Positioned as a Leader in Gartner Cloud HCM Suites for Midsize and Large Enterprises Magic Quadrant. Germany Software and IT.

Bersin, J., Enderes, K., & Ioannidou, S. (2022). *Best Practices for HCM Excellence: SAP SuccessFactors Edition.* The joshbersin company.

Cattermole, G. (2019). Developing the employee lifecycle to keep top talent. *Strategic HR Review, 18*(6), 258–262. https://doi.org/10.1108/SHR-05-2019-0042

ChatGPT. (2023). *HCM for Large Businesses.* OpenAI. Accessed November 4-6, 2023.

Engelsrud. (n.d.). *Managing PeopleSoft on the Oracle Cloud: Best Practices with PeopleSoft Cloud Manager.* Apress. https://doi.org/10.1007/978-1-4842-4546-0

Jordan, A. (2019). PeopleSoft to be replaced by Workday System. In *University Wire*. Uloop, Inc.

Kharroubi, D. (2021). Global Workforce Diversity Management: Challenges across the world. *Economic and Managerial Spectrum, 15*(1), 28–37. https://doi.org/10.26552/ems.2021.1.28-37

NewsRX, LLC (2022). Oracle Named a Leader in the 2022 Gartner® Magic Quadrant[TM] for Cloud HCM Suites for 1,000+ Employee Enterprises. Information Technology Weekly.

Rawat, C. (2023). Role of ERP Modernization in Digital Transformation: PeopleSoft Insight. *arXiv.org.* https://doi.org/10.48550/arxiv.2303.03224

Traynor, Wellens, M. A., & Krishnamoorthy, V. (2021). *An Introduction to SAP SuccessFactors Talent Modules. In SAP SuccessFactors Talent: Volume 1* (pp. 1–6). Apress L. P. https://doi.org/10.1007/978-1-4842-6600-7_1

Traynor, Wellens, M. A., & Krishnamoorthy, V. (2021). *SAP SuccessFactors Talent: Volume 1: A Complete Guide to Configuration, Administration, and Best Practices: Performance and Goals* (Vol. 1). Apress. https://doi.org/10.1007/978-1-4842-6600-7

Workday. (2023). *Why We're Different.* Retrieved on November 4, 2023 from: https://www.workday.com/en-us/why-workday/why-different.html

Chapter 8
Small & Medium Sized Business Solutions

Table of Contents

Photo by Dmitry Zvolskiy from pexels.com

Chapter 8: Small & Medium Sized Business Solutions

Introduction

Our focus in this chapter will be on Small to Medium sized Businesses (SMBs) who operate on a local or regional scale. There's a wide variety and scale of businesses classified as SMBs. The reader will need to interpret and adjust this content for any given space that they are considering. Don't get caught up in the numbers used in this section, such as number of employees, number of locations, etc. An organization should let their requirements gathering determine system sizing and scalability.

Regardless of the size or industry of a business, effective Human Capital Management (HCM) is vital. What constitutes "effective" can change considerably among different SMBs. Compared to large businesses, SMBs have unique needs for managing their workforces. This chapter examines critical aspects of HCM systems and technology directed to the SMB. It explores how SMB requirements differ from large businesses, and it compares HCM providers. Unique to the SMB space is the topic of Professional Employment Outsourcers (PEO.) Additionally, this chapter reviews the advantages and risks of partnering with PEOs. Finally, the capabilities of several prominent HCM system providers are reviewed.

Unique Needs of Small to Medium Sized Businesses

Small to medium-sized businesses operate on a local or regional scale, with a footprint that could be as small as a single city or as large as a country. The range in size of SMBs is vast. The Small Business Administration in the United States reports that 99.9% of all businesses are SMBs (Main, 2024.) That percentage translates into 33.3 million businesses, and these are just U.S. numbers. Other various sources report that approximately half of the U.S. workforce is employed by SMBs. Here are some other interesting statistics regarding SMBs in the United States:

- Most businesses are small, comprising 99.9% of U.S. businesses.
- There are 33,185,550 small businesses in the United States.
- Small businesses employ 61.7 million people in the United States, totaling 46.4% of private sector employees.
- From 1995 to 2021, small businesses created 17.3 million net new jobs, accounting for 62.7% of net jobs created since 1995.
- Small businesses pay 39.4% percent of private sector payroll.
- Small businesses generate 32.6% percent of known export value.
- About 38% of small businesses use specialized software in their business operations. (Office of Advocacy, 2023).

As small businesses launch and develop in their early stages, they have relatively simple and straightforward needs in the HCM space. As they grow and become larger, they encounter challenges and needs approaching those of larger businesses. It's this continuum of size, scale, and growth that makes the provision of HCM solutions especially diverse for SMBs. To be considered "small," these organizations are often regarded as having 100 or fewer employees. To be considered "medium," these organizations are often regarded as having 100-999 employees. These numbers and ranges are certainly not rules. The picture becomes more dynamic when revenue is considered. Even in the case of small businesses with no employees, the average revenue is just under $50,000. Small business revenue ranges from $0 to $50 million, and medium sized businesses range from $50 million to less than $1 billion (Gartner, 2024).

SMBs face a complex and varied landscape of HCM that offers many more solution possibilities than what exists for large businesses. The sheer number of possibilities presents its own challenges and generates unique needs, especially when looking toward future endeavors and growth projections. Let's examine each of the five categories of unique needs of small to medium sized businesses.

Scalability and Budget

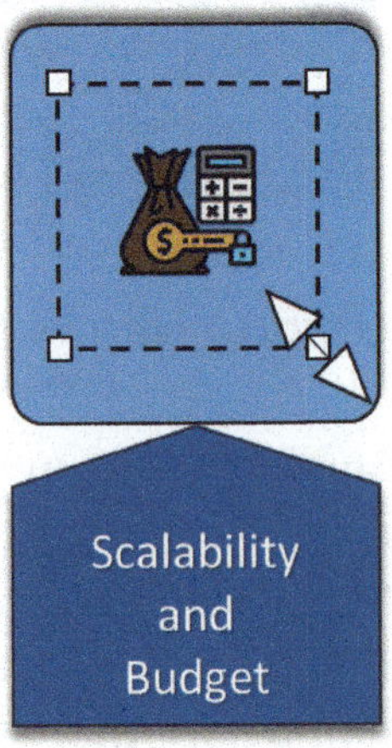

SMBs typically have smaller budgets and a smaller workforce compared to large businesses. This means that the cost of HCM systems and technology can be a more significant concern for SMBs, especially earlier in their lifecycle. They need solutions that are cost-effective and provide best possible value. SMBs are smaller; however, many still aim for growth and expansion. Consequently, their HCM systems need to also be scalable. Scalability enables the best possible balance between current-state cost conscientiousness and future-state workforce growth. The right HCM solution can help a company achieve this balance without causing disruptions or requiring frequent migrations to new systems. Additionally, many SMBs do not need the extensive customization capabilities that large enterprises do, which enables them to select from more budget friendly "off-the-shelf" options.

Simplicity

It's highly unlikely that a decision maker in a large business would tell you that they don't want simplicity. However, the reality of large businesses is that their systems often require customizations which add complexity. Contrast that with SMBs. SMBs rally around simplicity from several perspectives.

The first perspective is on technical support and is closely related to budget. From budget it extends to the fact that SMBs often don't have the number or type of dedicated IT or HR resources required for more complex system solutions. Therefore, a simple system solution is desirable because it requires few resources with a lower degree of specialization. SMBs often require HCM systems that are easy to implement, user-friendly, and do not require extensive customization or technical expertise.

The second perspective is around usability. SMBs often don't have resources dedicated to support extensive user training on systems. Consequently, procuring a HCM system that is intuitive and simple to use pays dividends in usability and satisfaction. From a system supplier standpoint, those vendors that offer excellent customer support and training resources can be especially valuable for SMBs and have an edge when it comes to system selection.

The third perspective is around business processes. SMBs, especially early-stage businesses, are in a unique position to benefit from decades of research and system design. Where business processes do not offer a competitive advantage, it makes much more sense to keep things simple and follow the processes that are already embedded in the system design and system workflow.

Integration

Many SMBs rely on a mix of software solutions for various business functions. Their HCM systems need to be able to integrate with other software, such as accounting, payroll, and time-tracking systems, to streamline processes and avoid duplicate data entry. The subject of integration continues to be a unique need of SMBs as they grow. If the core HCM system is built for integrations, the company is much more likely to be able to adapt and grow using add-on's, extensions, and other third-party system solutions.

Self-Service

SMBs often have limited HR staff, so it's essential for employees and managers to access and manage their own information. HCM systems for SMBs should provide self-service portals for employees to update personal information, request time off, and access pay stubs and benefits information. They should also provide managers with the ability to approve workflows, schedule their workforce, perform talent acquisition, manage employee performance, administer compensation, and more.

Compliance and Data Security

SMBs may face different compliance challenges and regulations than larger corporations. They need HCM systems that can help them manage compliance with labor laws, tax regulations, and industry-specific requirements. They also need HCM systems that proactively help them navigate changing compliance requirements. These changes are commonly driven by growth/size and location. For example, if a company has 40 employees, and in the next year it grows to 55 employees, they may need to comply with the Family Medical Leave Act (FMLA.) FMLA has a 50-employee threshold for compliance, and there are a couple of other conditions surrounding the need to comply. A good HCM system will enable compliance as the SMB grows and matures over time.

HCM systems for SMBs should be cost-effective, user-friendly, and adaptable to growth. They should also assist with compliance, integrate with other software, and offer strong support and training options. An organization's specific needs will vary based on the industry, location, and size of the SMB, so it's essential to select an HCM solution that aligns with the unique requirements of the business both today and in the future.

System Provider Characteristics for SMB's

When small and medium-sized businesses (SMBs) are evaluating HCM system providers, they will want to consider characteristics and capabilities that are tailored to their unique needs. In many respects, these are different from those of large enterprises. The categories themselves aren't necessarily different, but there are several nuances within each that vary for SMBs. The following are characteristics of system providers that are relevant:

Affordability
SMBs often have more limited budgets compared to large corporations. HCM system providers should offer pricing models that are affordable for SMBs. This might include lower upfront costs, subscription-based pricing, and scalable pricing structures that grow with the business.

Ease of Implementation
SMBs typically have smaller IT departments or, in some cases, none at all. HCM providers should offer solutions that are easy to implement and require minimal technical expertise. Cloud-based systems that don't demand extensive on-premises infrastructure can be advantageous.

Scalability
Many SMBs aspire to grow, so they need HCM systems that can scale with them. Providers should offer solutions that can accommodate a growing workforce without major disruptions or expensive upgrades.

User-Friendly Interface

SMBs often lack dedicated HR staff or IT professionals. HCM systems should have an intuitive and user-friendly interface that doesn't require extensive training. This is particularly important for SMBs where employees may be tasked with HR functions through self-service. The best user interfaces help to reduce dependency on customer support and training.

Compliance Expertise

HCM providers should have a good understanding of the compliance requirements that are specific to SMBs. This might include labor laws, tax regulations, and industry-specific compliance needs. Providers should offer tools and features to help SMBs stay compliant. Compliance can be a major determinant of which providers are considered during the system selection process. Often SMBs will select a provider whose base of operation is within the same country, helping to ensure proper legal and regulatory coverage.

Integration Capabilities

SMBs often rely on a mix of software tools for various business functions. HCM systems should have robust integration capabilities to work seamlessly with other software, such as accounting, payroll, and time-tracking systems. Reviewing potential providers for their approach to integrations, with a specific review of programming interfaces may be warranted. HCM providers should offer affordable add-ons or modules that address these specific needs.

Data Security

While SMBs may not have the same resources for cybersecurity as larger enterprises, data security is still crucial. HCM providers should offer robust security features and safeguards to protect sensitive employee data. Often this need for data security extends beyond just the HCM system provider and needs to be validated across providers where data is moved/shared between them. For example, between HCM and Finance/Accounting systems.

Payroll and Tax Features

Payroll and taxes are often the first areas of need related to HCM systems, and these needs are encountered early in the lifecycle of a business. HCM systems for SMBs should have comprehensive payroll and tax features to simplify these tasks and be capable of future expansion.

In summary, HCM system providers catering to SMBs should be reviewed for their focus on affordability, ease of use, scalability, compliance, integrations, customer support, data security, and other potential features tailored to the unique needs of smaller businesses. The specific characteristics and capabilities required will vary depending on the industry and the specific SMB's needs.

Professional Employment Outsourcers

A PEO, or Professional Employer Organization, is a company that provides comprehensive HR and employment-related services to other businesses. SMBs) often turn to PEOs to outsource various HR functions and responsibilities. PEOs act as co-employers, sharing certain employer responsibilities with the client company.

Here are some key aspects of PEOs:

- **Co-Employment:** When a business partners with a PEO, they enter into a co-employment arrangement. The PEO takes on certain HR and employment-related responsibilities, such as payroll, benefits administration, workers' compensation, and compliance, while the client company maintains control over its day-to-day operations, employees' work, and business strategy. Some PEO providers will move a company's employees to the Employer Identification Number (EIN) of the PEO to leverage economies of scale when providing services such as benefits and healthcare.

- **HR Services:** PEOs offer a wide range of HR services, including payroll processing, employee benefits administration (health insurance, retirement plans, etc.), HR compliance management, risk management, and workers' compensation support. This allows SMBs to access HR expertise and services they might not have in-house.

- **Cost Savings:** Due to economies of scale related to bundling employees together, PEOs can often negotiate better rates for employee benefits and workers' compensation insurance due to their collective size. These savings can be passed on to their client companies and respective employees. This can be a cost-effective option for SMBs.

- **Compliance and Legal Support:** One of the value propositions of a PEO is that they stay up to date with employment laws and regulations, helping client companies remain compliant. They can provide legal support and guidance to mitigate potential HR-related risks.

- **Focus on Core Activities:** By outsourcing HR functions to a PEO, SMBs can focus on their core business activities and growth strategies, knowing that their HR needs are being professionally managed. Outsourcing can delay the need to staff a HR team or mitigate the need to grow the HR team.

- **Access to Expertise:** This is another function of economies of scale. Since PEOs specialize in providing these services, they typically have HR professionals and experts on staff who can provide guidance on various HR matters. Companies can tap into these experts on an as-needed basis, only paying for the services when they need them.

- **Recruitment and Onboarding Support:** PEOs may assist with recruitment, hiring, and onboarding processes to help client companies find talent. This can be as simple as providing Applicant Tracking System (ATS) capability, or it can be more extensive such as providing full Recruitment Process Outsourcing (RPO) services.

These advantages can make partnering with a PEO a strategic choice for small companies that want to streamline HR functions, save costs, access professional HR expertise, offer competitive benefits, and focus on their core business operations. However, the decision to use a PEO should be based on a thorough analysis of the specific needs and goals of the company, as well as a careful review of the terms of the PEO agreement. It's important to note that PEOs are not suitable for every business. Many SMBs find PEOs to be valuable partners, especially when they want to offload HR responsibilities and focus on their core operations.

Comparing Some of the more Predominant PEO's

Automatic Data Processing (ADP,) Insperity, and Paychex are well-established and reputable Professional Employer Organizations (PEOs) that offer a range of HR and employment-related services. While they share some common features, they also have differences in their capabilities, service offerings, and target markets. Here's a comparison and contrast of these PEO providers:

ADP:

- Size and Scale: One of the largest HR and payroll service providers globally, serving a wide range of businesses, from small to large enterprises.
- Service Offerings: Offers a comprehensive suite of HR services, including payroll processing, benefits administration, time and attendance, talent management, HR management, and compliance services.
- Industry Specialization: Caters to a wide variety of industries and can provide tailored solutions for specific business needs.
- Technology: Provides its own HCM software and solutions, including ADP Workforce Now, which is highly regarded for its usability and features.

- Global Reach: Has a significant global presence, making it a suitable choice for companies with international operations.
- Support and Resources: Offers robust customer support and resources, including training and educational materials.

Insperity:

- Service Focus: Specializes in providing HR solutions and services to small and mid-sized businesses, with a particular focus on delivering HR expertise and support.
- Comprehensive HR Services: Offers a wide array of HR services, including payroll, benefits administration, HR consulting, risk management, and recruitment support.
- PEO Expertise: Known for its expertise in PEO services, making it a strong choice for businesses looking for comprehensive HR outsourcing.
- Technology: Offers its proprietary HCM system, Insperity Premier, as well as other HR software and tools.
- Compliance and Legal Support: Places a strong emphasis on HR compliance and provides legal support for its clients.

Paychex:

- Size and Market Focus: A leading HR and payroll service provider that primarily targets small and medium-sized businesses.
- Service Offerings: Offers a broad range of HR and payroll services, including payroll processing, benefits administration, time and attendance, and HR solutions.
- Technology: Provides its HCM platform, Paychex Flex, which includes features for payroll, HR, and benefits management.
- Industry Specialization: Serves businesses across various industries, making it suitable for companies with diverse needs.
- Customer Support: Known for its customer support, offering 24/7 assistance and a user-friendly client portal.

While ADP, Insperity, and Paychex all provide comprehensive HR and PEO services, they have differences in terms of their target markets, industry specialization, and proprietary technology offerings. The choice between these providers should be based on the specific needs, size, and goals of the business, as well as the level of HR expertise and support required. Additionally, considering factors such as cost, contract terms, and the quality of customer support is crucial when deciding.

Comparing System Providers in the SMB Market

The first thing to be said here is that there are hundreds of system providers around the world targeting SMBs. We'll focus on a few of them to provide example comparisons; however, this is a good place to reemphasize the need to do a thorough requirements analysis and system selection process. BambooHR, UKG (Ultimate Kronos Group), and Ceridian are well-known Human Capital Management (HCM) system providers, and they each have unique capabilities, strengths, and weaknesses. Here's a comparison of these four HCM systems in the SMB market:

BambooHR:

Capabilities:

- Offers core HR functions, including employee self-service, HRIS (Human Resource Information System), applicant tracking, onboarding, time tracking, and performance management.
- It has user-friendly interface and mobile apps.
- Provides customizable reporting and analytics.

Strengths:

- Well-suited for small businesses due to its ease of use.
- Strong onboarding and employee self-service features.
- Excellent customer support and extensive educational resources.

Weaknesses:

- Lacks advanced features like benefits administration, which may require integration with other systems.
- May not be as suitable for larger enterprises with complex HR needs.

UKG (Ultimate Kronos Group):

Capabilities:

- Offers a wide range of HCM solutions, including workforce management, HR and payroll, talent management, and HR service delivery.
- It includes features like time and attendance, payroll, benefits administration, talent acquisition, and learning management.

Strengths:

- Comprehensive suite of HR and workforce management tools, suitable for SMBs and especially medium sized businesses or larger.
- Strong in payroll and workforce management functions.
- Offers industry-specific solutions and compliance support.
- Offers tiered product platforms, enabling a more seamless migration as the company grows.

Weaknesses:

- May be more complex and costly for smaller SMBs that do not require the full range of features.
- Implementation and training can be time-consuming.

Ceridian:

Capabilities:

- Offers Dayforce, a unified HCM platform covering HR, payroll, benefits, talent management, and workforce management.
- Features include payroll processing, workforce scheduling, performance management, and employee self-service.

Strengths:

- Highly configurable and adaptable to various business needs.
- Strong payroll capabilities with global payroll support.
- Good at workforce management, including time and attendance.

Weaknesses:

- May have a steeper learning curve for users due to its extensive customization options.
- Can be a higher-cost option, especially for smaller businesses.

Choosing an HCM system for a SMB depends on the specific needs and priorities of the business. BambooHR is well-suited for smaller businesses looking for a straightforward, user-friendly solution. UKG is ideal for organizations seeking a comprehensive HCM suite, especially those with more complex needs. Ceridian is highly configurable and adaptable, making it a good fit for SMBs willing to invest in customization. The decision should consider factors like company size, budget, and the importance of various HR functions in your organization.

Summary

Managing human capital effectively is a fundamental need which can drive business success. For SMBs, this task can be unique and challenging. In this chapter, we explored the distinct needs of SMBs compared to large enterprises when it comes to HCM systems and technology. We highlighted factors such as budget constraints, simplicity, scalability, and industry-specific compliance. We also compared three HCM system providers: BambooHR, UKG, and Ceridian, shedding light on their capabilities, strengths, and weaknesses. Additionally, we examined the benefits of partnering with Professional Employer Organizations (PEOs) and the characteristics that make them suitable for SMBs.

Discussion Questions

How do the specific HR and workforce management needs of Small and Medium-Sized Businesses (SMBs) differ from those of large enterprises, and what considerations should SMBs keep in mind when selecting HCM systems?

In the context of HCM providers for SMBs, what are some of the key factors businesses should consider when choosing between providers such as BambooHR, UKG, and Ceridian? How do providers differ in their ability to cater to SMB needs?

What are the primary advantages and potential drawbacks of SMBs partnering with Professional Employer Organizations (PEOs) to manage their HR functions and responsibilities? Under what circumstances does it make the most sense for an SMB to choose a PEO solution?

How important is data security and compliance for SMBs when selecting an HCM system, and what strategies should they employ to ensure they meet regulatory requirements?

In the evolving landscape of remote work and mobile workforces, how can HCM systems best support SMBs in accommodating flexible work arrangements and providing employee self-service options? What trends do you foresee in HCM technology for SMBs in the future?

Chapter References

ADP (2022). *A Guide to Early-Stage Business Success.* Retrieved on November 5, 2023 from: https://www.adp.com/resources/articles-and-insights/articles/e/early-stage-business-success-guide.aspx

BambooHR (2023). *How Do BambooHR & ADP Compare?* Retrieved on November 5, 2023 from: https://www.bamboohr.com/why-bamboohr/compare/adp/

Ceridian (2023). The 2023 *Gartner Magic Quadrant for Cloud HCM Suites for 1,000+ Employee Enterprises.* Retrieved on November 5, 2023 from: https://www.ceridian.com/resources/gartner-magic-quadrant-hcm-2023

Cattermole, G. (2019). Developing the employee lifecycle to keep top talent. *Strategic HR Review, 18*(6), 258–262. https://doi.org/10.1108/SHR-05-2019-0042

ChatGPT. (2023). *HCM for SMBs.* OpenAI. Accessed November 4-6, 2023.

Cornerstone. (2023). *The Force Behind Limitless Potential: A talent experience platform designed to unlock the limitless potential of your workforce and streamline how you do it.* Retrieved November 5, 2023 from: https://www.cornerstoneondemand.com/why-cornerstone/

Gartner (2024). *Small And Midsize Business (SMB).* Gartner Glossary. Retrieved from: https://gartner.com/en/information-technology/glossary/

Kharroubi, D. (2021). Global Workforce Diversity Management: Challenges across the world. *Economic and Managerial Spectrum, 15*(1), 28–37. https://doi.org/10.26552/ems.2021.1.28-37

Main, K. (2024). *Small Business Statistics of 2024 (January 31, 2024.)* Forbes Advisor. Retrieved from https://forbes.com/advisor/business/small-business-statistics/

Office of Advocacy (2023). *Frequently Asked Questions About Small Business 2023 (March 7, 2023).* U.S. Small Business Administration, Office of Advocacy. Retrieved from: https://advocacy.sba.gov/

Rawat, C. (2023). Role of ERP Modernization in Digital Transformation: PeopleSoft Insight. *arXiv.org.* https://doi.org/10.48550/arxiv.2303.03224

Chapter 9
HCM System Implementation

Table of Contents

Photo by fauxels from pexels.com

Chapter 9: HCM System Implementation

Introduction

In this chapter we will explore the process of implementing a HCM system. The successful implementation, integration, and adoption of a HCM system is crucial for streamlining HR processes, enhancing workforce management, and improving overall organizational efficiency. We will explore the stages of system implementation, the roles and responsibilities of key stakeholders, and the critical aspects of post-implementation support. This chapter is written from the perspective of implementing a new system; however, the same approach, processes, and considerations are also applicable in system upgrades and migrations. The larger the system and organization, the more likely that a systems integrator will be used. Systems integrators are usually well-equipped to guide an organization's HR team through the system implementation process.

The Implementation Process

Implementing a HCM system is a multifaceted process that involves many stages and considerations. Refer to Figure 08.01 in conjunction with this overview of a typical 8-stage process in HCM system implementations:

1. **Requirements Gathering and System Sizing:**

   Earlier in the book, a chapter is dedicated to this first stage of the process. It may seem a bit out of place to go deep on this stage so early in this book. The reason this is an early focus area is due to its criticality. If this stage is done correctly, it sets up the organization for success. If this stage is done incorrectly (or incompletely,) it sets up the organization for a failed initiative, cost overruns, and extended timelines and delays. The importance of this first stage cannot be overstated.

   - See chapter 3 for details on requirements gathering.

2. **Vendor Selection:**

   Vendor evaluation and selection is the process of identifying, assessing, and choosing a supplier of the system. This process is critical for businesses to make informed decisions about which supplier to engage with, whether it involves software, hardware, or services. Where system integrators are used to create the requirements document, they often continue through this part of the process.

   - See chapter 3 for details on requirements gathering.
   - Identify potential HCM software providers and evaluate their offerings, considering factors like features, scalability, cost, and customer support.

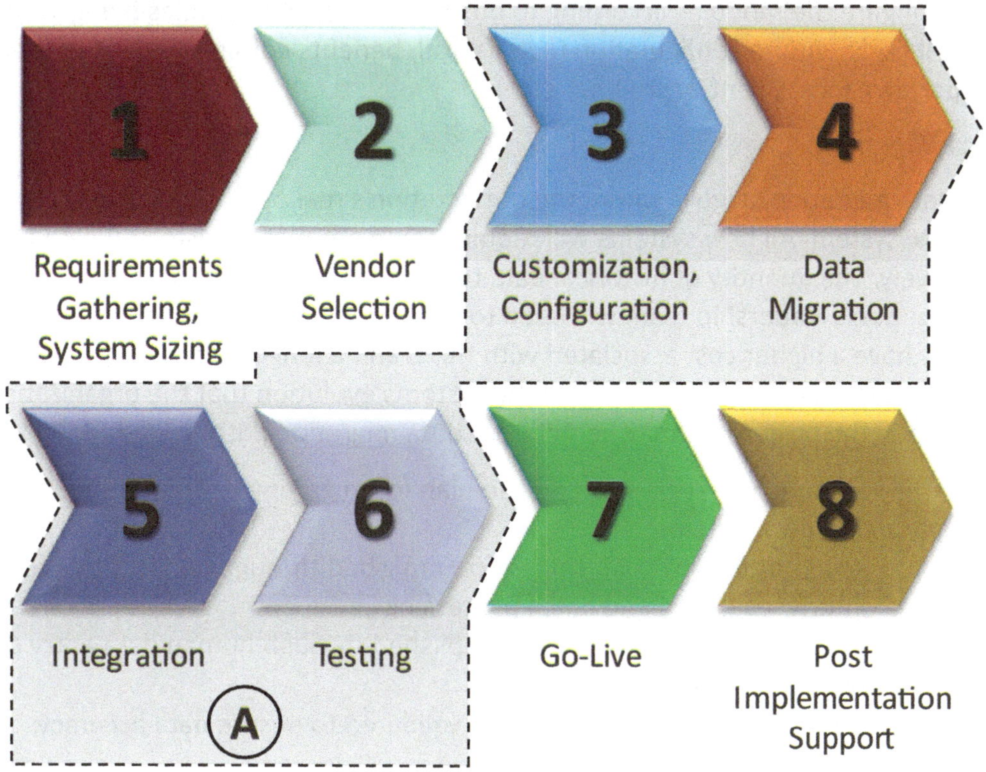

Figure 08.01
HCM System Implementation Process Diagram
The 8 stages of a HCM system implementation, including a carry-over stage after the system is live and being used by the organization. A) These steps are repeated as necessary.

- Create an RFP and invite bids from suppliers to gather detailed information about their products and services.
- Review supplier demos, check references, and assess capabilities.
- Select the best supplier which aligns with the needs of the organization.

3. **Customization and Configuration:**

   These two activities get bundled into the same implementation stage, but they are very different things. **Customization** is changing the software design, features, and functionality. It usually requires software developers to either re-code or to newly-code objects and modules which are then integrated. The operative word is "customize." The system supplier is customizing the HCM system to meet specific requirements of the organization. In stark contrast, **configuration** is working within the software design to setup parameters which are meant to be changed and adapted on a customer-by-customer basis.

- Customize the HCM system to align with your organization's unique workflow and process requirements.

- Configure the modules according to business needs. All modules being implemented will likely require configuration (e.g. payroll, benefits administration, self-service, performance, talent, recruiting, etc.)

4. **Data Migration:**

   The data migration stage is where the organization's real operational data is loaded into the new system. All new systems will require some amount of historical data to operate effectively. The quantity of historical data to be loaded is a decision that the organization's leadership team will need to make. Higher volumes of historical data usually have a higher cost associated with them and a longer amount of time needed to execute the migration. Depending on the systems evolution that the organization's been through in the past, there may be different data migration paths required.

   - Develop a data migration strategy and plan for migrating existing HR and employee data to the new system.
     - *Automated* data migration is accomplished through application programming interfaces (API's) and batch processing.
     - *Manual* data migration is accomplished through human data entry on a record-by-record basis.
   - Once migrated, the data is cleaned and validated to ensure data accuracy, consistency, and integrity before use.

5. **Integration:**

   Systems need to interconnect to move work and information between them and to facilitate the flow of work through the organization. Even in the case of large-scale ERP systems, where the entire ERP system's modules are already interconnected, there's likely still going to be ancillary systems that will require integration. At a minimum, integration requires connecting through API's so data can flow properly. At a maximum, integration requires custom (see stage 3) coding and data mapping. Often, there are integrations needed with other third-party systems. These integrations will have special considerations including data security and protection.

   - Integrate with existing systems: Connect the HCM system with other applications through defined API's.
   - Connect the HCM system with other applications through custom data mapping.
   - Connect the HCM system with third-party applications as needed.
   - Ensure data security and protection with all integrated applications.

6. **Testing:**

   The testing stage is vitally important to a successful implementation. All system functionality and source data are tested to ensure that the system functions as defined in Stage 1 when requirements were established. What was written in Stage 1 is what's tested in Stage 6. Again, taking the time to do Stage 1 thoroughly establishes a foundation for the rest of the implementation. Testing is often done through workflow scenarios. For example, a workflow scenario could be "Creating a new employee record manually." Another workflow scenario could be "Creating a new employee record automatically with data input from the third-party Applicant Tracking System (ATS.)" Both scenarios are testing new record creation, but the data sources vary. The testing stage is extensive because every workflow should be tested prior to Stage 7 and going live.

- Test all HCM workflows and operations which were identified, listed, and defined in Stage 1.
- For each workflow, confirm that data moves seamlessly within the HCM system and between integrated applications to avoid errors.
- Ensure the HCM system performs reliably, securely, and accurately.
- Involve all system roles in testing, including end-users to identify and resolve any issues or bugs.
- Keep all stakeholder groups informed about the progress of the system implementation. Active communication in the testing phase helps to prepare the organization for the next stage, go-live.

7. **Go-Live:**

   This stage probably doesn't need much of a description. The transition/go-live date is selected, and on that day, everyone does their work in the new system. To mitigate potential business disruption, one strategy that's used successfully is to keep both the old system and the new system running in parallel for a period of time. This allows for a "warm" switch-back if something goes wrong. To use this kind of a fail-safe requires advance planning starting back in Stage 2 and going throughout the implementation.

   - Schedule the launch and coordinate efforts to minimize disruptions.
   - Monitor both system *and team* performance during the initial period and address issues promptly.
   - Leverage system roles such as super-users and administrators to be key points of contact as the workforce begins using the new system. These various roles have been involved in the implementation of the HCM system, and they each possess advanced knowledge/skills about the new system's operation.

8. **Post-Implementation Support:**

   It's beneficial to define a limited post-implementation support period where a higher-level of support is provided compared to the future-state of run-time. Common durations range from a couple weeks to a few months, depending on the degree of change for the organization and the anticipated potential for issues. When this post-implementation support period is over, the project transitions into the run-state and the organization uses the normal support methods that were defined in Stage 1, requirements, and more specifically any Service Level Agreements (SLA's) that were agreed upon between the organization and the supplier.

   - Continue to actively communicate system implementation and operational status updates to the organization during this higher-level of support timeframe. This helps the workforce feel better about the system because they have confidence that any questions or issues can be addressed quickly.

- Assist, troubleshoot, and fix systems workflow and configuration issues as needed.
- Regularly assess the system's performance and gather feedback to make improvements.

An important note regarding the system implementation process. Refer to Figure 08.01. Steps 3 through 6 can be done iteratively and repeatedly depending on needs. The more complex the customization and configuration, the more likely it is that these steps will be repeated.

There are two activities which are worth calling out. Both of these are critical to the success of the systems implementation process, and both activities are conducted throughout a project. Training and change management are required through the entirety of the system implementation process. They're activities that begin immediately and continue for several months after the go-live. Successful implementations use these activities extensively to ensure transformation and adoption by the various departments, managers, and employees.

Change Management:

Every organization is a little different regarding the level of support needed from a change management standpoint. However, one thing is very consistent: every organization is best served by giving this topic due consideration. People react differently to change, and our responses range from proactive adoption to active resistance. Careful consideration helps the organization mitigate resistance and accelerate adoption, thereby accelerating the return on investment and the achievement of the organization's goals. Some principles of change management to keep in mind:

- Drive **awareness** through communication and participation. Start as early as possible to generate awareness across all employee groups and ensure that the workforce not only understands *what's* being changed but that they also understand the reasons *why* the organization will go through the change. Continue proactive communications throughout the entire implementation process.
- One of the goals of proactive communication and participation is to generate a **desire** in the workforce for the system change. This borrows from a marketing term, "push versus pull." The best case is to switch from a "pushed" change to a "pulled" change. A "pushed" change is something that the leadership team pushes or forces down through the organization. From the employee's perspective, this is something that is done ***to*** them. A "pulled" change is something that the employees/workforce want to have happen; they ask for the change. From the employee's perspective, this is something that is done ***with*** them. Being able to achieve a state of desire (for the new system) in the workforce makes the rest of the implementation process much easier!

Training:

- Train the Project Team: The project team's training begins in Stage 1. Each person who participates in requirements identification and definition is learning about the organization's needs. These foundational knowledge points are built upon throughout the entire project. This team learns a tremendous amount during Stage 2 when supplier demos are conducted. The project team is primarily learning-by-doing, and their experience is invaluable to the rest of the organization, especially as the project approaches go-live in Stage 7.

- Users need comprehensive training so they will be able to perform their daily jobs in the new system.
- Training materials are a point of consideration. The extent to which manuals, guides, and online resources need to be created is going to depend on a couple things. 1) How much of this is available through the supplier selected, and 2) How much has customization and configuration changed how the system was intended to operate and function from the supplier's standard product.

A new HCM system is a substantial undertaking that requires careful planning, collaboration, and ongoing support to ensure successful implementation. Done well, it can help an organization by streamlining HR processes and enhancing workforce management. It also helps an organization move to a more/fully integrated suite of business applications and tools which are used to operate the business.

Run-Time Support

Run-time support, often referred to as ongoing support, is a critical phase in the life cycle of any system, including Human Capital Management (HCM) systems. It involves providing assistance, troubleshooting, and continuous improvement after the system has been successfully implemented, gone live, and is in daily use. Here are some key aspects of post-implementation support:

- **Service Level Agreements:** A Service Level Agreement (SLA) is a contract or agreement between a service provider and a customer that outlines the level of service the provider is obligated to deliver. Often these are negotiated and included in the purchase agreement, and it's wise to negotiate the terms, conditions, and performance requirements of a SLA prior to committing to purchase a system. Example performance metrics (SLA's) are system uptime/availability, response time to issues, and meantime to repair.
- **Roles and Responsibilities:** The capabilities of both companies and service providers vary. Some large companies may have extensive ability to support their own systems operations. In circumstances like this a company may direct all of their users to their own support team, while using suppliers for highly technical issues. In contrast, small companies may have little ability to support system operations; therefore, they require day-to-day customer support from their suppliers. The support strategy along with roles and responsibilities will need to be established early, and it's recommended that this is negotiated as part of the purchase agreement along with establishing SLA's.
- **Issue Resolution:** Run-time support involves addressing and resolving any issues, glitches, or bugs that may arise in the HCM system after it's in use. This includes technical problems, data discrepancies, and user concerns. Metrics should be established in the SLA and reviewed on a regular basis between the organization and the supplier.

- **User Assistance:** Providing ongoing assistance to system users is a crucial part of run-time support. Users, including HR professionals, managers, and employees, may encounter questions or challenges using the system effectively. Support may come in the form of helpdesk services, user guides, training, or online resources.
- **Software Updates and Maintenance:** Over time, software vendors release updates, patches, and new versions of their systems to enhance functionality, security, and address known issues. The type of system implementation chosen impacts this activity dramatically. A cloud based/SAAS implementation is likely to receive updates automatically. An on-premise implementation will require special planning to conduct updates and maintenance.
- **Data Management:** Managing and maintaining the integrity of data within the HCM system is an ongoing task. This includes data backup, data cleansing, and data retention. Run-time support teams are responsible for ensuring data is accurate, secure, and available when needed. Who does this is part of the roles and responsibilities negotiation and potentially part of the contract/SLA. It's within scope of the contract and SLA if the organization is contracting with the supplier to provide data management services.
- **Performance Monitoring:** Continuous monitoring of the HCM system's performance is essential to identify any performance degradation. This is an accountability item. Most suppliers will track performance metrics on their own; however, it's useful for companies to do the same. These metrics should be anchored in the terms and conditions of the SLA and they should be reviewed on a regular basis by a joint meeting between the organization and the supplier.
- **Training and Documentation Updates:** As the system evolves, training materials and documentation will need to be updated to reflect changes and improvements. This ensures that users have access to accurate and up-to-date resources. The extent of work that's reflected here is heavily dependent on the type of implementation and the degree to which the system was changed during customization and configuration. The closer to "off-the-shelf"/"vanilla" an implementation is, the more the organization will be able to leverage supplier provided resources.
- **Security and Compliance:** Ongoing security monitoring and compliance checks are vital to protect sensitive HR and employee data. Who does this is part of the roles and responsibilities negotiation and should be part of the contract/SLA. It's within scope of the contract and SLA if the organization is contracting with the supplier to provide data security and compliance services. It's also common practice for companies to contract with a neutral third-party to perform data security and compliance audits. A security and compliance strategy should be developed early in the implementation process, as early as Stage 1 during requirements gathering.

- **Scalability and Growth:** Businesses change and grow over time, and the HCM system must be able to adapt. Scalability is a significant point of consideration in Stage 2 during vendor selection. See chapter 3 for additional details. Run-time support may include supporting additional modules as they're turned on in the future.

Overall, run-time support ensures that the HCM system continues to function effectively, meets the needs of the organization, and it remains aligned with evolving business requirements. It plays a crucial role in maximizing the return on investment and ensuring the long-term success of the system and the organization.

Role of the Systems Integrator

The role of systems integrator is worth a deeper exploration because of its deep specialization. They are an entity which plays a crucial, albeit temporary, part in the system implementation process. The primary responsibility of the Systems Integrator is to ensure that different software applications, systems, and technologies work together cohesively to meet the organization's needs. Refer to Figures 08.01 and 08.02 for this section. The organization or company is involved in (A), which is the entirety of the implementation and extending for the entire lifecycle of the system. Here is an overview of the Systems Integrator role in each stage of the implementation process:

Stage 1, Requirements Gathering and System Sizing:

Systems integrators are usually brought in during (B) Stage 1. It's common for the chosen integrator to manage the requirements gathering process for the organization. They also perform preliminary assessments of the organization's existing systems and work processes. If a company is concerned about biases during Stage 2, Vendor Selection, they may choose to use another third party who works on only Stage 1. In this case, the systems integrator is chosen at the same time as the system supplier during Stage 2.

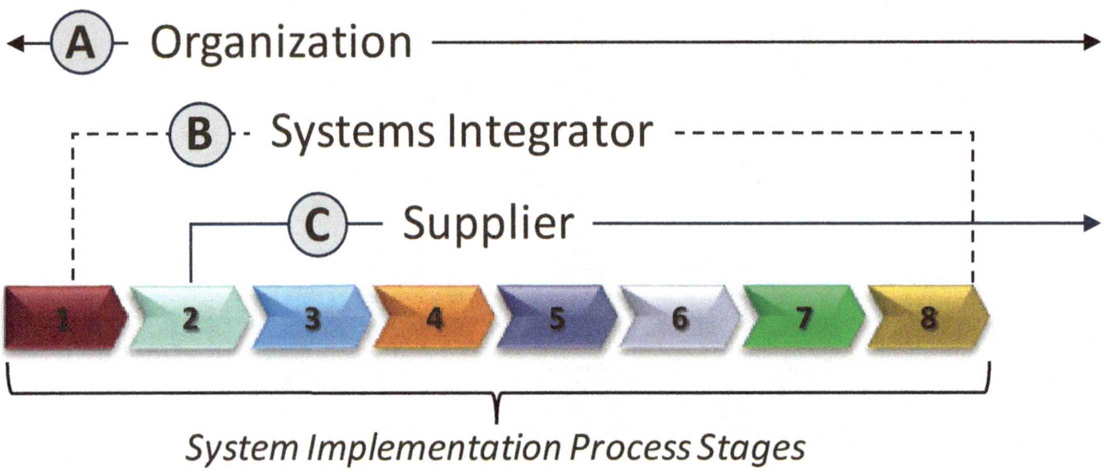

Figure 08.02
System Integrator Relationship
Shows the relationship between the Organization, Systems Integrator, and System Supplier.

Stage 2, Vendor Selection:

If involved in the prior stage, Systems integrators may assist the organization in the selection *decision* regarding the HCM software vendor. From a *decision-making* standpoint, the role of the systems integrator is to recommend the suppliers which can meet the needs of the organization based on a thoroughly researched business case. Systems Integrators facilitate engagement, demonstrations, and detailed Q&A between suppliers and the organization. Ultimately, they help evaluate options to ensure the chosen solution aligns with the organization's needs.

Stage 3, Customization and Configuration:

Stages 3-6 are where the systems integrators "earn their pay" so to speak. A Systems Integrator often performs the customization and configuration of the HCM system to meet the organization's specific requirements. They ensure that the software is tailored to the organization's work processes. It's important to mention that this is not the exclusive domain of integrators. Many system suppliers will provide customization and configurations services, and when they do, the systems integrator then fulfills more of a program/project management role.

Stage 4, Data Migration:

Systems integrators are often responsible for planning and executing the data migration process. They ensure that existing HR and employee data is accurately and securely transferred to the new system using either automated or manual transfer techniques.

Stage 5, Integration:

Systems Integrators facilitate the connectivity (integration) of the HCM system with other existing business systems, such as accounting, salesforce automation, and enterprise resource planning. They ensure data flows seamlessly between them, avoiding redundancies and errors.

Stage 6, Testing:

Systems Integrators facilitate the testing stage. They will develop the workflow scenarios to be tested, schedule participants, setup sandbox instances of the system, and track completion and results. They create tracking logs to identify, track, and resolve any design, customization, configuration, migration, and integration issues. The completion of this stage is driven by the entire system functioning correctly and reliably according to the requirements. When issues are discovered, it is normal for the implementation process to loop-back through prior stages until the issues are resolved.

Stage 7, Go-Live:

At this stage, the role of the System Integrator starts to ramp down. Many integrators will encourage the organization to take a prominent role in their own communication and training of employees. This helps with change and organizational adoption of the new system. If an organization is especially resource constrained, an integrator may provide these services.

Stage 8, Post Implementation Support:

For a limited period, Systems integrators may continue to monitor the system's performance after implementation. If issues arise, they identify and address them, working as an intermediary between the organization and the supplier.

Referring to Figure 08.02, it is important to note that the Systems integrator role (B) is temporary; however, the involvement between the (A) organization and the (C) supplier is on-going. The best Systems Integrators know that the relationship which will drive on-going success is between the organization and supplier, and they will work to ensure that this is on solid footing before they close their portion of the engagement. Since the (B) integrator is heavily involved with the (A) organization on a day-to-day basis during stages 2-8, it's common for productive professional relationships to develop. It's paramount that equally strong relationships develop between the (A) organization and the (C) supplier.

Ultimately, the Systems Integrator acts as a technical expert who bridges the gap between the organization's specific needs and the technology solutions offered by suppliers. They play a pivotal role in the implementation, ensuring that the system functions optimally, integrates well with other business systems, and meets the organization's requirements. Their expertise is valuable in achieving a successful and well-maintained HCM system.

Role of the Internal Integrations Teams

There are several key roles that are fulfilled by internal team members. Don't get this confused with the prior chapter on *system* roles. The roles being discussed here are project-based roles, and in many cases these roles are assumed temporarily and only for the duration of the implementation. In larger system implementations, people are rotated away from their normal jobs and are assigned to the implementation team, often taking their direction from the Systems Integrator. The roles that we'll examine are HCM Lead and Super Users. There are a couple other support roles which are served on an as-needed basis during the project. These include Subject Matter Experts (SME's) and Usability Test Groups.

The HCM lead plays a crucial role in the system implementation process. Their responsibilities include overseeing and coordinating the implementation in conjunction with the integrator, ensuring that the HCM system meets the organization's needs, and facilitating communication between various stakeholders. Here's an overview of the HCM lead's role and their interactions:

Responsibilities of the HCM Lead:

- **Team Management:** The HCM lead acts as the interface between the implementation team and those who are running the day-to-day HR operations. They are responsible for team scheduling, communications, and tracking progress to ensure that the project stays on course.

- **Requirements Gathering:** The HCM lead works closely with HR stakeholders and other relevant departments to gather and document the organization's specific requirements for the HCM system. They ensure that the system aligns with the organization's HR processes and objectives.

- **Vendor Selection:** The HCM lead may be involved in the vendor selection process, helping to evaluate potential HCM software providers, and ensuring that the chosen solution meets the organization's needs.

- **Collaboration with Integrator:** The HCM lead interacts closely with the systems integrator, providing them with a clear understanding of the organization's requirements and expectations. They facilitate collaboration and communication between the integrator and the organization. The become a crucial link for the facilitation of effective decision making. In the context of systems implementations, that often means that both speed and quality of decisions are critical.

- **Customization and Configuration:** The HCM lead will often spend the bulk of their time in customization and configuration meetings. With large scale implementations, these can last for months or even years. They oversee and manage the involvement of team members during this stage, helping to optimize the use of resources to balance between normal operational needs and project needs.

- **Data Migration:** The HCM lead coordinates the data migration process, working with the integrator to ensure that existing HR and employee data is transferred accurately and securely to the new system. This is not usually an individual contribution of the HCM lead; rather, it's a collaboration between the HCM lead and the relevant Subject Matter Experts (SME's.)

- **Testing and Quality Assurance:** The HCM lead is involved in user acceptance testing (UAT) and quality assurance efforts to identify and resolve issues, ensuring that the integrated system functions correctly. They coordinate with Super-Users and other team members to ensure that the right people are testing workflows through the new system.

- **Training and Change Management:** The HCM lead will often serve as the leader of all training and change management efforts. Doing so helps to ensure the best possible transition through go-live because the HCM lead is in the best position to leverage both project and team resources in the preparation of the workforce.

Overall, the HCM lead is a central figure in the HCM system implementation process. They are responsible for ensuring the successful deployment of the system and maintaining alignment with the organization's goals and work processes. They act as a bridge between stakeholder groups, ensuring effective communication, collaboration, and resource management.

Super-users, also known as power users, play a critical role during system implementation. These individuals are typically employees within the organization who are especially knowledgeable about the *current* system and its functionalities. They are often "early adopters" with a high degree of technical acumen. Consequently, they learn new systems quickly. They are responsible for a range of tasks that help ensure the successful implementation of the HCM system and its effective use within the organization. Here's an overview of what super-users do and their interactions with the integrator and system provider:

Responsibilities of Super-Users:

- **System Expertise:** Super-users are expected to become experts in the new system. They invest time to become proficient with the system's features, capabilities, and configuration options.
- **User Training:** They often take on the role of trainer, helping other employees learn how to use the new system. This often includes providing training sessions, creating user guides, and answering questions.
- **User Support:** Super-users serve as a first point of contact for their colleagues when they have questions or encounter issues with the system. They assist with troubleshooting and problem resolution. This provides an important "stop-gap" for issues during go-live at stage 7. A large percentage of the operational issues at this stage are often driven by knowledge and skills, and the super-user can resolve these directly. This allows the integrator to focus on any technical issues that arise.
- **Testing and Validation:** During testing, stage 6, super-users are involved in workflow tests on the new system. Their expertise of workflow in the current system, along with acquired skills on the new system, places them in a uniquely valuable position to perform testing. They help identify and report issues, ensuring that the system aligns with user requirements and organizational processes.

Subject Matter Experts (SMEs) also play a crucial role during system implementation. SMEs are individuals within the organization who possess specialized knowledge and expertise in operational work domains. The SME knows how the business operates. Their role is typically more oriented to contributing on an as-needed basis, and they serve as valuable resources to guide and inform the implementation process. Here's an overview of what SMEs do and their interactions:

Responsibilities of SMEs:

1. **Domain Knowledge:** SMEs provide in-depth expertise in specific areas. Within HR this would be sub-domains such as payroll, benefits administration, recruiting, learning and development, employee relations, policies, compliance, and more. They have a deep understanding of how the work is accomplished within the organization.

2. **Requirements Gathering:** SME participation is particularly heavy during Stage 1, gathering requirements. They are often the best sources to identify and define the requirements associated with their areas of expertise. A change management note: Getting SMEs bought-in early is vital. Without their early buy-in, they may not give the requirements identification stage enough effort or attention. It's not uncommon for SMEs to check-out, or even walk out, of these early-stage meetings because they don't believe in the project and/or don't want to participate. Yet, their tacit knowledge is exactly what's vital to the success of the implementation. Taking the time to properly engage SME's is a critical success item for system implementations.

Usability test groups play an important role in the system implementation process, particularly testing in Stage 6. These groups are responsible for evaluating the system's user interface and overall user experience to ensure that it meets the organization's needs and expectations of the end-users. Their primary focus is on usability and user satisfaction. Here's an overview of the purpose of usability test groups and their interactions:

Purpose of Usability Test Groups:

- **User Interface:** Usability test groups are responsible for assessing the HCM system's user interface and how easily users can navigate and perform tasks within the system.

- **User Experience:** They evaluate the overall user experience, including factors like efficiency, effectiveness, learnability, and user satisfaction. The goal is to ensure that the system is intuitive and user-friendly.

- **Issue Identification:** Usability test groups identify usability issues, pain points, and areas of improvement within the system. This can include issues related to design, navigation, terminology, and accessibility.

- **Feedback and Recommendations:** They provide feedback and recommendations to improve the user interface, streamline workflows, and enhance the overall user experience. This feedback helps make the system more user centric.

Interactions with the Integrator, System Provider, and Project Team:

- **Integrator:** Usability test groups may work closely with the systems integrator during testing in Stage 6. The usability testing that's done would likely be related to any customizations and configurations.

- **System Supplier:** Many system suppliers will offer the opportunity for select employees to participate in usability test groups. These groups can operate for specific releases or exist for longer durations. The system provider uses this feedback to inform future design updates or enhancements to the user interface.

The usability test groups are beneficial for ensuring that the HCM system is user-friendly and meets the needs of the end-users. Their interactions with the systems integrator and system provider help identify and resolve usability issues, leading to a more effective and user-centric implementation. Their feedback can result in system adjustments that enhance the overall user experience.

Summary

The implementation of an HCM system involves a structured approach that encompasses the assessment of organizational needs, vendor selection, system customization, data migration, integration, testing, training, and change management. Post-implementation support is equally essential, encompassing activities such as issue resolution, software updates, data management, security, and performance monitoring. Throughout the process, key roles, including the HCM lead, super-users, SMEs, and usability test groups, contribute to the successful adoption and use of a system. Effective collaboration between the system supplier, systems integrator, and the organization's HR department is vital for achieving seamless implementation and ongoing effective operation. Ultimately, a well-executed HCM system implementation empowers a business to manage their human capital effectively and adapt to evolving workforce challenges.

Discussion Questions

What are the primary objectives a business should define when considering the implementation of an HCM system? How do these objectives influence the implementation process?

What are some key factors to consider when selecting an HCM software vendor, and how can organizations ensure they choose the right solution for their needs?

How does the role of the HCM lead evolve across the stages of system implementation?

What are the specific responsibilities of super-users during a HCM system implementation? How can their expertise be leveraged most effectively?

What are the specific responsibilities of SMEs during a HCM system implementation? How can their expertise be leveraged most effectively?

What's the difference between customization and configuration? Which is more expensive? Which presents more challenges for software updates?

Chapter References

Almase, G. G. C. (2023). *Managing Change in Human Capital Management Systems Implementations in Multinational Companies: Modified e-Delphi Study.* ProQuest Dissertations Publishing.

ChatGPT. (2023). *HCM System Implementation.* OpenAI. Accessed November 5, 2023.

Ganesh, K. (2014). *Enterprise resource planning : fundamentals of design and implementation.* Springer. https://doi.org/10.1007/978-3-319-05927-3

Ganesh, K.S., & Wishkerman, A. (2014). *SAP HCM - a complete tutorial : deploy and implement the diverse functionalities of SAP HCM* (1st edition). Packet Publishing.

Pugh, K. (2011). *Lean-agile acceptance test driven development : better software through collaboration* (1st edition). Addison Wesley Professional.

Reitsma, E., & Hilletofth, P. (2018). Critical success factors for ERP system implementation: a user perspective. *European Business Review, 30*(3), 285–310. https://doi.org/10.1108/EBR-04-2017-0075

Samara, T. (2015). *ERP and information systems : integration or disintegration* (1st edition). ISTE.

Chapter 10
Environmental, Social, Governance, and Data Privacy

Chapter Table of Contents

Chapter 10: Environmental, Social, Governance, and Data Privacy

Introduction

In today's business landscape, Environmental, Social, and Governance (ESG) principles have emerged as important considerations for businesses aiming to achieve sustainable growth and positive societal impact. Within the realm of human capital management, integrating ESG factors includes aligning HR practices with environmental sustainability, social responsibility, and ethical governance standards. Simultaneously, data privacy has become a paramount concern, particularly with the increasing digitization of HR processes and the accumulation of vast amounts of sensitive employee data. Data breaches and privacy violations not only jeopardize individuals' privacy rights but also erode trust and damage organizational reputation.

Terminology to be familiar with:

ESG stands for Environmental, Social, and Governance. It's a set of criteria used by investors to evaluate a company's impact beyond just financial returns.

CSR stands for Corporate Social Responsibility. This involves businesses integrating social and environmental concerns in their operations and interactions with stakeholders.

Environmental Factors in Human Capital Management

Sustainable HR practices encompass various initiatives aimed at reducing the environmental footprint of organizations while promoting employee well-being and engagement. A large part of the focus on environmental issues in supply chain and on manufacturing practices. However, there are considerations for back-office support functions like human resources. This includes implementing energy-efficient workplace solutions, reducing paper usage through digitalization, and adopting eco-friendly options wherever they're feasible. Furthermore, organizations can cultivate a culture of environmental awareness and responsibility among employees through educational programs, waste reduction campaigns, and sustainable procurement practices. By integrating environmental considerations into HR strategies, organizations can demonstrate their commitment to sustainability while fostering a healthier, more environmentally conscious workplace. Sustainable HR practices can include things such as:

Electronic Waste (e-Waste): HCM systems rely on electronic devices, such as computers, and servers. The disposal of obsolete hardware contributes to electronic waste, which poses environmental hazards due to the presence of hazardous materials. Organizations should implement responsible e-waste management practices to minimize environmental impact. Hosted/SAAS implementations can provide an improvement compared to on-premise.

Paper Usage: While many HR processes have transitioned to digital platforms, paper-based workflows persist in many organizations. Printing paper-based documents, such as handbooks, training materials, and performance reviews, contributes to waste generation. Implementing paperless practices, such as electronic document management and digital signatures, can help reduce paper consumption and promote sustainability.

Social Responsibility and Human Capital Management

Social responsibility in a business context refers to the ethical obligation of businesses to act in ways that benefit society beyond their primary goal of production and profits. It encompasses a range of actions and initiatives aimed at addressing social concerns while balancing the interests of various stakeholders. These stakeholders include employees, management, customers, shareholders, investors, governments, and communities.

At the forefront of social responsibility is Diversity, Equity, and Inclusion (DEI). DEI initiatives lie at the heart of socially responsible human capital management. Organizations must actively promote diversity in their workforce, address systemic biases, and create an inclusive workplace culture where every employee feels valued and respected. Additionally, investing in employee well-being programs, such as mental health support, flexible work arrangements, and employee assistance programs, not only enhances employee satisfaction and retention but also contributes to the organization's long-term performance. Moreover, corporate social responsibility extends beyond the workplace, encompassing community engagement, philanthropy, and volunteering initiatives that positively impact society at large.

There can be material concerns with HCM systems in terms of social responsibility and Diversity, Equity, and Inclusion (DEI). Here are a few considerations:

Biases: HCM systems, especially in the areas of recruiting and performance management, may inadvertently perpetuate biases if they are not designed with DEI principles in mind. For example, algorithms used in resume screening or candidate evaluation may unintentionally favor certain demographics or perpetuate stereotypes, leading to discriminatory outcomes in hiring and promotion decisions. These are two areas which will likely see near-term use of artificial intelligence, and there's been much research and commentary about biases being present in the currently used algorithms.

Accessibility and Inclusivity: HCM systems must be accessible and inclusive to all employees, including those with disabilities and diverse needs. Accessibility considerations may include providing alternative formats for content, ensuring compatibility with assistive technologies, and designing user interfaces that are intuitive and user-friendly for everyone. One of the early promises of artificial intelligence is that it will help with accessibility issues by providing more natural language interactions with systems. This will be an interesting area to watch develop.

Transparency and Accountability: Socially responsible HCM systems prioritize transparency and accountability in decision-making processes, particularly concerning workplace policies. Employees should have access to information about how HCM systems operate, how data is collected and used, and how decisions are made regarding their employment. Transparent communication fosters trust and empowers employees to hold organizations accountable for upholding DEI principles and social responsibility standards.

Training and Awareness: Organizations must invest in training and awareness initiatives to ensure that employees understand the importance of social responsibility. HCM systems are often the platform for communicating, distributing, and tracking training programs. These can cover topics such as unconscious bias, cultural competency, inclusivity, and respectful workplace behaviors. By promoting awareness and fostering a culture of inclusivity and social responsibility, organizations can mitigate the risk of discriminatory practices and promote equity and fairness in the workplace.

Overall, addressing material concerns related to social responsibility and DEI in HCM systems requires a multifaceted approach that encompasses technological solutions, organizational policies and practices, and cultural norms and values. By prioritizing DEI principles and social responsibility standards in HCM systems, organizations can create more equitable, inclusive, and socially responsible workplaces.

Governance Practices in Human Capital Management

Ethical leadership and corporate governance are foundational to responsible human capital management. HR leaders must prioritize transparency, accountability, and ethical decision-making in all aspects of workforce management, from recruitment and performance management to employee relations and conflict resolution. Compliance with labor laws and regulations is essential to safeguarding employee rights and ensuring fair and equitable treatment for all individuals within the organization. Moreover, protecting employee data privacy is a critical aspect of governance, requiring organizations to implement robust data protection measures, uphold privacy regulations, and provide clear guidelines on data handling and consent.

Governance practices in HCM systems involve identifying and mitigating risks associated with workforce and organizational processes, such as data breaches, compliance violations, and unethical conduct. Organizations should implement robust internal controls, risk management frameworks, and compliance monitoring mechanisms to detect and prevent potential issues before they escalate. HCM systems should support risk management efforts by providing analytics, reporting tools, and compliance checks to proactively identify and mitigate areas of concern.

Global Data Privacy, Security and Compliance

In Human Capital Management (HCM) systems, addressing global data privacy, information security, and compliance is vital to successfully operating a business. Here are some concerns in data privacy, security, and compliance which need to be addressed:

- **Global Data Privacy Regulations:** Compliance with the General Data Protection Regulation (GDPR) in Europe remains a top concern. Additionally, as more countries adopt similar data protection regulations, HCM systems need to adapt to these global compliance requirements.

- **Cross-Border Data Transfers:** Many countries are enacting laws that require personal data to be stored within their borders. HCM systems must facilitate compliance with these data sovereignty requirements while ensuring seamless cross-border data transfers.

- **Consent Management:** HCM systems should enable organizations to efficiently manage data consent processes, including capturing, storing, and updating user consents, especially in the context of marketing and HR data.

- **Data Encryption and Security:** As cyber threats continue to evolve, HCM systems need to implement advanced encryption, multi-factor authentication, and other security measures to protect sensitive employee data.

- **Data Retention and Deletion:** HCM systems should allow organizations to easily identify and delete employee data in compliance with data protection regulations like the right to be forgotten under GDPR.
- **Data Breach Notification:** HCM systems should support quick and effective data breach response, including identifying and notifying affected individuals and authorities as required by law.
- **Industry-Specific Regulations:** HCM systems serving regulated industries, such as healthcare or finance, should be tailored to comply with sector-specific regulations.
- **Employee Training and Awareness:** HCM systems can include features for employee training and awareness programs to ensure that all staff understand their role in data protection and information security.
- **Third-Party Vendor Compliance:** HCM systems must address the risk associated with third-party vendors by assessing their compliance with data privacy and security standards.
- **Incident Response Planning:** HCM systems should assist in creating, managing, and testing incident response plans to mitigate data breaches and security incidents.
- **Secure Remote Work Environments:** In a world where remote work is increasingly prevalent, HCM systems must facilitate secure access to HR data and ensure remote employees' adherence to security protocols.
- **Regular Compliance Updates:** HCM systems should provide automated updates and notifications to ensure that organizations remain compliant with evolving regulations.

Addressing these concerns and focus areas is critical for HCM systems to maintain the privacy and security of employee data while navigating the complex landscape of global data privacy, information security, and compliance regulations. Staying up to date with these evolving requirements is an ongoing responsibility for HR and IT teams.

Integration of ESG and Data Privacy into HCM Systems

Integrating ESG and data privacy principles into human capital management (HCM) systems requires a holistic approach that spans people, processes, and technology. Organizations must align their business strategies with ESG goals, embedding sustainability, social responsibility, and ethical governance considerations into every aspect of every workflow. Within human resources, this involves incorporating ESG metrics into performance evaluations, establishing sustainability goals for recruitment and talent development, and fostering a culture of accountability and transparency regarding ESG initiatives. Moreover, integrating data privacy principles into HCM systems involves implementing privacy by design principles, and ensuring that data protection measures are embedded into HR work processes from the beginning.

Technological solutions play a pivotal role enabling organizations to integrate ESG and data privacy into HCM systems. HR technology platforms can facilitate data-driven decision-making by providing insights into ESG performance metrics, employee engagement levels, and diversity metrics. Additionally, these platforms can incorporate features such as encryption, access controls, and audit trails to enhance data privacy and security. Collaboration between departments is essential to ensure that systems are implemented in compliance with ESG standards and data privacy regulations. Through collaboration, organizations can create systems that uphold ESG principles and safeguard employee data privacy.

Ethical Considerations

As HR professionals navigate the evolving landscape of technology and human capital management, they must also be acutely aware of ethical considerations and concerns. Here are some of the predominant ethical items that HR professionals should be prepared to handle:

- **Data Privacy and Consent:** HR professionals need to prioritize the privacy of employee data and ensure that individuals have given informed consent for data processing. This includes transparency about what data is collected and how it will be used.

- **Bias and Fairness:** Guarding against bias in workforce management processes is a significant ethical concern. HR professionals must ensure that technology solutions are fair and do not discriminate.

- **Candidate Experience:** Treating job candidates with respect, fairness, and transparency is essential. HR professionals must ensure that the candidate's experience, from application to onboarding, aligns with the organization's values and standards.

- **Ethical Use of AI:** As AI becomes more integrated into processes and systems, HR professionals must ensure that AI is used ethically and transparently. This includes explaining AI-driven decisions and addressing potential biases.

- **Handling Employee Complaints:** HR professionals must be prepared to handle employee complaints, including those related to harassment, discrimination, and unethical behavior. Providing a safe and confidential channel for reporting issues is critical. As AI is embedded into processes and systems, it is likely that HR will need to address complaints arising from its usage.

- **Continuous Learning and Development:** Offering opportunities for employee development and growth is not just a business necessity but also an ethical commitment to employees' career aspirations and job satisfaction. As AI is embedded into processes and systems, there will be a greater need for continuous learning and development so the workforce can maintain skills.

- **Global Compliance:** Navigating international labor laws and regulations while maintaining ethical standards is a complex challenge. HR professionals must balance local compliance requirements with the organization's ethical values.

Ethical considerations are integral to HR's mission of creating a positive workplace culture, fostering trust, and ensuring the fair and respectful treatment of all employees. HR professionals should continuously educate themselves on these ethical issues, stay informed about relevant laws and regulations, and develop policies and practices that align with their organization's and community's ethical standards and values.

Summary

In today's dynamic business environment, integrating Environmental, Social, and Governance (ESG) principles and data privacy considerations into human capital management (HCM) systems is important for businesses to achieve sustainable long-term growth and operation. By embracing sustainable practices, promoting diversity and inclusion, and upholding ethical governance standards, organizations can cultivate a thriving workplace culture. Concurrently, prioritizing data privacy and security ensures the protection of sensitive employee information and upholds individuals' privacy rights. Leveraging technology solutions and fostering organizational collaboration, businesses can effectively integrate ESG and data privacy into their business systems. These efforts will drive organizational success while fostering a culture of integrity and accountability.

Discussion Questions

How can organizations effectively integrate ESG principles into their human capital management strategies?

What are the key challenges and opportunities associated with implementing data privacy measures in human capital management systems? How can organizations balance the need for data security with employees' privacy rights?

What role does leadership play in driving the adoption of ESG principles and data privacy measures within organizations?

How do ESG and data privacy considerations impact employee engagement, retention, and overall organizational performance?

What are the potential benefits of prioritizing sustainability, social responsibility, and ethical governance in human capital management?

What are some key performance indicators (KPIs) and metrics that organizations can use to track progress and demonstrate impact?

What are some best practices for fostering a culture of continuous learning and improvement around ESG and data privacy in human capital management?

How can organizations encourage employees to stay informed and engaged with evolving trends and regulations?

Chapter References

ChatGPT. (2023). *HCM Future Trends.* OpenAI. Accessed November 5, 2023.

Just, V. (2020). *Sustainable Business Processes in Global Companies: Current Perspectives and Future Trends in Regard to Efficiency and Risk Management* (1st ed. 2020.). Springer Fachmedien Wiesbaden. https://doi.org/10.1007/978-3-658-28196-0

OpenAI. (2024, April 27). ChatGPT conversation on *ESG, Diversity, Inclusion, and Data Privacy in Human Capital Management.* Accessed April 27, 2024.

Shin, J., Moon, J. J., & Kang, J. (2023). Where does ESG pay? The role of national culture in moderating the relationship between ESG performance and financial performance. *International Business Review, 32*(3), 102071. https://doi.org/10.1016/j.ibusrev.2022.102071

Ratten, V. (2020). Entrepreneurial ecosystems: Future research trends. *Thunderbird International Business Review, 62(*5), 623–628. https://doi.org/10.1002/tie.22163

Read, Colin. (2023). *Understanding Sustainability Principles and ESG Policies : A Multidisciplinary Approach to Public and Corporate Responses to Climate Change* (1st ed. 2023.). Springer International Publishing. https://doi.org/10.1007/978-3-031-34483-1

Chapter 11
Future Technology Trends Impacting Human Capital Management

Table of Contents

Photo by Pixabay from pexels.com

Chapter 11: Future Technology Trends Impacting Human Capital Management

Introduction

In this chapter on future technology trends impacting HCM, we explore the ever-evolving landscape of the workplace and technologies that may impact it. Human resources is one of many functions within an enterprise which must continually adapt to emerging trends to maximize the benefits to employees and companies. We'll identify and define prominent future trends that may impact human capital management. This chapter examines specific anticipated trends. The next chapter describes some recommended approaches for how you can adapt to technological changes throughout your career.

Employee Experience & the Employer Value Proposition

In the area of employee experience (EX), several trends are likely to continue to develop. They could have significant implications for the workplace and HCM systems, ultimately impacting the Employer's Value Proposition (EVP) to the workforce and the communities where they operate. An Employer Value Proposition (EVP) is a set of unique offerings and benefits that an employer provides to its employees in exchange for their skills, experience, and contributions to the organization. It's essentially what an employer promises to deliver to its workforce in terms of the overall employment experience. An EVP includes a combination of tangible and intangible elements, such as compensation, benefits, work culture, and career development opportunities. Here are some of these trends and their implications:

Remote and Hybrid Work Arrangements:

- **Trend:** Remote and hybrid work arrangements, which gained prominence during the COVID-19 pandemic, are likely to continue. The technologies that were adopted widely during this time enabled improvements in collaboration across geographic boundaries, which in-turn reduced business dependency on bricks-and-mortar office spaces.
- **Implications:** Workplace boundaries are becoming more flexible. Businesses are depending less on physical workspaces and depending more on virtual workspaces/teams. This will continue to require HCM systems to support dynamic scheduling, collaboration, and performance management for distributed teams.
- EX needs to consider the challenges of remote work, such as maintaining work-life balance and combating feelings of isolation.

Flexible Work Hours and Location:

- **Trend:** Remote and hybrid work arrangements, globalization, and the ubiquitous presence of technology have all erased the lines that used to exist between work time and personal time. Employees increasingly expect (and need) flexibility in their work hours and location.
- **Implications:** It's common in today's workplace that an individual's work time never stops. HCM systems will need to evolve with the changing expectations around flexible scheduling, time tracking, and location tracking.
- EVP is particularly fragile with this topic. A work environment which is perceived as "unrelenting" will erode the quality of an employer's workforce over time. Employees will leave and go to work for companies which have a better EVP. Management tools need to accommodate variable work hours and locations.

Wellness Programs:

- **Trend:** Employees need resources that focus on the wellness of the whole person including physical, mental, and emotional health.
- **Implications:** HCM systems should integrate wellness initiatives, track participation, and measure their impact on EX.
- Data analytics capabilities within HCM systems can be used to identify trends and suggest improvements. These can be combined with employee opinion surveys such as engagement, culture, and organizational performance.

Digital Employee Engagement:

- **Trend:** Digital platforms such as mobile apps and social collaboration tools are prevalent.
- **Implications:** HCM systems should provide integrated digital platforms for communication, recognition, and collaboration.
- These tools need to be user-friendly and accessible on various devices.

Learning and Development:

- **Trend:** Continuous learning is available to almost everyone now. This includes various online sources such as Massive Online Open Courseware (MOOC,) commercial learning content sites, and the proliferation of on-demand micro learning.
- **Implications:** HCM systems need to offer integrated and seamless learning solutions that support personalized learning paths and offer access to a variety of resources.
- Integrating microlearning, on-the-job training, and AI-driven recommendations can enhance EX in this area.

Employees need to trust that their data is handled responsibly, which impacts EX.
These trends in employee experience have profound implications for HCM systems, as they require technological solutions that can adapt to the changing landscape of work. HCM systems will need to be agile, data-driven, and employee-centric to support and enhance the employee experience effectively.

Artificial Intelligence

Artificial intelligence (AI) is poised to significantly transform the work of human resources professionals. Here are several ways AI could change HR practices and how they can be integrated into Human Capital Management (HCM) systems:

AI-Driven Recruitment and Candidate Screening: AI can analyze resumes, applications, and candidate data to identify the most suitable candidates. It can predict a candidate's fit for a role by matching skills, experience, and cultural alignment. HCM systems can include AI-powered applicant tracking systems (ATS) that streamline recruitment by automating candidate screening and selection.

Chatbots for Employee Self-Service: HCM systems can incorporate AI-powered chatbots as part of their employee self-service portals, which would provide quick answers to common employee queries, such as benefits, leave policies, and HR procedures, reducing the HR team's workload.

Predictive Analytics for Employee Turnover: HCM systems can include predictive analytics modules that provide insights into employee turnover, such as the ability to analyze historical data and predict which employees are at risk of leaving the company. This allows HR to proactively address retention issues.

AI-Powered Learning and Development Recommendations: AI can recommend personalized learning and development opportunities based on an employee's role, performance, and career goals. This would enable learning management systems to tailor training and development plans for each employee.

Performance Management and Feedback: AI can provide continuous performance feedback by analyzing data from various sources, including peer reviews and project outcomes. HCM systems can then provide real-time feedback and insights.

Compensation Analysis and Pay Equity: AI can help identify compensation disparities and provide recommendations to ensure pay equity across demographics. Job analysis, design, and the production of job descriptions can be greatly accelerated.

Employee Sentiment Analysis: AI can analyze employee feedback, sentiment, and employee opinion surveys to gauge overall employee satisfaction and well-being.

Workforce Planning and Succession Management: AI can analyze workforce data to forecast future talent needs and identify potential future leaders within the organization. HCM systems dynamically and instantly address workforce planning and succession management to help organizations make decisions that impact their future direction.

These AI-driven advancements in HR can (and likely will) be seamlessly integrated into HCM systems, making them more data-driven, efficient, and employee-centric. The best HCM platforms will have the flexibility to incorporate AI modules and offer a unified interface that allows HR professionals to access these enhanced capabilities while managing various aspects of human capital across the employment lifecycle.

Artificial Intelligence of Things

Artificial Intelligence of Things (AIoT) refers to the integration of artificial intelligence algorithms into the Internet of Things (IoT). These technologies become embedded into devices which enhance their capabilities by providing users with predictive maintenance and intelligent automation. AIoT can enable HCM systems to collect and analyze vast amounts of data from IoT devices, such as wearables, sensors, and smart devices in the workplace. By applying AI algorithms to this data, HCM systems can identify patterns, trends, and correlations related to employee performance, productivity, and well-being. Predictive analytics can help HR professionals anticipate workforce needs, identify potential risks, and make data-driven decisions to optimize workforce management strategies.

AIoT-enabled health and wellness monitoring solutions can track employee health metrics, such as heart rate, sleep patterns, and stress levels, using wearable devices and biometric sensors. By leveraging AI algorithms to analyze this data in real-time, HCM systems can identify signs of burnout, fatigue, or health-related issues among employees and provide proactive interventions, such as wellness programs, mental health resources, and work-life balance initiatives. This proactive approach to employee well-being can improve overall health outcomes, reduce absenteeism, and enhance workforce engagement and retention.

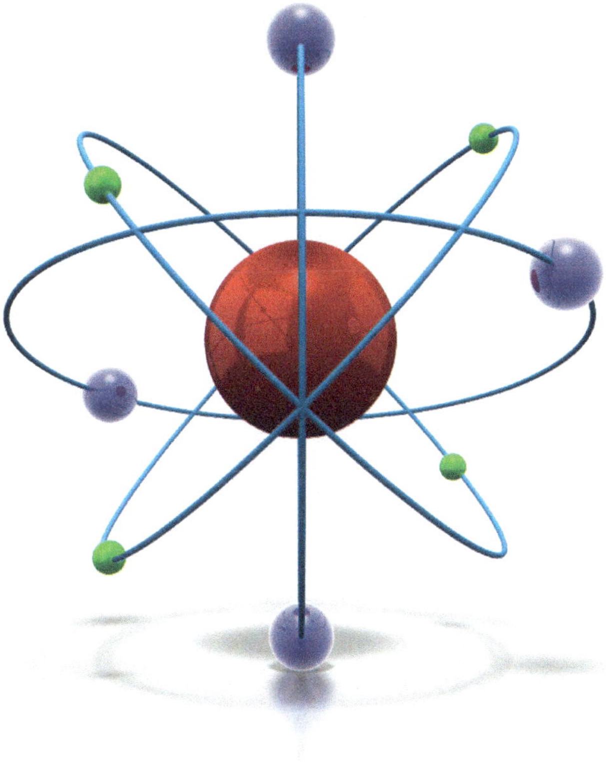

Quantum Computing

Quantum Computing: Quantum computing involves the use of quantum-mechanical phenomena, such as superposition and entanglement, to perform operations on data. It has the potential to solve complex problems much faster than classical computers. In simple terms, quantum computing is a revolutionary type of computing that uses the principles of quantum mechanics to perform computations. Unlike classical computers, which use bits to represent information as either 0s or 1s, quantum computers use quantum bits, or qubits, which can represent both 0s and 1s simultaneously due to a phenomenon called superposition. This allows quantum computers to process and manipulate vast amounts of data in parallel, potentially enabling them to solve complex problems much faster than classical computers.

As for when we might see quantum computing become mainstream in the workplace, it's difficult to predict. It's certainly not here yet. Significant progress is being made in research and development every year. Some experts estimate that practical, commercially viable quantum computers capable of solving real-world problems could be available within the next decade.

Edge Computing

Edge computing is a decentralized computing paradigm that brings data processing and storage closer to the source of data generation, rather than relying solely on centralized data centers or cloud servers. Instead of sending all data to a distant data center for processing, edge computing distributes computational tasks to local devices or "edge" nodes located closer to where the data is generated, such as IoT devices, sensors, or edge servers. Think back to an earlier chapter when we explored client-server computing structures. Edge computing reduces latency, improves responsiveness, and enables real-time data analysis and decision-making at the network's edge.

Edge computing is already mainstream in some industries, and its adoption is expected to continue growing rapidly. In hosted/SaaS implementations, edge computing is likely to complement cloud-based solutions rather than replace them entirely. Edge computing can enhance the performance, reliability, and scalability of hosted/SaaS implementations by offloading computational tasks to edge nodes. Additionally, edge computing can help address concerns related to data sovereignty, compliance, and regulatory requirements by processing data locally, closer to where it is generated, while still leveraging the benefits of centralized cloud infrastructure for storage, management, and collaboration.

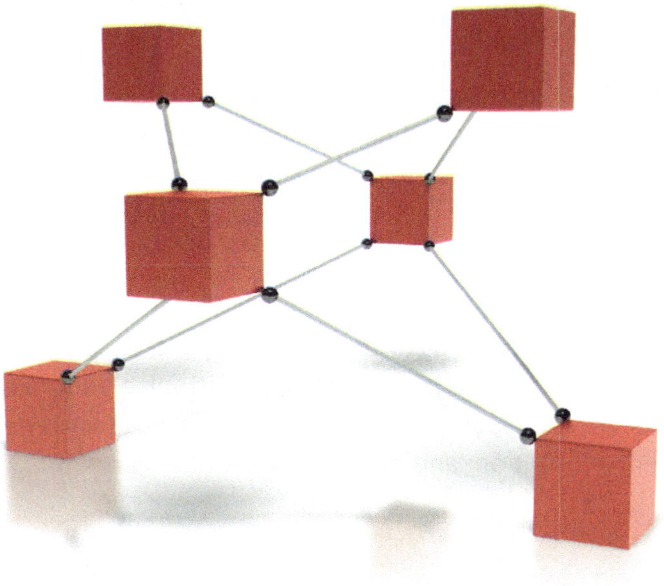

Blockchain

Blockchain computing is a decentralized, distributed ledger technology that records transactions across multiple computers in a way that makes them secure, transparent, and tamper resistant. Instead of relying on a central authority to validate and authenticate transactions, blockchain uses a network of computers (nodes) to verify and add transactions to a shared digital ledger. Each transaction, or "block," is linked to the previous one, forming a chain of blocks, hence the name blockchain.

Regarding its impact on human capital management (HCM) systems, blockchain technology has the potential to transform various aspects of HR processes and workforce management:

- **Credential Verification:** Blockchain can streamline the verification of employee credentials, such as degrees, certifications, and licenses, by providing a secure and immutable record of academic and professional achievements. This can simplify the hiring process, reduce the risk of credential fraud, and ensure the integrity and authenticity of employee qualifications.
- **Payroll and Benefits Management:** Blockchain-based payroll systems can automate and streamline payroll processing, ensuring accurate and timely payments to employees. Smart contracts can be used to automate payroll calculations, deductions, and payments based on predefined rules and criteria, reducing administrative errors and delays.
- **Talent Acquisition and Recruitment:** Blockchain-based platforms can facilitate decentralized talent marketplaces, where employers and job seekers can connect directly, without the need for intermediaries. This can create more efficient and

transparent recruitment processes, reduce recruiting costs, and enable organizations to access a broader pool of talent.

- **Employee Data Privacy and Security:** Blockchain technology can enhance employee data privacy and security by providing a decentralized and tamper-resistant way to store and manage sensitive HR data. Employees can have greater control over their personal information with cryptographic techniques ensuring data integrity and confidentiality.

Blockchain technology is becoming mainstream in business, and it's already being adopted in various industries. Its use is expected to continue growing and accelerating in the coming years. Overall, blockchain technology has the potential to revolutionize human capital management systems by providing secure, transparent, and efficient solutions for credential verification, payroll processing, talent acquisition, and data management.

Internet of Behaviors

The Internet of Behaviors (IoB) is a concept that involves using data collected from various sources, such as IoT devices, AIoT devices, social media platforms, and online interactions, to analyze and understand human behaviors. By leveraging advanced analytics and machine learning algorithms, organizations can gain insights into how individuals behave, make decisions, and interact with digital technologies. The impact of the IoB on human resources, workplace culture, and human capital management systems can be significant:

- **Employee Monitoring and Productivity:** IoB technologies enable organizations to monitor employee behaviors and activities, such as time spent on tasks, digital interactions, and communication patterns. While this can provide valuable insights into productivity levels and work habits, it also raises concerns about privacy, autonomy, and the potential for surveillance in the workplace.
- **Personalized Employee Experiences:** IoB allows organizations to personalize employee experiences based on individual behaviors, preferences, and needs. By analyzing data on employee behaviors, HCM systems can deliver tailored learning and development opportunities, recognition programs, and wellness initiatives that resonate with employees and enhance engagement and satisfaction.
- **Workforce Analytics and Decision-Making:** IoB provides HR professionals with data-driven insights into workforce trends, behaviors, and performance metrics. By analyzing patterns and correlations in employee data, HR systems can identify areas for

improvement, predict future trends, and make informed decisions about talent management, recruitment, and retention strategies.

- **Culture and Employee Well-Being:** IoB can impact workplace culture and employee well-being by influencing organizational norms, values, and behaviors. By fostering a culture of transparency, accountability, and respect for privacy, organizations can build trust and confidence among employees and mitigate concerns about intrusive monitoring and surveillance practices.
- **Ethical and Legal Considerations:** IoB raises ethical and legal considerations related to data privacy, consent, and transparency. Organizations must establish clear policies and guidelines for collecting, storing, and analyzing employee data, ensuring compliance with relevant regulations and protecting individuals' rights to privacy and autonomy.

Overall, while the Internet of Behaviors offers opportunities to improve workforce management and culture, it also poses challenges related to privacy and ethics. By balancing the benefits of IoB technologies with ethical considerations and respect for individual rights, organizations can harness the power of behavioral data to create positive and inclusive workplace environments that foster employee well-being, engagement, and success.

Robotic Process Automation

Robotic Process Automation (RPA) is a technology that uses software robots or "bots" to automate repetitive, rule-based tasks and processes typically performed by humans. This is the office version of robotics in manufacturing. These bots are programmed to mimic human actions and interactions with digital systems, such as logging into applications, entering data, copying information, and performing calculations. RPA enables organizations to streamline workflows, improve efficiency, and reduce human error by automating mundane and time-consuming tasks.

The impact of Robotic Process Automation on human resources, workplace performance, and human capital management systems can be significant:

- **Process Efficiency and Productivity:** RPA can enhance process efficiency and productivity by automating routine HR tasks, such as employee onboarding, payroll processing, benefits administration, and time tracking. By eliminating manual interventions and reducing processing times, RPA enables HR professionals to focus on more strategic initiatives and value-added activities that require human judgment and creativity.
- **Accuracy and Compliance:** RPA helps ensure accuracy and compliance in HR processes by minimizing errors and deviations from established rules and regulations. Bots can perform tasks with precision and consistency, reducing the risk of data entry errors, compliance violations, and audit findings. This improves data quality, integrity, and reliability in HR systems and processes.
- **Cost Savings and Resource Optimization:** RPA can generate cost savings and optimize resource allocation by reducing the need for manual labor and reallocating human resources to higher-value tasks. By automating repetitive tasks, organizations can lower

labor costs, improve operational efficiency, and achieve faster ROI on their investments in HR technology and systems.

- **Scalability and Flexibility:** RPA offers scalability and flexibility by adapting to changing business needs and demands. Bots can be quickly deployed, scaled up or down, and reconfigured to accommodate fluctuations in workload, seasonal peaks, or business expansions. This agility enables organizations to respond rapidly to evolving HR requirements and market dynamics.
- **Strategic Insights and Decision-Making:** RPA can generate valuable data and insights that inform strategic decision-making and workforce planning initiatives. By analyzing process metrics, performance indicators, and workflow patterns, organizations can identify opportunities for optimization, innovation, and continuous improvement in HR systems and practices.

Overall, Robotic Process Automation has the potential to transform human resources, workplace performance, and human capital management systems by improving efficiency, accuracy, compliance, and employee experience. By harnessing the power of automation, organizations can unlock new levels of productivity, agility, and value creation, driving business success and competitive advantage in the digital age.

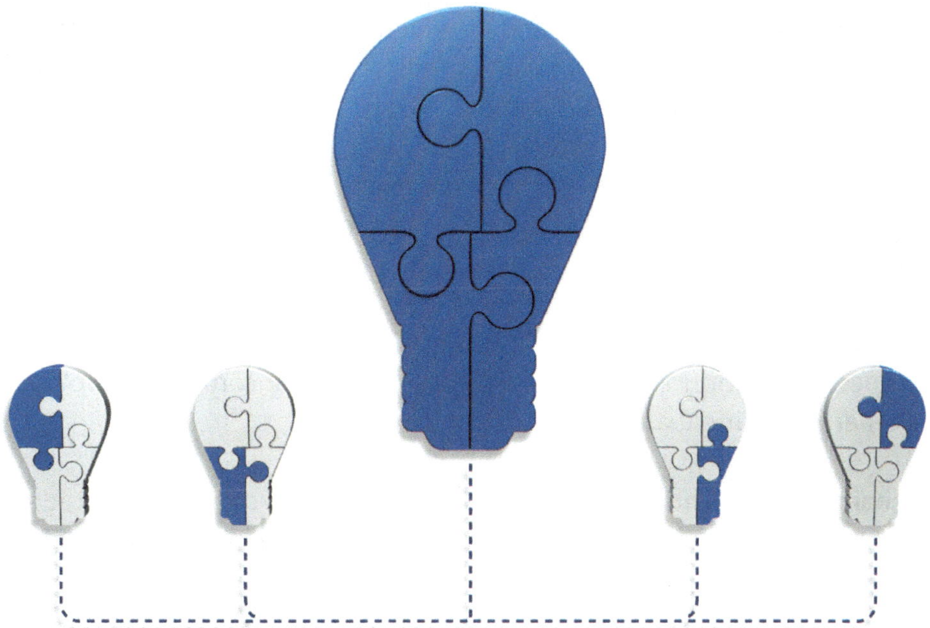

Industry Segment Consolidations

The HR systems space has seen significant company consolidations over the past few decades. Looking forward, additional consolidations in the HR tech industry could make sense to address evolving needs and deliver more comprehensive solutions. Here are some potential consolidation scenarios:

- **End-to-End HR Solutions:** We may see mergers and acquisitions between companies specializing in different HR functions, such as recruitment, talent management, payroll, and workforce analytics, to provide seamless end-to-end HR solutions. This would reduce the need for multiple standalone systems and improve data integration.

- **HCM and Learning Management:** Integration of Human Capital Management (HCM) systems with Learning Management Systems (LMS) can provide a holistic approach to talent development and management. Consolidations between HCM and LMS providers could create comprehensive platforms for talent development.

- **HCM and Workforce Management:** Merging HCM systems with Workforce Management (WFM) solutions can lead to more efficient scheduling, time tracking, and labor cost management, creating a comprehensive workforce management suite.

- **Recruitment and Employee Engagement:** Combining recruitment and employee engagement platforms can lead to a more cohesive talent acquisition and retention strategy. This consolidation can help organizations maintain a consistent candidate and employee experience.

- **HR Analytics and AI:** HR analytics and AI-driven solutions could be integrated to provide comprehensive data-driven insights and predictions. This consolidation could streamline decision-making and workforce planning.

- **AI and HR Tech Startups:** Larger HR tech companies might acquire or collaborate with startups specializing in AI-driven HR innovations to enhance their offerings with cutting-edge technology.

- **Employee Experience Platforms:** HR tech companies could merge with Employee Experience (EX) platforms to offer a unified solution that combines employee engagement, sentiment analysis, and feedback tools.

- **Blockchain and Credential Verification:** Integrating blockchain-based credential verification solutions with HR systems can reduce the risk of fraud and ensure the accuracy of employee records.

These consolidations can result in more comprehensive and efficient HR solutions that better meet the evolving needs of organizations. However, it's essential for organizations to carefully consider the compatibility, interoperability, and ethical implications of these consolidations to ensure successful integration and alignment with their HR strategies.

Summary

In this chapter on future trends in HCM, we discussed a multitude of current and potential trends. These have the potential to reshape the way organizations manage their workforces. From the integration of AI and automation to the ever-increasing focus on employee experience, the HCM landscape is evolving rapidly. These trends are influencing recruitment, training, performance management, and the overall employee journey. As HCM systems continue to evolve, they will need to adapt to changing data privacy regulations, global compliance requirements, and the ethical imperatives of creating inclusive, fair, and transparent work environments. HR professionals play a crucial role in harnessing these trends and navigating the challenges to foster an environment where employees can thrive and organizations can excel.

Discussion Questions

How can AI and automation improve the efficiency of HR processes, and what challenges might arise from their integration into HCM systems?

What are the key components of an effective employee experience, and how can HCM systems contribute to enhancing it?

In what ways do data analytics and people analytics benefit HR decision-making, and how can organizations leverage these tools within their HCM systems?

What challenges and opportunities do remote work and hybrid work models present for HCM systems and HR professionals, and how can they address them effectively?

How can HCM systems support the development of a diverse, equitable, and inclusive workplace, and what role should HR professionals play in promoting diversity and inclusion?

How can HCM systems improve learning and development opportunities for employees, and what role should they play in personalized training and upskilling?

How might blockchain technology impact the verification of employee credentials, and what are the potential benefits and challenges in implementing this technology in HCM systems?

In a rapidly changing work environment, how can HR professionals use HCM systems to adapt to future workforce planning and employee well-being needs, while ensuring compliance with evolving labor laws and regulations?

Chapter References

Ahlemann, F., Schütte, R., & Stieglitz, S. (Eds.). (2021). *Innovation Through Information Systems : Volume II: A Collection of Latest Research on Technology Issues* (1st ed. 2021.). Springer International Publishing. https://doi.org/10.1007/978-3-030-86797-3

Bavdaz, M. (Ed.). (2023). *Advances in business statistics, methods and data collection.* John Wiley and Sons, Inc.

ChatGPT. (2023). *HCM Future Trends.* OpenAI. Accessed November 5, 2023.

Dhavse, Rasika., Kumar, Vinay., & Monteleone, Salvatore. (Eds.). (2023). *Emerging Technology Trends in Electronics, Communication and Networking : Select Proceedings of the Fourth International Conference, ET2ECN 2021* (1st ed. 2023.). Springer Nature Singapore. https://doi.org/10.1007/978-981-19-6737-5

Landeta Echeberria, A. (Ed.). (2022). *Artificial Intelligence for Business: Innovation, Tools and Practices* (1st ed. 2022.). Springer International Publishing. https://doi.org/10.1007/978-3-030-88241-9

Liatsis, Panos., Hussain, Abir., Mostafa, S. A., & Al-Jumeily, Dhiya. (Eds.). (2022). *Emerging Technology Trends in Internet of Things and Computing : First International Conference, TIOTC 2021, Erbil, Iraq, June 6–8, 2021, Revised Selected Papers* (1st ed. 2022.). Springer International Publishing. https://doi.org/10.1007/978-3-030-97255-4

Loureiro, S. M. C., Guerreiro, J., & Tussyadiah, I. (2021). Artificial intelligence in business: State of the art and future research agenda. *Journal of Business Research, 129*, 911–926. https://doi.org/10.1016/j.jbusres.2020.11.001

Chapter 12
Future Proofing: A Guide to Continuous Learning in Technology

Table of Contents

Photo by Cristian Cativo from pexels.com

Chapter 12:
Future Proofing: A Guide to Continuous Learning in Technology

Introduction

In an era defined by rapid technological advancement and digital transformation, the ability to future-proof one's career through continuous learning has never been more critical. The landscape of technology is constantly evolving, with emerging trends reshaping industries and creating new opportunities for innovation. In this dynamic environment, individuals must cultivate a mindset of lifelong learning and adaptability to stay ahead of the curve, remain relevant in their fields, and thrive in the digital economy. This chapter serves as a comprehensive guide to continuous learning in technology, offering practical strategies, resources, and insights to empower individuals to navigate the ever-changing technology landscape, develop new skills, and future-proof their careers.

Mindset of Continuous Learning

Continuous learning is not just a practice, it's a mindset. It's a fundamental orientation towards growth and development that extends beyond formal education and training programs. At its core, the mindset of continuous learning embodies *curiosity* in life and work, characterized by a willingness to embrace new challenges, seek out opportunities for learning, and adapt to change. It's about recognizing that knowledge is dynamic and ever changing, and that the pursuit of learning is a lifelong journey rather than a destination.

The importance of the mindset of continuous learning cannot be overstated in today's rapidly changing world, particularly in the technology sector. With the pace of technological innovation accelerating exponentially, the skills and knowledge that are in demand today will become obsolete quickly. By cultivating a mindset of continuous learning, individuals can keep pace, remain relevant, and thrive in an increasingly competitive and dynamic job market. Moreover, continuous learning fosters adaptability, resilience, and agility.

Developing new behaviors to embrace the mindset of continuous learning requires a deliberate and proactive approach. It begins with a commitment to self-reflection and self-awareness. One needs to be able to recognize strengths, weaknesses, and areas for growth. From there, individuals can set learning goals that align with their personal and professional aspirations. It's also essential to cultivate habits of curiosity, exploration, and experimentation, seeking new experiences and perspectives from diverse domains.

Effective Learning Strategies with Technology

One of the most effective learning strategies for mastering business systems and technology is **hands-on practice** and application. This approach involves actively engaging with software applications, platforms, and tools in real-world scenarios to gain practical experience and proficiency. By immersing oneself in hands-on activities, individuals can develop a deeper understanding of how business systems and technology work in day-to-day operation. Whether it's navigating a new software application, configuring a database, or designing a workflow automation process, hands-on practice allows learners to apply theoretical knowledge in context. This reinforces concepts through repetition and builds confidence in their technical skills.

Project-based learning is another effective strategy for mastering business systems and technology, as it provides people with opportunities to tackle complex challenges, solve problems, and create tangible outcomes. This approach involves defining and executing projects that require the application of business systems and technology to achieve goals and objectives. Whether it's developing a custom software application, implementing an enterprise resource planning (ERP) system, or optimizing business processes, project-based learning encourages active participation, collaboration, and critical thinking. By working on real-world projects, employees can gain hands-on experience, develop practical skills, and demonstrate abilities.

Professional Groups and Associations often provide rich opportunities to explore the latest technologies in their associated fields. Many of the groups host regular conferences and expositions, where technology providers showcase the latest trends and capabilities. These tradeshows can contribute strongly to a person's ability to stay current within their profession.

Peer Learning and Collaboration

Peer learning and collaboration involves the exchange of knowledge, skills, and experiences between individuals within a group or community. Unlike traditional forms of learning that are instructor-led or self-directed, peer learning emphasizes mutual support, shared learning goals, and active participation among peers. This collaborative approach to learning fosters a sense of camaraderie, trust, and collective ownership of the learning process. As individuals collaborate, share insights, and learn from each other's perspectives. Peer learning can take various forms, including tutoring, study groups, collaborative projects, and professional groups/associations, each providing unique opportunities for growth.

Developing peer learning opportunities requires intentional effort on the individual's part to find, design, or facilitate an environment conducive to collaboration and mutual support. One way to foster peer learning is to establish formalized learning communities or study groups, where individuals with similar interests come together to exchange ideas, resources, and feedback. Collaborative projects and group assignments can provide opportunities for individuals to work together towards common goals and solve problems collectively. Ultimately, by creating opportunities for peer learning and collaboration, individuals are empowered to own their learning journey, build meaningful connections with others, and cultivate their own mindset of continuous learning.

Cross-Disciplinary Studies

Cross-disciplinary studies are incredibly important for keeping up with current technology and anticipating future trends. Technology is becoming increasingly interconnected and complex, often transcending traditional disciplinary boundaries. It is likely that the advent of AI will accelerate the blending of technologies across disciplines. As such, a multidisciplinary approach allows individuals to gain insights from diverse fields and perspectives, enabling them to better understand the broader implications of technological advancements and anticipate emerging trends.

Reading and studying about technologies in varied industries is of paramount importance in today's interconnected world. Technological advancements have far-reaching implications across diverse sectors. Encouraging individuals to read broadly and outside their comfort zone not only expands their knowledge base but also fosters a deeper understanding of the broader technological landscape and its potential impact on society. By exploring insights from different industries, ranging from healthcare and finance to agriculture and manufacturing, individuals can gain valuable perspectives, identify common patterns, and uncover innovative ideas that may not be immediately apparent within their own field. Moreover, exposure to diverse technologies and industries encourages interdisciplinary thinking, creativity, and problem-solving skills. This enables individuals to draw connections, bridge gaps, and drive innovation at the intersection of multiple disciplines. Ultimately, reading broadly empowers individuals to stay informed, adaptable, and prepared to navigate the complex challenges and opportunities presented by the ever-evolving world of technology.

Below are a couple examples of new technologies that were developed from cross-disciplinary approaches:

Wearable Health Monitoring Devices

Wearable health monitoring devices, such as fitness trackers, smartwatches, and biosensors, are prime examples of innovative developments that integrate insights from various disciplines, including electronics, materials science, biomedical engineering, and data analytics. These devices combine miniature sensors, wireless connectivity, and data processing capabilities to monitor vital signs, track physical activity, and provide real-time feedback on health and wellness metrics. By integrating biometric data with machine learning algorithms, wearable health monitoring devices can analyze patterns, detect anomalies, and provide personalized insights and recommendations for improving health outcomes. This convergence of technology from different disciplines has led to the development of wearable solutions that empower individuals to take control of their health and well-being, revolutionizing preventive healthcare and personalized medicine.

Autonomous Vehicles

Still developing, autonomous vehicles represent another groundbreaking technological development that results from the merging of technology from multiple disciplines. This includes robotics, artificial intelligence, computer vision, and automotive engineering. These vehicles leverage a complex array of sensors, cameras, Light Detection and Ranging (LiDAR,) radar, and Global Positioning System (GPS.) These are coupled with advanced algorithms to perceive the environment, interpret sensory data, and make real-time driving decisions without human intervention. By integrating insights from robotics and AI, autonomous vehicles can navigate complex traffic scenarios, predict, and respond to dynamic road conditions, and optimize driving routes for safety and efficiency. This interdisciplinary approach to automotive technology has the potential to transform transportation systems, improve road safety, reduce traffic congestion, and enhance mobility for individuals worldwide.

Summary

Futureproofing one's career through continuous learning in technology is essential for success in today's business world. By embracing a mindset of lifelong learning, individuals can adapt to changing technologies, anticipate emerging trends, and remain agile in the face of uncertainty. This chapter has provided a guide to continuous learning, exploring various strategies, resources, and approaches for staying informed, and acquiring new skills. Whether through structured learning paths, hands-on projects, peer collaboration, or professional development opportunities, individuals have the power to chart their learning journey, unlock their full potential, and thrive in the digital age. By committing to continuous learning, individuals can future-proof their careers, seize new opportunities, and make meaningful contributions to their profession.

Discussion Questions

What are some of the key challenges around technology that individuals face while trying to stay relevant and future-proofing their careers?

How do you think the mindset of continuous learning can impact personal and professional growth in the area of technology?

What role do you believe formal education (e.g. degrees or certifications) plays in future-proofing one's career around technology? How does it complement informal learning and self-directed study?

In what ways can organizations support and promote a culture of continuous learning among their employees, particularly in the context of technology-driven changes?

How might you balance the need for continuous learning with other demands and responsibilities in your personal and professional life?

What are some emerging trends or technologies that you believe will significantly impact the future of work? How are you preparing to adapt and stay ahead of these trends?

How can individuals leverage peer learning and collaboration to enhance their continuous learning around technology?

Chapter References

Ball, L. J., Christensen, B. T., & Halskov, K. (Eds.). (2017). *Analysing design thinking : studies of cross-cultural co-creation.* CRC Press/Balkema. https://doi.org/10.1201/9781315208169

ChatGPT. (2023). *HCM Future Trends.* OpenAI. Accessed November 5, 2023.

Elstein, K., & Driver, K. (2007). Fostering a Continuous-Learning Mindset in a Federal Research Organization. *Organization Development Journal, 25*(2), P93-.

Nanda, J.D. (2024). Agency life has taught me to embrace a mindset of continuous learning. Exchange4media.

Wheeler, L. B., Thompson, K. V., Marbach-Ad, G., Sheehan, P., Bortiatynski, J. L., & Ghent, C. (2023). Factors Predicting the Extent to which STEM Students Value Cross-Disciplinary Skills: A Study across Four Institutions. *CBE Life Sciences Education, 22*(2), ar20–ar20. https://doi.org/10.1187/cbe.22-06-0101

Consolidated References

ADP (2022). *A Guide to Early-Stage Business Success.* Retrieved on November 5, 2023 from: https://www.adp.com/resources/articles-and-insights/articles/e/early-stage-business-success-guide.aspx

Al Hayek, W. Y., & Abu Odeh, R. A. (2020). Cloud ERP VS On-Premise ERP. *International Journal of Applied Science and Technology, 10(4).*

Albrecht, D.J. (2021). *Strategic Human Resources: The business context. (Whitepaper).* Alonos Corporation.

Albrecht, D.J., & Albrecht, M.G. (2020). *DECIDE to Thrive: Improving business performance through decision effectiveness.* Dallas, TX: Alonos Corporation.

Almase, G. G. C. (2023). *Managing Change in Human Capital Management Systems Implementations in Multinational Companies: Modified e-Delphi Study.* ProQuest Dissertations Publishing.

Ahlemann, F., Schütte, R., & Stieglitz, S. (Eds.). (2021). *Innovation Through Information Systems : Volume II: A Collection of Latest Research on Technology Issues* (1st ed. 2021.). Springer International Publishing. https://doi.org/10.1007/978-3-030-86797-3

Athanur, A., Ingram, M., & Wellens, M. A. (2022). *Innovative SAP SuccessFactors Recruiting : A Guide to Creating Custom Integration and Automation* (1st ed. 2022.). Apress. https://doi.org/10.1007/978-1-4842-7425-5

Aquisdata, Inc. (2019). SAP (NYSE: SAP) - SAP SuccessFactors Solutions Positioned as a Leader in Gartner Cloud HCM Suites for Midsize and Large Enterprises Magic Quadrant. Germany Software and IT.

Bain News Service, P. (ca. 1915) *First Typewriter.*, ca. 1915. [Between and Ca. 1920] [Photograph] Retrieved from the Library of Congress, https://www.loc.gov/item/2014704116/.

Ball, L. J., Christensen, B. T., & Halskov, K. (Eds.). (2017). *Analysing design thinking : studies of cross-cultural co-creation.* CRC Press/Balkema. https://doi.org/10.1201/9781315208169

BambooHR (2023). *How Do BambooHR & ADP Compare?* Retrieved on November 5, 2023 from: https://www.bamboohr.com/why-bamboohr/compare/adp/

Bard, Google AI. (2023). A History of Business Systems. Bard, Google AI. Accessed October 22, 2023.

Bard, Google AI. (2023). History of HR Systems and Technology. Bard, Google AI. Accessed October 25, 2023.

Bavdaz, M. (Ed.). (2023). *Advances in business statistics, methods and data collection.* John Wiley and Sons, Inc.

Consolidated References

Beech, S. (2023). *Ancient construction plans from 9,000 years ago unearthed: 'Oldest in human history'* (November 4, 2023). StudyFinds. Retrieved December 28, 2023 from https://studyfinds.org/ancient-construction-plans/

Bersin, J., Enderes, K., & Ioannidou, S. (2022). *Best Practices for HCM Excellence: SAP SuccessFactors Edition.* The joshbersin company.

Bhuiyan, F., Chowdhury, M. M., & Ferdous, F. (2014). *Historical evolution of human resource information system (HRIS): An interface between HR and computer technology.* Human Resource Management Research, 4(4), 75-80.

Cattermole, G. (2019). Developing the employee lifecycle to keep top talent. *Strategic HR Review, 18*(6), 258–262. https://doi.org/10.1108/SHR-05-2019-0042

Ceridian (2023). The 2023 *Gartner Magic Quadrant for Cloud HCM Suites for 1,000+ Employee Enterprises.* Retrieved on November 5, 2023 from: https://www.ceridian.com/resources/gartner-magic-quadrant-hcm-2023

ChatGPT. (2023). *Finding Business Systems Information.* OpenAI. Accessed November 2, 2023.

ChatGPT. (2023). *HCM Future Trends.* OpenAI. Accessed November 5, 2023.

ChatGPT. (2023). *HCM for Large Businesses.* OpenAI. Accessed November 4-6, 2023.

ChatGPT. (2023). *HCM for SMBs.* OpenAI. Accessed November 4-6, 2023.

ChatGPT. (2023). *HCM Modules.* OpenAI. Accessed November 3, 2023.

ChatGPT. (2023). *HCM System Business Uses.* OpenAI. Accessed November 2, 2023.

ChatGPT. (2023). *HCM System Implementation.* OpenAI. Accessed November 5, 2023.

ChatGPT. (2023). *HCM System Roles.* OpenAI. Accessed November 3, 2023.

ChatGPT. (2023). History of Business Systems. OpenAI. Accessed October 22, 2023.

Cornerstone. (2023). *The Force Behind Limitless Potential: A talent experience platform designed to unlock the limitless potential of your workforce and streamline how you do it.* Retrieved November 5, 2023 from: https://www.cornerstoneondemand.com/why-cornerstone/

Curumsing, F.N., Abdelrazek, M., Vasa, R., Mouzakis, K., & Grundy, J. (2019). Understanding the impact of emotions on software: A case study in requirements gathering and evaluation. *The Journal of Systems and Software, 147*, 215–229. https://doi.org/10.1016/j.jss.2018.06.077

Dhavse, Rasika., Kumar, Vinay., & Monteleone, Salvatore. (Eds.). (2023). *Emerging Technology Trends in Electronics, Communication and Networking : Select Proceedings of the Fourth International Conference, ET2ECN 2021* (1st ed. 2023.). Springer Nature Singapore. https://doi.org/10.1007/978-981-19-6737-5

Duan, J., Faker, P., Fesak, A., & Stuart, T. (2013). Benefits and drawbacks of cloud-based versus traditional ERP systems. *Proceedings of the 2012-13 course on Advanced Resource Planning.*

Consolidated References

Elbardan, H., & Kholeif, A. O. (2017). *Enterprise Resource Planning, Corporate Governance and Internal Auditing : An Institutional Perspective.* Springer International Publishing. https://doi.org/10.1007/978-3-319-54990-3

Elstein, K., & Driver, K. (2007). Fostering a Continuous-Learning Mindset in a Federal Research Organization. *Organization Development Journal, 25*(2), P93-.

Engelsrud. (n.d.). *Managing PeopleSoft on the Oracle Cloud: Best Practices with PeopleSoft Cloud Manager.* Apress. https://doi.org/10.1007/978-1-4842-4546-0

Ferreira, D. (2013.). Evolution of Enterprise Systems. In Enterprise Systems Integration (pp. 3–14). Springer Berlin Heidelberg. https://doi.org/10.1007/978-3-642-40796-3_1

Fowinkel. (2014). *Human resource management systems in new business creation : an exploratory study.* Springer Gabler. https://doi.org/10.1007/978-3-658-05982-8

Ganesh, K. (2014). *Enterprise resource planning : fundamentals of design and implementation.* Springer. https://doi.org/10.1007/978-3-319-05927-3

Gartner (2024). *Small And Midsize Business (SMB).* Gartner Glossary. Retrieved from: https://gartner.com/en/information-technology/glossary/

Hartono, S., Tjahyadi, Td., & Cassandra, C. (2021). Analysis of Employee and Manager Self Service Module on SAP Portal (A Case Study Approach). 2021 *International Conference on Information Management and Technology (ICIMTech), 1*, 93–98. https://doi.org/10.1109/ICIMTech53080.2021.9535090

Hirschheim, R., & Heinz K. (2012) "A Glorious and Not-So-Short History of the Information Systems Field," Journal of the Association for Information Systems, 13(4), DOI: 10.17705/1jais.00294 Available at: https://aisel.aisnet.org/jais/vol13/iss4/5

Jacobs, R., & Weston, F. C. (2007). Enterprise resource planning (ERP)—A brief history. Journal of Operations Management, 25(2), 357–363. https://doi.org/10.1016/j.jom.2006.11.005

Jatav, P. K., Nagar, N., Singh, A., & Sharma, Y. Comparative study of various tools of On-Premises ERP and Cloud based ERP.

Jordan, A. (2019). PeopleSoft to be replaced by Workday System. In *University Wire*. Uloop, Inc.

Just, V. (2020). *Sustainable Business Processes in Global Companies: Current Perspectives and Future Trends in Regard to Efficiency and Risk Management* (1st ed. 2020.). Springer Fachmedien Wiesbaden. https://doi.org/10.1007/978-3-658-28196-0

Karuppan, C.M., & Karuppan, M. (2008). Resilience of super users' mental models of enterprise-wide systems. *European Journal of Information Systems, 17*(1), 29–46. https://doi.org/10.1057/palgrave.ejis.3000728

Kazakov, O.D., & Azarenko, N.Y. (2019). The Model of Human Capital Management in Decision Support Systems. *Vestnik Voronežskogo gosudarstvennogo universiteta inženernyh tehnologij, 81*(3), 290–298. https://doi.org/10.20914/2310-1202-2019-3-290-298

Kharroubi, D. (2021). Global Workforce Diversity Management: Challenges across the world. *Economic and Managerial Spectrum, 15*(1), 28–37. https://doi.org/10.26552/ems.2021.1.28-37

Konradt, U., Christophersen, T., & Schaeffer-Kuelz, U. (2006). Predicting user satisfaction, strain and system usage of employee self-services. *International Journal of Human-Computer Studies, 64*(11), 1141–1153. https://doi.org/10.1016/j.ijhcs.2006.07.001

Landeta Echeberria, A. (Ed.). (2022). *Artificial Intelligence for Business: Innovation, Tools and Practices* (1st ed. 2022.). Springer International Publishing. https://doi.org/10.1007/978-3-030-88241-9

Lane, S., O'Raghallaigh, P., & Sammon, D. (2016). Requirements gathering: the journey. *Journal of Decision Systems, 25*(sup1), 302–312. https://doi.org/10.1080/12460125.2016.1187390

Liatsis, Panos., Hussain, Abir., Mostafa, S. A., & Al-Jumeily, Dhiya. (Eds.). (2022). *Emerging Technology Trends in Internet of Things and Computing : First International Conference, TIOTC 2021, Erbil, Iraq, June 6–8, 2021, Revised Selected Papers* (1st ed. 2022.). Springer International Publishing. https://doi.org/10.1007/978-3-030-97255-4

Lindenfors, P., Wartel, A., & Lind, J. (2021). *'Dunbar's Number" deconstructed.* Royal Society Publishing. https://doi.org/10.1098/rsbl.2021.0158

Lorincz, P. (2007). Evolution of Enterprise Systems. 2007 International Symposium on Logistics and Industrial Informatics, 75–80. https://doi.org/10.1109/LINDI.2007.4343516

Loureiro, S. M. C., Guerreiro, J., & Tussyadiah, I. (2021). Artificial intelligence in business: State of the art and future research agenda. *Journal of Business Research, 129,* 911–926. https://doi.org/10.1016/j.jbusres.2020.11.001

Main, K. (2024). *Small Business Statistics of 2024 (January 31, 2024.)* Forbes Advisor. Retrieved from https://forbes.com/advisor/business/small-business-statistics/

Mahdavian, M., & Mostajeran, F. (2013). Studying key users' skills of ERP system through a comprehensive skill measurement model. *International Journal of Advanced Manufacturing Technology, 69*(9-12), 1981–1999. https://doi.org/10.1007/s00170-013-5144-1

Marler, J.H., Fisher, S.L., & Weiling, KE. (2009). Employee Self-Service Technology Acceptance: A comparison of pre-implementation and post-implementation relationships. *Personnel Psychology, 62*(2), 327–358. https://doi.org/10.1111/j.1744-6570.2009.01140.x

Mayer, J.H., & Quick, R. (Editors) (2015). *Self-Service Management Support Systems: Findings from a New-Generation Manager Perspective. In Business Intelligence for New-Generation Managers* (pp. 113–136). Springer International Publishing AG. https://doi.org/10.1007/978-3-319-15696-5_9

Milani. (2019). *Digital Business Analysis.* Springer International Publishing. https://doi.org/10.1007/978-3-030-05719-0

Miller, T. (2017). *HR analytics and innovations in workforce planning* (First edition.). Business Expert Press.

Mondal, S.R., Di Virgilio, F., & Das, S. (2021). *HR Analytics and Digital HR Practices: Digitalization Post COVID-19.* Palgrave Macmillan. https://doi.org/10.1007/978-981-16-7099-2

Nanda, J.D. (2024). Agency life has taught me to embrace a mindset of continuous learning. Exchange4media.

Nestell, J.G., & Olson, D. L. (2018). Successful ERP systems : a guide for businesses and executives. Business Expert Press.

NewsRX, LLC (2022). Oracle Named a Leader in the 2022 Gartner® Magic Quadrant[TM] for Cloud HCM Suites for 1,000+ Employee Enterprises. Information Technology Weekly.

Office of Advocacy (2023). *Frequently Asked Questions About Small Business 2023 (March 7, 2023).* U.S. Small Business Administration, Office of Advocacy. Retrieved from: https://advocacy.sba.gov/

Onore, J. (2022). *Asking Effective Questions During Requirements Elicitation.* (Linked-In Learning Course.) linkedin.com.

OpenAI. (2024, April 27). ChatGPT conversation on *ESG, Diversity, Inclusion, and Data Privacy in Human Capital Management.* Accessed April 27, 2024.

Porancea-Răulea, A.S., & Cofaru, N.F. (2021). *The need and implications of the human capital management system.* MATEC Web of Conferences, 343, 5004–. https://doi.org/10.1051/matecconf/202134305004

Prencipe. A., Davies, A., & Hobday, M. (2003). The business of systems integration. Oxford University Press.

Pugh, K. (2011). *Lean-agile acceptance test driven development : better software through collaboration* (1st edition). Addison Wesley Professional.

Rashvanlouei, K.Y., Thome, R., & Yazdani, K. (2015). *Functional and technological evolution of enterprise systems: An overview.* 2015 IEEE International Conference on Industrial Engineering and Engineering Management (IEEM), Singapore, 2015, pp. 67-72, doi: 10.1109/IEEM.2015.7385610.

Rasmussen, T., & Ulrich, D. (2015). Learning from practice: how HR analytics avoids being a management fad. *Organizational Dynamics, 44*(3), 236–242. https://doi.org/10.1016/j.orgdyn.2015.05.008

Ratten, V. (2020). Entrepreneurial ecosystems: Future research trends. *Thunderbird International Business Review, 62(*5), 623–628. https://doi.org/10.1002/tie.22163

Rawat, C. (2023). Role of ERP Modernization in Digital Transformation: PeopleSoft Insight. *arXiv.org.* https://doi.org/10.48550/arxiv.2303.03224

Read, Colin. (2023). *Understanding Sustainability Principles and ESG Policies : A Multidisciplinary Approach to Public and Corporate Responses to Climate Change* (1st ed. 2023.). Springer International Publishing. https://doi.org/10.1007/978-3-031-34483-1

Reitsma, E., & Hilletofth, P. (2018). Critical success factors for ERP system implementation: a user perspective. *European Business Review, 30*(3), 285–310. https://doi.org/10.1108/EBR-04-2017-0075

Samara, T. (2015). *ERP and information systems : integration or disintegration* (1st edition). ISTE.

Sharma, C., Sakshi, Sharma, S., & Kondal, N. (2023). Role and impact of human resource information system (HRIS) on organizational activities. *AIP Conference Proceedings, 2558(*1). https://doi.org/10.1063/5.0123335

Shin, J., Moon, J. J., & Kang, J. (2023). Where does ESG pay? The role of national culture in moderating the relationship between ESG performance and financial performance. *International Business Review, 32*(3), 102071. https://doi.org/10.1016/j.ibusrev.2022.102071

Strause, S. (2010). Selecting and partnering with a vendor for a qualified software product. *Journal of Validation Technology, 16*(3), 43–46.

Sun, W., Zhang, X., Guo, C. J., Sun, P., & Su, H. (2008, September). Software as a service: Configuration and customization perspectives. In 2008 *ieee congress on services part ii (services-2 2008)* (pp. 18-25). IEEE.

Traynor, Wellens, M. A., & Krishnamoorthy, V. (2021). *An Introduction to SAP SuccessFactors Talent Modules. In SAP SuccessFactors Talent: Volume 1* (pp. 1–6). Apress L. P. https://doi.org/10.1007/978-1-4842-6600-7_1

Traynor, Wellens, M. A., & Krishnamoorthy, V. (2021). *SAP SuccessFactors Talent: Volume 1: A Complete Guide to Configuration, Administration, and Best Practices: Performance and Goals* (Vol. 1). Apress. https://doi.org/10.1007/978-1-4842-6600-7

United States Office Of War Information, Hollem, H. R., photographer. (1942) *Conversion. Floor waxer plant. These twenty-year-old lathes are producing equipment for Uncle Sam's armed forces twenty-two hours a day. Alive to the possibilities of converting old equipment to defense usage, the owner of this small Eastern factory bought and remodelled old equipment which is proving its mettle in . Note overhead power-driven machinery. Floorola Products Inc., York, Pennsylvania.* Pennsylvania United States York County York, 1942. Feb. [Photograph] Retrieved from the Library of Congress, https://www.loc.gov/item/2017690336/.

Valcik, N.A., Sabharwal, M., & Benavides, T. J. (2021). *The History and Evolution of HRIS. In Human Resources Information Systems* (pp. 19–32). Springer International Publishing AG. https://doi.org/10.1007/978-3-030-75111-1_2

Valcik, N.A., Sabharwal, M., & Benavides, T. J. (2021). *Human Resources Information Systems : A Guide for Public Administrators* (1st ed. 2021.). Springer International Publishing. https://doi.org/10.1007/978-3-030-75111-1

Vladimir, Yulia, Tatyana, Aleksandra, & Veronika. (2017). *Formation of Human Resource Management System in Organizations. European Research Studies, XX*(Issue 3A), 408–421. https://doi.org/10.35808/ersj/712

Walterbusch, M., Martens, B., & Teuteberg, F. (2013). Evaluating cloud computing services from a total cost of ownership perspective. *Management Research Review, 36*(6), 613–638. https://doi.org/10.1108/01409171311325769

Weske, M. (2012.). Evolution of Enterprise Systems Architectures. In Business Process Management (pp. 25–69). Springer Berlin Heidelberg. https://doi.org/10.1007/978-3-642-28616-2_2

Wheeler, L. B., Thompson, K. V., Marbach-Ad, G., Sheehan, P., Bortiatynski, J. L., & Ghent, C. (2023). Factors Predicting the Extent to which STEM Students Value Cross-Disciplinary Skills: A Study across Four Institutions. *CBE Life Sciences Education, 22*(2), ar20–ar20. https://doi.org/10.1187/cbe.22-06-0101

Workday. (2023). *Why We're Different.* Retrieved on November 4, 2023 from: https://www.workday.com/en-us/why-workday/why-different.html

Wu, C., & Rajkumar, B. (2015). Cloud data centers and cost modeling : A complete guide to planning, designing and building a cloud data center (Green, Ed.; 1st edition). Morgan Kaufmann.

Zhang, L. L., Chen, X., Falkner, A. A., & Chu, C. (2014, September). Open Configuration: a New Approach to Product Customization. *In Configuration Workshop* (pp. 75-79).

Glossary of Terms

Agile Methodology: A software development approach that emphasizes iterative development, collaboration, and flexibility in response to changing requirements.

Application Programming Interface (API): A set of protocols, tools, and definitions that allow different software applications to communicate and interact with each other.

API Economy: The ecosystem of APIs and developers that drive the creation of value-added services, products, and experiences by enabling integration and innovation.

Applicant Tracking System (ATS): Software that streamlines recruitment processes by managing job postings, applications, and candidate data.

Application: A program or software designed to perform specific tasks on a computer or mobile device.

Artificial Intelligence of Things (AIoT): The integration of AI algorithms and techniques with IoT devices to enhance their capabilities.

Artificial Intelligence: The simulation of human intelligence processes by machines, particularly computer systems.

Augmented Reality (AR): A technology that overlays digital information or imagery onto the real world, enhancing the user's perception and interaction with their environment.

Big Data: Extremely large and complex datasets that traditional data processing applications are inadequate to handle, often requiring specialized tools and techniques for analysis.

Blockchain: A decentralized digital ledger technology that records transactions across multiple computers in a way that is transparent, secure, and tamper resistant.

Business Intelligence (BI): Technologies, applications, and practices for collecting, analyzing, and presenting business information to support decision-making and strategic planning.

Business Systems: Infrastructure and processes that facilitate business operations, including management, information flow, resource utilization, and decision-making.

Chatbot: A computer program designed to simulate conversation with human users, typically over the internet or within an application.

Client-Server: A network architecture where tasks or requests are distributed between clients and servers, enabling resource sharing and centralized data management.

Closed Architecture: A computing system or software environment where the source code is proprietary and not openly available for modification or redistribution.

Cloud Computing: The delivery of computing services, including servers, storage, databases, networking, software, and analytics, over the internet (the cloud) often on a pay-per-use basis.

Cloud-Based: Software or services that are hosted and accessed over the internet instead of on local servers or personal computers.

Co-Employment: A relationship where two or more entities share responsibility and liability for the same employee.

Compliance: Adherence to laws, regulations, standards, and guidelines relevant to an organization's industry, operations, and geographic locations.

Configuration: The arrangement of settings for software, hardware, or systems to meet specific requirements or preferences.

Continuous Learning: A process of ongoing education or skill development to adapt to changing circumstances or advancements in knowledge.

Corporate Social Responsibility (CSR): A business practice that involves initiatives to assess and take responsibility for a company's impact on the environment and social well-being.

Customer Relationship Management (CRM): Strategies, practices, and technologies for managing and analyzing customer interactions and data throughout the customer lifecycle.

Customization: Tailoring through redesign or redevelopment of products, services, software, or systems to meet the specific needs or preferences of individual users or clients.

Cybersecurity: Measures and practices implemented to protect computer systems, networks, and data from unauthorized access, cyber attacks, and data breaches.

Data Center: A facility used to house computer systems and associated components, such as servers, storage systems, and networking equipment.

Data Governance: The framework of policies, processes, and controls for managing and ensuring the availability, integrity, and security of data assets.

Data Migration: The process of transferring data from one system, format, or location to another, typically during system upgrades or platform changes.

Data Privacy: The protection of sensitive or personal information from unauthorized access, use, or disclosure.

Data Security: Measures and practices implemented to protect digital data from unauthorized access, corruption, or theft.

Database: A structured collection of data organized for efficient retrieval, storage, and manipulation, typically stored in electronic format.

Descriptive Analytics: Analysis of past data to understand historical patterns, trends, and relationships.

DevOps: A set of practices that combines software development (Dev) and IT operations (Ops) to shorten the development lifecycle and improve deployment frequency and reliability.

Diagnostic Analytics: Analysis of data to identify the root causes of past events or behaviors.

Digital Marketing: Marketing strategies and techniques that leverage digital channels, such as websites, social media, email, and search engines, to reach and engage with customers.

Digital Transformation: The process of integrating digital technologies into all aspects of business operations to fundamentally change how organizations operate and deliver value to customers.

Disk Storage Device: A hardware device used to store digital data, typically in the form of magnetic or optical storage media.

Document Management: The process of organizing, storing, and managing documents in a digital environment to facilitate access, retrieval, and collaboration.

Dumb Terminal: A computer terminal or device that relies on a central server or mainframe for processing and storage, with minimal local processing capability.

E-commerce: The buying and selling of goods or services over the internet, encompassing online retail, electronic payments, and digital marketing.

Edge Computing: A distributed computing paradigm that brings computation and data storage closer to the location where it is needed to improve response times and save bandwidth.

Electronic Waste (e-Waste): Discarded electronic devices and equipment that are no longer functional or useful, posing environmental and health risks if not properly disposed of.

Employee Self Service (ESS): A system or portal that allows employees to access and manage their own employment-related information, such as benefits, time-off requests, and personal details.

Enterprise Resource Planning (ERP): Integrated software systems that facilitate business process management and automate back-office functions related to technology, services, and human resources.

Environmental, Social, and Governance (ESG): Criteria used by investors to evaluate a company's sustainability and ethical impact.

Financial Capital: Resources in the form of money or assets that a company can use to generate income or sustain operations.

Global Workforce Management: Strategies and technologies for managing a geographically dispersed workforce.

Hard Disk Drive: A storage device that uses magnetic storage to store and retrieve digital data on spinning disks.

Hardware: Physical components of a computer system, including devices such as processors, memory modules, and input/output peripherals.

Hosting: Providing and maintaining servers or resources for storing and serving digital content or applications over the internet.

Human Capital Lead: A person or role responsible for managing and optimizing an organization's human resources software to achieve strategic goals.

Human Capital Management (HCM): Strategies, processes, and technologies for effectively managing an organization's workforce and culture.

Human Capital Management Systems (HCMS): Software platforms designed to streamline HR processes, including recruitment, payroll, performance management, and training.

Human Capital: The collective skills, knowledge, and abilities possessed by employees that contribute to the productivity and value of an organization.

Human Resource Information Systems (HRIS): Software systems that automate the management of HR processes and employee data.

Human Resource Management Systems (HRMS): Integrated software solutions for managing HR processes, including recruitment, payroll, benefits administration, and employee development.

Hybrid Work: A work arrangement that combines remote and in-person work, allowing employees to work from home or in the office as needed.

Internet of Behaviors (IoB): The use of data from various sources, including IoT devices and online interactions, to influence or modify behavior.

Internet of Things (IoT): The network of interconnected devices embedded with sensors, software, and other technologies that enable them to collect and exchange data.

Knowledge Management: The process of capturing, organizing, storing, and sharing knowledge and information within an organization to enhance learning, decision-making, and innovation.

Learning Content Management System (LCMS): Software platforms for creating, managing, and delivering digital learning content, such as courses, modules, and assessments.

Learning Management System (LMS): Software platforms for administering, delivering, and tracking educational courses and training programs.

Machine Learning: A subset of artificial intelligence that enables computer systems to learn from data and improve their performance without being explicitly programmed.

Mainframe: A large, powerful computer system typically used by large organizations for critical applications requiring high reliability, scalability, and security.

Manager Self Service (MSS): Systems or portals that enable managers to access and manage employee-related information, such as performance reviews, scheduling, and approvals.

Microservices: Architectural approach to software development that structures an application as a collection of loosely coupled, independently deployable services.

Network Security: Measures and protocols implemented to protect computer networks from unauthorized access, misuse, or disruption.

On Premise: Software or systems installed and operated on the premises of the organization, rather than hosted remotely or in the cloud.

Open Architecture: A computing environment or system that allows for interoperability and customization through open standards and interfaces.

Open Source: Software or technology with source code that is freely available for modification, redistribution, and collaboration within a community of developers.

Operating System: Software that manages hardware resources and provides services for computer programs, enabling them to execute tasks and interact with users.

Packaged Business System: Pre-built software solutions designed to address specific business needs or processes, typically customizable to some extent.

Pay Grades: A system for categorizing and defining salary levels within an organization based on factors such as job responsibilities, skills, and experience.

Performance Management: Processes and systems for setting goals, evaluating performance, providing feedback, and improving employee effectiveness.

Performance Monitoring: Tracking and assessing the performance of systems, processes, or individuals to ensure they meet predetermined standards or objectives.

Personal Computer: A small, single-user computer typically used for general computing tasks such as word processing, web browsing, and email.

Personal Computing: The use of personal computers by individuals for various tasks and activities.

Physical Capital: Tangible assets such as buildings, equipment, and infrastructure that contribute to the production of goods and services.

Predictive Analytics: Analysis of data to forecast future trends, behaviors, or outcomes using statistical algorithms and machine learning techniques.

Prescriptive Analytics: Analysis of data to recommend actions or decisions based on predicted outcomes and optimization algorithms.

Professional Employment Outsourcer (PEO): A company that provides HR outsourcing services, including payroll, benefits administration, and compliance management.

Quantum Computing: A computing paradigm that uses quantum-mechanical phenomena, such as superposition and entanglement, to perform operations on data.

Remote Work: Work performed outside of a traditional office environment, typically from home or another location away from the employer's premises.

Request For Information (RFI): A formal request for details or clarification on products, services, or projects issued by a buyer to potential suppliers or vendors.

Request For Proposal (RFP): A formal solicitation document used by organizations to request bids from potential vendors or suppliers for products or services.

Requirements Gathering: The process of identifying, documenting, and prioritizing the needs and expectations of stakeholders for a software or system project.

Risk Management: The process of identifying, assessing, and mitigating risks to minimize their impact on business operations and objectives.

Robotic Process Automation (RPA): The use of software robots or "bots" to automate repetitive and rule-based tasks traditionally performed by humans.

Scalability: The ability of a system, network, or process to handle increasing amounts of work or users without significantly impacting performance or functionality.

Small to Medium Sized Businesses (SMB): Businesses that fall within a certain size range, typically defined by factors such as revenue, number of employees, or market share.

Software As A Service (SAAS): A software delivery model where applications are hosted by a third-party provider and accessed over the internet on a subscription basis.

Software: Programs or instructions that control the operation of computer hardware and enable users to perform specific tasks or functions.

Solid State Drive: A storage device that uses flash memory to store and retrieve digital data, offering faster access times and lower power consumption than traditional hard disk drives.

Subject Matter Expert (SME): An individual with specialized knowledge, expertise, or experience in a particular subject or field.

Succession Planning: The process of identifying and developing internal candidates to fill key leadership positions within an organization.

Super User: A highly skilled and knowledgeable user of a software system or application who provides support, training, and assistance to other users.

Supply Chain Management: The oversight and coordination of materials, information, and finances as they move from supplier to manufacturer to wholesaler to retailer to consumer.

Sustainability: The practice of meeting present needs without compromising the ability of future generations to meet their own needs, encompassing environmental, social, and economic factors.

Switching Barrier: Factors or conditions that make it difficult or costly for customers to switch from one product or service provider to another.

System Integrator: A company or individual responsible for integrating various subsystems or components into a unified system that meets specified requirements.

System Lifecycle: The stages through which a system passes, including planning, development, implementation, operation, maintenance, and retirement.

System Provider: An entity that supplies or provides a system, software, or service to meet the needs of an organization.

System Scaling: The ability of a system to handle increased workload or user demand by adding resources or expanding capacity.

System Sizing: Determining the appropriate capacity or configuration of a system to meet current and future needs based on factors such as usage patterns and growth projections.

Systems Integration: The process of combining different subsystems or components into a single, cohesive system that functions effectively and efficiently.

Talent Acquisition: The process of identifying, attracting, and hiring qualified candidates to fill job vacancies within an organization.

Talent Card: A digital profile or portfolio that showcases an individual's skills, experience, and qualifications for employment or other opportunities.

Talent Lifecycle Management: The strategic management of an organization's talent from recruitment and onboarding through development, retention, and succession planning.

Talent Management: Strategies and practices for attracting, developing, and retaining skilled employees to meet current and future business needs.

Talent Profile: A comprehensive record of an individual's skills, qualifications, performance, and career progression within an organization.

Total Rewards: The sum of all the rewards and benefits offered to employees in exchange for their work, including compensation, benefits, recognition, and career development opportunities.

Usability Group (UG): A team or committee responsible for evaluating and improving the user experience and usability of products, systems, or services.

User Acceptance Testing (UAT): The process of testing a software application or system to ensure it meets the needs and requirements of end-users before deployment.

User Experience: The overall experience of a person using a product, system, or service, encompassing aspects such as usability, accessibility, and satisfaction.

User Interface: The means by which users interact with a computer system or software application, including graphical elements, controls, and navigation menus.

User Persona: A fictional representation of a target user group, based on research and data, used to guide design and development decisions.

User Story: A concise, informal description of a feature, requirement, or need from the perspective of an end-user, used in Agile development methodologies.

Virtual Private Network (VPN): A secure network connection that allows users to access resources and services securely over a public network, such as the internet.

Virtual Reality (VR): An immersive computer-generated environment that simulates physical presence and allows users to interact with 3D objects and environments.

Workflow Automation: The use of technology to automate repetitive tasks, processes, or workflows to improve efficiency, productivity, and accuracy.

Year 2000 (Y2K): The term used to describe the potential computer bug or glitch related to the rollover of dates from 1999 to 2000, which was a concern for many computer systems and applications at the turn of the millennium.

Index

Made in the USA
Coppell, TX
22 January 2025

44767952R00155